The Rise of Modern Business

Mansel G. Blackford

THE RISE OF MODERN BUSINESS

GREAT BRITAIN, THE UNITED STATES, GERMANY, JAPAN, AND CHINA

THE UNIVERSITY OF NORTH CAROLINA PRESS ■ CHAPEL HILL

Third Edition ■ Revised and Updated

© 2008 The University of North Carolina Press
All rights reserved
Designed and typeset in Arnhem, Officina Sans,
and Russell Square by Eric M. Brooks
Manufactured in the United States of America

The paper in this book meets the guidelines
for permanence and durability of the Committee
on Production Guidelines for Book Longevity
of the Council on Library Resources.

Library of Congress Cataloging-in-Publication Data
Blackford, Mansel G., 1944–
The rise of modern business: Great Britain, the United States,
Germany, Japan, and China / Mansel G. Blackford. — 3rd ed.,
rev. and updated.
    p. cm.
Includes bibliographical references and index.
ISBN 978-0-8078-3210-3 (cloth: alk. paper)
ISBN 978-0-8078-5886-8 (pbk. alk. paper)
1. Industries — Great Britain — History. 2. Industries —
United States — History. 3. Industries — Japan — History.
4. Industries — Germany — History. 5. Industries —
China — History. I. Title.
HC255.B59   2008
338.09 — dc22   2007044527

cloth   12 11 10 09 08   5 4 3 2 1
paper   12 11 10 09 08   5 4 3 2 1

With thanks to my students

for pushing me to explore new

topics and ideas, and

With love for my grandsons,

Jasper and Liam

Contents

Maps and Figures

Acknowledgments

I have benefited greatly from the help of many people in preparing the third edition of *The Rise of Modern Business*. I especially would like to thank those scholars who read and commented on various editions of this work: James Bartholomew, Cynthia Brokaw, Philip Brown, William Childs, Michael Dintenfass, James Kraft, and Christopher Reed. I would also like to thank my wife, Vicki, for her careful proofreading of the manuscript. More generally, I would like to thank my colleagues in the Department of History at The Ohio State University for a congenial environment in which to work. I would like to thank as well the College of Humanities at The Ohio State University for a grant-in-aid, which helped in the preparation of this study. I owe thanks to Chuck Grench, the Assistant Director and Senior Editor of the University of North Carolina Press, for his encouragement and thoughts as I prepared this edition. I remain, of course, solely responsible for any errors this study may still contain.

The Rise of Modern Business

Introduction

Business errors resulting from uninformed views of foreign cultures and histories abound. In the mid-1960s the Japanese purchased lots of Western-style cakes from bakeries, because few Japanese stoves possessed ovens. Executives at General Mills thought that they had an ideal new product for the Japanese market, a Betty Crocker cake mix that could be baked in the electric rice cookers found in every Japanese household. However, the cake mix did not sell well and was soon withdrawn from the market. The most fundamental problem was cultural. Historically, the Japanese placed an almost religious value on the purity of clean, white rice. They did not want to risk the contamination of their rice by cake crumbs that might be left in their rice cookers. By the same token, a lack of knowledge of foreign cultures sometimes hindered the Japanese in opening up overseas markets. Even language could be a problem. When the Japanese tried to export a soft drink with the name Calpis, the name of the beverage killed sales. Similar problems resulted in efforts to export a coffee creamer called Creap and a snack named Krap.

By examining business developments worldwide, this book seeks to help readers avoid such missteps in the future. The book grew out of the needs I encountered in teaching comparative business history to mixed groups of undergraduates at The Ohio State University. No text on this subject was suitable for that purpose, and I found myself in perennial difficulty when selecting readings for the course. I originally wrote this book, first published in 1988, to try to fill that void. Over the next decade interest in comparative (international) business history greatly increased, as did my own involvement in the field, resulting in the publication of a second edition in 1998. Business history has continued to move in new directions since then, as has my teaching and writing, leading to my preparation of this third edition.

As a work in business history, this study examines the history of the business firm and its management. This book looks especially at the rise of modern forms of business worldwide but does so in the full context of traditional business developments and, indeed, shows that the line between modern and traditional was often a blurred one. By focusing on the firm, business history differs from economic history, which looks more at the entire economy of a nation, at the big macroeconomic picture of economic booms and contractions. Nonetheless, the external environment, including politics, culture, social norms, and law, has influenced the firm; and this book deals with the evolution of the business firm in relationship to the environment within which business has developed.

This book compares the evolution of business in five of the most important and economically dynamic nations on three continents: Great Britain and Germany in Europe, the United States in North America, and Japan and China in Asia. There are compelling reasons to study the business history of these nations. First of all, businesses in these nations have accounted for the lion's share of global economic production in recent times. In 1870 the United States, Great Britain, and Germany produced 68 percent of the world's industrial goods, and in 1938 they still accounted for 52 percent of it. In 2006 those three nations, joined by Japan and China, accounted for well over one-half of the globe's gross domestic product—that is, over one-half of the world's reported, measurable economic output.

Moreover, a study of businesses in these countries reveals the most important changes that have occurred in the nature of the business firm and its management. Industrialization was *the* big event in the economic and business history of the world. Great Britain was the first country to industrialize. It makes sense, then, to examine British firms as the first to be affected by industrialization. A study of business in Great Britain also permits an investigation of European business. So does a look at business in Germany, which successfully industrialized a bit later than Great Britain. Several reasons call for an examination of the history of American business. Even though the United States, like Germany, industrialized somewhat later than Great Britain, it was in the United States where business leaders worked out many new forms of company structures and management methods. Americans were the first to develop big businesses in a major way, along with new ways to run them. Some American business structures and methods were later dispersed to other nations. Moreover, studying the United States offers a chance to examine business in a New World country. Japan deserves investigation as a latecomer to industrialization and as a nation with a culture very different from those of Western nations. Looking at business in Japan permits an examination of the first Asian nation to successfully modernize its economy. More recently, China has emerged as a substantial economic power, a situation calling for an examination of that Asian nation's businesses.

I hope this study will prove valuable to several audiences. History students will, I think, find business history a major key to understanding the past; and comparative business history can be especially useful. Through comparative business history we can begin to uncover what has been universal and what has been specific to the development of business in different nations and cultures. Business and international studies students will also, I hope, find this sketch of the evolution of major aspects of world business valuable. Today's business scene is an international one, and to work effectively in it business people need to understand business practices beyond their nations' boundaries. Comparative business history can lend an international perspective to business developments.

In its largest sense, this book is a comparison of capitalistic evolution in five different nations (except for China in the 1950s, 1960s, and early 1970s). In capitalistic societies people produce and sell goods and services through privately owned businesses and means of production. They invest in factories and stores, hoping that their sales will generate profits for themselves. In capitalistic economies people interact through markets, most obviously through the markets in which business people sell their goods, but also in labor markets through which workers arrange with management the terms of their employment. Capitalistic business systems reduced the roles of custom, royal decrees, and arbitrary decisions characteristic of earlier feudal business systems in determining how exchanges of goods, services, and labor would occur. Far from uniform or static, capitalism, this book shows, varied from nation to nation and from one time period to the next.

This book argues that similarities in the development of businesses across national boundaries resulted mainly from certain economic and technological imperatives that all five nations shared. Thus, industrialization led to the rise of big businesses in some fields in all of the nations studied in this volume. Conversely, this book also argues that many of the differences in the businesses of the nations were the results of the different political, social, and cultural environments of the countries. Those differences, within a general capitalistic framework, could be substantial. The big businesses that grew up with industrialization developed at different paces and assumed different forms in each nation. Moreover, smaller firms played different roles in different nations. No nation can escape its history, and national business forms remain varied down to the present day, despite the development of a global economy.

The basic narrative organization of this book remains the same as in the earlier editions. Chapter 1 looks at preindustrial business, especially the world of the merchant. Stable political frameworks generally allowed the growth of thriving commercial economies even before industrialization. However, when compared to what would come with industrialization, the pace of business was slow, and the output of business was low, permitting merchants to conduct business by time-honored, traditional methods. Industrialization, the topic of chapter 2, changed this situation. As shown in chapters 3, 4, and 5, industrialization accelerated the speed of doing business and increased the output of business firms, changes that led some executives to alter their ways of doing business. Yet, as these three chapters also illustrate, not everything changed in the business world of industrializing nations. Newly formed big businesses did not sweep away all the institutions and practices that stood before them, even in the United States. Chapters 6 and 7 examine alterations in the political environment of business in the years between the First World War and the Second World War and the impacts of those changes upon the nature of business. The final two chapters and the conclusion look at the development of business since the Second World War, a time of growing international trade, and assess whether businesses around the globe are becoming more and more similar or increasingly different.

Within the same general framework that existed in the first two editions, the third edition contains important alterations. There has been an explosion of writing in business history over the past decade, and this edition incorporates the most recent scholarship in the field. It also provides coverage of business evolution in China, a topic not dealt with in the earlier editions. Moreover, this edition speaks clearly to relationships between business development and environmental changes, a topic not present in the first or second editions.

Finally, I should mention linguistic matters. I have followed Japanese and Chinese conventions in name usage: I have placed family names first and given names second throughout this text. I have employed italics to indicate foreign words and terms not in common English usage.

Suggested Readings

Specific suggested readings, books and articles in English available at university libraries, appear at the end of each chapter. However, several particularly important studies deserve mention at the outset. Alfred D. Chandler Jr., *Scale and Scope: The Dynamics of Industrial Capitalism* (Cambridge, Mass.,

1990), has stimulated tremendous interest in comparative business history through its examination of the development of large industrial firms in Great Britain, the United States, and Germany. See also Alfred D. Chandler Jr., Franco Amatori, and Takashi Hikino, eds., *Big Business and the Wealth of Nations* (Cambridge, Mass., 1997). The many volumes of essays collected in *The International Conference on Business History* (the Fuji Conference), edited by various Japanese scholars (Tokyo, the mid-1970s to the early 2000s), offer solid introductions to major topics in comparative business history. Thomas K. McCraw, *Creating Modern Capitalism: How Entrepreneurs, Companies, and Countries Triumphed in Three Industrial Revolutions* (Cambridge, Mass., 1997), is a valuable collection of case studies dealing with business developments in Great Britain, the United States, Japan, and Germany. Mannari Hiroshi, *The Japanese Business Leaders* (Tokyo, 1974), compares the socioeconomic backgrounds of business leaders in Japan, the United States, and Europe over time. For an introduction to the study of business history around the globe, see Franco Amatori and Geoffrey Jones, eds., *Business History Around the World* (Cambridge, 2003).

National histories are valuable. On Great Britain, see David J. Jeremy, *A Business History of Britain, 1900–1990s* (Oxford, 1998), and John F. Wilson, *British Business History, 1720–1994* (Manchester, 1995). For a comparative study, see Youssef Cassis, *Big Business: The European Experience in the Twentieth Century* (Oxford, 1997). On the United States, see Mansel G. Blackford and K. Austin Kerr, *Business Enterprise in American History* (Boston, 1994). On Japan, see Johannes Hirschmeier and Yui Tsunihiko, *The Development of Japanese Business, 1600–1973* (Cambridge, Mass., 1975), and W. Mark Fruin, *The Japanese Enterprise System* (Oxford, 1994). Peter Zarrow, *China in War and Revolution, 1895–1949* (London, 2005), is a valuable overview. David Faure, *China and Capitalism: A History of Business Enterprise in Modern China* (Hong Kong, 2006), is concise and provocative. See also R. Bin Wong, *China Transformed: Historical Change and the Limits of European Experience* (Ithaca, 1997).

Preindustrial Businesses
The Time of the Merchant

Directions to clerks in the London merchant house of Herries & Company in 1766 required that they keep the business fully informed of where they lived and ate so that they could be summoned immediately to the merchant house in times of emergencies, such as fires or other accidents, at any time of the day or night. As this directive suggested, the world of the preindustrial merchant, in whatever land, was a world of personal business. Merchants, their clerks, their competitors, and their customers were bound together by personal and kinship connections. Merchants like those at Herries & Company were the leading business people of preindustrial times. Through their control of foreign and domestic trade, the merchants provided much of the direction for the economic growth of their nations and regions. For all the similarities, however, there also existed important differences in how merchants operated in various lands.

In many ways, the preindustrial business world was vastly different from the business world of industrial and modern times. In the preindustrial era the pace of business activity was relatively slow, and the volume of goods produced and distributed was relatively low. In this situation traditional business methods, based on ties of friendship and family, dominated the business scene. Such ties were needed to overcome the tremendous risks of doing business in preindustrial years. With communications generally slow and unreliable, merchants had to rely on connections of blood and friendship to do business, especially if they sought to conduct trade beyond their localities. With market information spotty and uncertain, they had to rely on the judgment of friends and relatives beyond their local regions to make decisions on the buying and selling of goods.

Yet the preindustrial economies of Great Britain, North America, Japan, and China were anything but stagnant. They were vibrant commercial economies whose expansion prepared the way for further economic changes during industrialization. Government policies and actions were important in this economic growth. Throughout the world, economic, political, and cultural changes have always been intertwined. Business has never, and does not today, exist in a vacuum. Rather, business has always been influenced, and has influenced, its external environment. Thus, the development of preindustrial business can best be understood by first examining the political and economic frameworks within which it grew up, ones favorable to business development.

Political Frameworks

Great Britain, North America, Japan, and China were all characterized by growing degrees of political unity and domestic tranquility in preindustrial times, which in turn stimulated economic growth and business development. Conversely, a lack of political unity retarded economic growth in Germany.

Great Britain and Germany

Great Britain has had a long existence as a unified nation ruled by one crowned monarch. However, civil wars shattered this political unity on several important occasions in preindustrial times. Most divisive was the English Revolution, a civil war in the mid-1600s. This major conflict had both religious and political origins, pitting the king against Parliament and Anglican (the Church of England) against Nonconformist (Puritan). It was a bloody conflict that sorely divided Englishmen, but the Restoration Settlement of 1689 reunified the country. Never again would England be divided by civil war. The Restoration Settlement had several major terms. First, at the invitation of Parliament, William, Prince of Orange, the leader of the military forces of the Dutch Republic, became king of England and his wife, Mary, became the queen. England acquired political unity under one set of monarchs. However, a Bill of Rights clearly subordinated monarchs to Parliament. The king now ruled "in Parliament." Second, the Toleration Act of 1689 began healing religious differences. Religious toleration, the right to hold their own public services and so forth, was given to Nonconformists by this law.

Great Britain also began building an empire in the late 1600s and early 1700s. By an Act of Union in 1707 Scotland became part of Great Britain (England already controlled much of Ireland). England acquired the origins of an overseas empire as well. British control of this empire was either direct, as in the case of many of the North American colonies, or indirect, as in the control the British East India Company exercised over India.

By way of contrast, there was no united German nation until the early

1870s. Instead, there were several large German principalities and many more small ones. Substantial economic growth took place in Prussia, a large northern German state, which in the nineteenth century became home to many railroads and much heavy industry. However, the economic growth of Germany as a whole was hindered for decades by the region's division into many states, which erected trade barriers against each other, making internal trade and market development difficult. Even after a customs union partially united the some of the German states in 1834, other principalities remained outside that union. And, of course, there existed no uniform laws, no commercial laws across national boundaries, again impeding business development.

North America: The British Colonies

In North America there existed some political unity, though not true national unity. The British colonies possessed the unity that derived from their membership in the expanding British Empire. Only later, with the American Revolution of 1776 and the adoption of the United States Constitution in 1789, was real national political unity achieved.

British merchants and investors established some of the most important colonies as profit-making enterprises. However, because of unexpected problems the colonies faced (none made a profit initially) and because of a desire by the British government to increase its power, most colonies had become royal colonies with governors directly responsible to the king and Parliament by the late 1600s and early 1700s. Or, they were proprietary colonies in which the English crown gave large grants of land in North America to various Englishmen in return for their friendships or favors. Of whatever type, the colonies were integrated into the British Empire.

The most important political mechanism unifying the British Empire was the Navigation Acts, pieces of legislation passed by Parliament in the mid-1600s. The goal of the Acts was to regulate trade — indeed, the entire economy — of the British Empire. The major terms of the Navigation Acts, which applied to all of the empire, not simply North America, were fourfold. First, most trade between England and its colonies had to be carried in English or colonial ships manned by English or colonial crews. Second, most goods going to the colonies had to pass through England, even if they originated elsewhere. Third, many goods exported from the colonies had to pass through England, even if bound somewhere else. Finally, many forms of manufacturing were restricted in the colonies, for the colonies were supposed to act as sources of raw materials for British industry and as markets for English manufactured goods. The object of the Acts was to build up the economic and military might of the British Empire, at the expense of its rivals, France and Spain.

Japan and China

Like Great Britain, Japan has long existed as an independent nation. The Japanese traditionally date the origin of their nation to 660 B.C., with the accession of their first emperor Jimmu, reputedly the great-grandson of the Sun Goddess. By the third century A.D. the Chinese, who received tribute-missions from Japan, reported that the Empress Pimiko was unifying Japan from her base in Kyushu. By the sixth and seventh centuries much of Japan was unified under one emperor, who ruled as both the religious and political leader of the nation. Yet, as in Great Britain, this was a fragile unity. Different families and clans struggled for control of Japan and in doing so reduced the real power of the emperor, so that the emperor often ruled in name only. After 1185 the real power rested with the leader of the most powerful military family, who became known as the shogun. Civil strife, common from the fourteenth century, reached an extreme during the Sengoku period, the years 1468 through 1573.

It was from this conflict between warring noble houses that Japan began to emerge as a unified nation. Tokugawa Ieyasu defeated his rivals in a climactic battle in 1600 and assumed the title of shogun in 1603. The years 1603 through 1867 are called the Tokugawa period, a time of relative unity and peace in Japan. In theory, the shogun was the military ruler of Japan, acting on behalf of the divine emperor, who lived in Kyoto. In practice, the emperor remained a figurehead with little political power.

The type of government established by Tokugawa is termed the *baku-han* system. Under this system the Tokugawa family ruled all of Japan. All the local lords, called *daimyo*, owed allegiance to the Tokugawa family. The *daimyo*, in turn, ruled their provinces, called *han* (or domains). There were about 260 domains. Both the Tokugawa family, which owned outright about one-quarter of Japan, and the *daimyo* depended on a rice tax amounting to about 40 percent of the crop for most of their income. To gather the rice and administer their lands the Tokugawa family and the *daimyo* relied on their former warriors, called samurai, now turned into administrators.

Throughout the Tokugawa period, there existed tension between the centralizing tendencies of the ruling Tokugawa family based in Edo and the decentralizing tendencies of the many *daimyo* striving to preserve their autonomy in their domains. Many of the stronger *daimyo* were able to maintain a high degree of independence from the shogun, and much of the political and military power of the nation continued to reside in the *daimyo*. *Daimyo* often maintained local governments, armies, and sometimes even currencies. Domain governments often promoted economic development in agriculture, crafts, and early-day industry. The Saga domain in southern Japan pioneered in the development of modern iron smelting, used in making guns. Centralization of government, while under way in the Tokugawa period, progressed slowly and was far from complete.

The *baku-han* was a personal form of government, based on bonds of allegiance and controls imposed on the personal behaviors of the *daimyo* more than upon institutions. The *daimyo* were required to take personal oaths of allegiance to the shogun and had to spend every other year living in Edo, where the shogun maintained his court and could watch over them. When the *daimyo* were absent from Edo, they had to leave family members as hostages. Only in the late Tokugawa period did a national government begin developing, as the shogun took responsibility for expanding regional coordination of flood control, putting down peasant revolts, and resolving regional disputes.

Unlike the situation in England or the North American colonies, Tokugawa Japan did not favor most foreign trade. Japan had long had a flourishing trade with the Asian mainland and, from 1543, a growing trade with the West. However, worried about outside political interference in Japan and the spread of Christianity, the Tokugawa government ended most trade with the West by 1640. Limited commerce continued through the southern Japanese city of Nagasaki.

Like Japan, China was a united nation in preindustrial times. Ruled by imperial dynasties, the Ming dynasty (1368–1644) and the Qing dynasty (1644–1911), China underwent a commercial revolution in the 1500s and 1600s and experienced something of an economic boom in the 1700s. China had a national real estate market from around 220 and a fully monetarized taxation and economic system by the mid-1500s, perhaps the first in the world. Engaging in foreign trade by land and sea, China also developed extensive internal commerce. However, Chinese merchants did not fully develop many of the legal and financial institutions important for economic development in the West. China lacked much in the way of commercial law (including incorporation laws), modern banks, and modern financial instruments until the twentieth century.

Even so, there was considerable customary law, which smoothed the way for business transactions and which, more specifically, permitted lineage estates to thrive from the time of the Song dynasty (960–1126). Lineage estates, basically extended families, were central to much of the business development in China. Thus, Chinese merchants contracted with each other more as members of lineage groups than as individuals. Whether as parts of lineage estates or on their own, traditional merchants sometimes established considerable enterprises. For instance, thirty major merchants oversaw extensive salt-making ventures in east-central China from their headquarters in Yang-Chou during the 1700s, with an additional thirty large merchants in charge of salt distribution and sales. They were accounted to be among the wealthiest people in China at that time.

Political Unity and Regionalism

By the late 1600s and early 1700s preindustrial Great Britain, North America, China, and Japan were either themselves becoming unified political bodies characterized by domestic tranquility or, as in the case of the North American colonies, parts of such a body. Political unity provided stable frameworks upon which economic growth and business development could be based. Yet there were differences. Political unity was most pronounced in Great Britain and China. In North America and Japan, local regions maintained considerable freedom from control by the central government, with attendant economic results. Disunity retarded economic growth in the region of Europe which later became Germany.

The Economic Setting

One major point stands out about the preindustrial economies of Great Britain, North America, Japan, and China: they were commercial rather than subsistence economies. That is, people lived to a significant degree by buying and selling goods in markets, not by simply consuming what they grew or made. Only on the farthest frontiers, such as the Kentucky country in America in the 1750s and 1760s, were subsistence economies dominant, and then only until political and transportation developments allowed localities to be linked into larger regions.

Several elements characterized these commercial economies. First, agriculture was becoming market-oriented. Second, both domestic and (except in Japan) foreign trade were growing. Third, this trade both resulted from and stimulated regional specialization. Fourth, urbanization, the growth of cities, was proceeding. These four characteristics were related to the development of political unity, for political unity and stability stimulated the spread of the commercial economies.

Commercial Agriculture and Regional Specialization

Agriculture became increasingly commercialized. No longer did farmers simply raise food for their own consumption. They sold significant portions of their crops in markets, and they were able to raise larger crops for their markets because of increases in land and labor productivity.

Some forms of commercial farming had existed in England from the Middle Ages — raising sheep for wool, with the wool being used in trade with continental Europe, for example. By the late 1600s and early 1700s wheat and livestock were being raised for consumption in Great Britain's expanding cities. Improvements in agricultural techniques — the drainage of swamps, increasing crop rotation, the use of manure for fertilizer, land enclosures that made land parcels larger and easier to farm, and the introduction of mechanical devices such as seed drills — increased the agricultural output of Great Britain fivefold between 1400 and 1700.

In the North American colonies the story was similar. The use of horses and improvements in agricultural implements boosted output. As in Great Britain, much of this growing output found urban markets, either in colonial cities and towns such as Philadelphia, New York, and Boston or abroad, with 10 to 20 percent of all of the crops grown in the colonies finding overseas markets.

Japanese and Chinese agriculture also became more and more market-oriented. In Japan the *daimyo* needed funds to cover their many expenses, especially their attendance on the shogun in Edo, and they sold the rice collected in their rice taxes through merchants in Osaka. Related to this point, the growth of cities as consumption centers stimulated the commercialization of agriculture. As in Great Britain and North America, productivity increases allowed agricultural development to proceed in Japan. Particularly important were the development of new strains of rice seeds, which allowed multiple plantings of rice each year in many areas, the spread of new farm implements, the use of night soil, plants, and fish cakes as fertilizers, improvements in irrigation and flood control techniques, and the development of better ways to plant rice. Similarly, Chinese agriculture was market-oriented and diversified from at least the 1500s onward.

In Great Britain and North America agriculture developed along the lines of regional specialization, as did industry at a later date. In England regional specialization was noticeable in agriculture as early as the years 1450 through 1650. Grain grown in Kent or East Anglia found markets in London, while cattle raised in the North and West were driven to fattening areas in the Midlands and South. This trend became more pronounced over the next century, 1650 through 1750. The West Country became famous for apples and pears, Kent for apples and cherries, Lancashire for potatoes, and the area around London for vegetables. Colonial American farmers also engaged in regional specialization. The southern colonies grew rice and indigo (a plant from which blue dye was made), the Chesapeake areas of Virginia grew tobacco, the middle colonies like Pennsylvania grew wheat, and New England specialized in fishing, shipbuilding, and producing naval stores.

Regional specialization also occurred in China and Japan. For example, in Japan rice was the main crop grown throughout much of nation. However, from the mid- and late 1600s peasants also grew mulberry bushes (whose leaves were food for silkworms), tea, lacquer trees, paper mulberry bushes, along with hemp, safflower, and indigo plants—according to the part of Japan in which they lived. In China, as well, different regions produced different goods, which were then exchanged in trade.

As regional specialization occurred, each nation's economy became more efficient and productive, and standards of living rose. Accompanying the commercialization and regional specialization of farming was the growing employment of farmers in nonagricultural tasks. For instance, Japanese peasants increasingly earned a considerable proportion of their income from making handicraft products, the forerunner of some forms of later industrialization, such as the weaving of tatami mats. In some areas village enterprises with five to twenty employees were common in the sugar, salt, oil, silk reeling and weaving, and cotton textile industries.

Trade

An increase in trade accompanied regional specialization. Trade both permitted regional specialization and was, in turn, stimulated by it. Great Britain, North America, Japan, and China were all fortunate in being able to carry on trade via coastal shipping, for until the coming of canals and railroads inland transportation was very expensive (and in Japan was constrained by mountainous topography). Trade allowed each area to develop its comparative advantage in economic development. Each region did what its resources best allowed and traded with other regions for that which it did not produce.

Britain's domestic commerce and foreign trade increased as time passed. Between 1720 and 1749 some 130 turnpike companies were established to build new roads, spurring the inland transportation of goods. Harbor improvements invigorated the coastal trade, which grew in volume and diversity. Foreign trade went beyond Europe, as English merchants joined in a general expansion of European trade with other parts of the world. As Great Britain's trade became oriented away from Europe, the commodities making up the trade changed. Raw wool declined in significance. Exports of manufactured goods — metal products, cotton textiles, and woolen textiles — to the colonies rose in importance, as did imports of raw materials from the colonies.

In the North American colonies internal trade was less important than in Great Britain, largely because of the poor state of inland transportation facilities. Even in the late colonial period there was four times as much trade between England and the American colonies as there was trade among the colonies themselves. Trade went overseas. In the 1760s Great Britain took 55 percent of all the exports of the North American colonies, and the British West Indies (British islands in the Caribbean) took another 27 percent. In return, Great Britain supplied the colonies with 80 percent of their imports. This situation was just as the framers of the Navigation Acts had intended.

China and Japan presented contrasts. Commerce carried on along camel caravan routes (the "Silk Road") connected China to other nations from about 200 B.C., as did ship-borne trade from about A.D. 1000 onward. Internal trade via land and water routes also linked different Chinese regions. Merchant networks held China's regions together economically. In Japan foreign trade was not very important after the early 1600s. More important was an increase in trade across domain boundaries, commerce facilitated by internal transportation improvements. Trade in rice, silk, and cotton developed, along with some commerce in sugar, indigo, and specialty fruits and vegetables, stimulated by the growth of consumption centers in Edo, Osaka, Kyoto, and domain castle towns. Throughout the Tokugawa period efforts were made to improve short-distance inland waterways, and from the mid-1600s coastal shipping routes around Honshu were greatly improved. A national road system converging on Edo was established, the Tokaido Road connecting Kyoto to Edo. By the early 1800s private messenger companies provided two-day service for letters and documents carried over the 300-mile-long route. Local roads also improved substantially in many areas. However, political considerations prevented the full economic integration of Japan in the Tokugawa period. Fearing the development of rival political power bases by leading *daimyo*, the shogun did not press for the complete development of internal commerce. Wheeled vehicles were not allowed for commoners, and as late as the 1860s road inspection sta-

Cassie LaVoie

Tuesdays

9 am - 3 pm

~~Roo~~   C-310
Room L

HC2545 WGB
         TGB

tions and guardhouses impeded the flow of trade between the domains on national highways.

The Growth of Cities

Urbanization characterized all five preindustrial economies. Cities and towns grew in importance, though their significance varied by nation and region. In terms of economic growth, the towns and cities were important as markets for agricultural goods, thus stimulating the commercialization of agriculture and the expansion of trade. Cities also became the locus for some early industry.

In Great Britain London was *the* city: the seat of government, the residence of the court, the head of England's overseas empire, the financial center, the location of much industry, and a social resort during the winter season. London's 1 million inhabitants, 11 percent of England's total population in 1801, made it a world-class city. However, regional market and manufacturing cities challenged London's supremacy; between 1750 and 1800 fourteen cities with a population of 10,000 or more doubled in population. By 1801 Manchester had 90,000 inhabitants and Liverpool 83,000. Great Britain as a whole was becoming more urbanized. People living in towns and cities of 2,500 or more made up 19 percent of the nation's population in 1700, and 30 percent one hundred years later. By 1801 Great Britain possessed sixteen cities with a population over 20,000, thirty-three with a population of 10,000 to 20,000, forty-five with a population of 5,000 to 10,000, and ninety-four with a population of 2,500 to 5,000.

If urban areas were important for Great Britain's economic growth, so were smaller villages and towns, especially as centers of early-day industry. Close to supplies of water and raw materials, small towns were, in fact, the backbone of nascent industrialization. Typical was Burslem in the Midlands, an area soon to be known as the Potteries. By 1730 two-thirds of the wage-earners in Burslem, which had a population of about 1,000, made their living in nonagricultural pursuits. Pottery production was most important, with about sixty small workshops, each employing a dozen or fewer men and children. In the shops master craftsmen and their assistants turned out butter-pots, pitchers, and mugs made of clays available locally. From these beginnings, Burslem emerged as a larger industrial district in the later 1700s and 1800s, the home for pottery made famous by Josiah Wedgwood.

Japan and China were also lands of towns and cities, as well as countryside. There were, for example, three major cities in Tokugawa Japan. Edo, the new political capital, became a city of 1 million in the early 1700s and was a major consumption center. By this time Kyoto and Osaka had about 300,000 people apiece. They, too, were consumption centers. They also were centers for some of Japan's early handicraft industry. Kyoto's western section had about 7,000 of Japan's finest textile looms, each requiring two operators. Altogether some 100,000 people—spinners and dyers, as well as weavers—were involved in textile production in the city. There were, as well, about forty substantial port towns lining Japan's coastline. In the domains, castle towns of the *daimyo* served as political and economic administration centers and in time became consumption centers like Edo on a smaller scale. About 200 castle towns dotted the landscape of Tokugawa Japan, some thirty to forty of which had populations of 10,000 or more. In 1707, for example, Okayama in southern Honshu possessed 38,000 inhabitants including 10,000 samurai. As a result of this urbanization, about 22 percent of the Japanese lived in towns or cities of 3,000 or more by 1750.

Even so, by the mid- and late Tokugawa years the castle towns and other urban centers were losing ground to smaller villages as the locus of much of Japan's economic activity. In fact, in the regions where economic development was most rapid, the large centers, primarily castle towns, lost population, contrary to what was occurring in Great Britain and America. A desire to avoid taxation and regulations easily imposed in large urban centers combined with a quest for raw materials, water power, and cheap labor, led handicraft manufacturers to spring up in the countryside. For example, the Izumi district near Osaka developed into a center for the production of cotton weaving. In 1843 nearly half of the households of Uda-otsu, one of the towns in Izumi, were engaged in weaving, with only 14 percent still working in agriculture.

Colonial America was less urbanized than Great Britain or Japan. In 1742 about 5.4 percent of the population lived in urban centers. Boston had 16,000 people, Philadelphia, 13,000, New York, 11,000, Charleston, 6,800, and Newport, 6,200. By 1820 the United States possessed one city with a population over 100,000, two in the 50,000 to 100,000 range, two in the 25,000 to 50,000 range, eight in the 10,000 to 25,000 range, twenty-two in the 5,000 to 10,000 range, and twenty-six in the 2,500 to 5,000 range. At that time about 7 percent of all Americans lived in towns or cities of 2,500 or more people.

Much early trade and economic specialization in America involved cities and their hinterlands, the areas surrounding cities. The evolving relationship between Philadelphia and the area within about fifty miles suggests the importance of such connections. As canals and, to a lesser extent, roads linked Philadelphia to nearby areas, the city became less reliant on overseas trade and commerce with distant American cities for its growth and more dependent on trade with nearby regions. Hinterland exports to Philadelphia tripled between the late 1810s and 1830. As trade back and forth between Philadelphia and nearby localities exploded, economic specialization occurred. Rural residents gave up handicraft manufacturing to people in Philadelphia, who worked in small shops or in early-day factories. More and more residents purchased industrial goods from Philadelphia with money earned in selling an increasingly varied range of specialized nonindustrial products to Philadelphians — coal, iron, and many agricultural goods (not simply their earlier major product, wheat). By the mid-1830s an integrated, growing regional economy had enveloped Philadelphia and its surrounding area.

Politics, Economics, and Society

Preindustrial Great Britain, North America, Japan, and China developed commercial economies within regional and national political frameworks. A major indication of the viability of their economies was that each supported increasing populations with rising standards of living. Great Britain's population rose from 2.1 million in 1430 to 3.8 million in 1603 to 6.9 million in 1700 to 7.8 million in 1760. Between 1700 and 1760 Great Britain's income per capita rose from £6.7 to £9.4. By 1776 the thirteen colonies later composing the United States had a population of about 2.5 million, including 500,000 blacks and 100,000 Native Americans. By this time the standard of living of the white colonists probably surpassed that of Englishmen, with their annual per capita income coming to about £13. Precisely comparable income figures are not available for Japan, but that nation's population rose from roughly 18 million in the early 1600s to about 30 million a century later, at which level it remained into the mid-1800s, probably due to the widespread adoption of population controls, including infanticide, as well as the catastrophic effect of three major famines. China had a population of about 150 million in 1700, and roughly 300 million a century later. China is generally regarded to have had the world's largest national economy as late as 1800, although solid per capita income figures are elusive.

A rough estimate of per capita income, expressed in 1965 American dollars, in various nations at the onset of industrialization is as follows: Great Britain, $227 (1765–85); the United States, $474 (1834–43); Germany, $302 (1850–59); France, $242 (1831–40); and Japan, $136 (1886).

The people in these nations were commercially oriented and well educated by the standards of their days. In Tokugawa Japan nearly 50 percent of the men and 15 percent of the women received some type of education in literacy, mainly in Buddhist temple schools. Most samurai and almost all merchants were literate. In China around 1700 about 25 percent of the men and 5 percent of the women were literate. Literacy improved in America throughout the eighteenth century; by the time of the American Revolution a majority of Americans could read and write. In Great Britain 50 percent of the men and about 25 percent of the women were literate in 1780, at least to the extent of being able to sign their names.

Merchants

The preindustrial period was, in business terms, the age of the merchant. Merchants were the business leaders in preindustrial Great Britain, North America, Japan, and China, and for good reason: their control over trade was the linchpin holding together the economies of their nations and regions. Moreover, as later chapters of this book show, it was merchants who often built up and dominated much of early industry.

British Merchants

Great Britain has often been labeled "a nation of shopkeepers," but the country could just as aptly be called a nation of merchants. It was merchants who, as much as explorers and the military, built the British Empire, and it was merchants who were most important in developing Great Britain's domestic economy. These merchants operated in a variety of ways: as members of joint-stock companies, as partners, and as single-owner proprietors.

Much of the expansion of Great Britain's overseas trade between 1550 and 1650 resulted from the actions of merchants linked in newly formed joint-stock companies. In chartered joint-stock companies the king granted a charter to a group of merchants to engage in trade in a certain commodity or region. The charter often granted the company of merchants monopoly privileges to attract merchants into risky ventures. As investors, the merchants bought shares in the joint-stock companies and expected to earn dividends on their shares. London merchants were the most important investors, and London was the center of England's overseas trade. Elected directors and a governor ran each company. Joint-stock companies permitted the pooling of capital for risky ventures and served the twin goals of expanding British power and increasing private profits. The most important were the Muscovy Company (1555), the Eastland Company (1579), the Africa Company (1588), the Levant Company (1592), the East India Company (1600), and the Virginia Company (1606).

The Muscovy Company was typical of the joint-stock companies. After financing several profitable voyages to Russia in the early 1550s, London merchants set up the Muscovy Company in 1555. Shares in the company cost £25 originally, but £200 from 1564 on. Sebastian Cabot, a well-known explorer, served as the governor of the company, and 28 of the 200 to 240 investors worked as his assistants in running the company's affairs. The Muscovy Company received monopoly rights to trade with Russia from the British government, and for some years the Russian government permitted the company to handle all of its foreign trade with Europe. The company exported tallow, furs, felt, cordage, ships' masts, and hemp from Russia and imported various English products into Russia. The company also opened a profitable trade with Persia in the late 1500s. In later years, however, problems — competition with the Dutch, the loss of the trade with Persia, and difficulties in controlling company representatives in Russia — mounted, and the Muscovy Company disbanded in 1620.

While first set up to develop foreign trade, joint-stock companies soon engaged in a wide variety of enterprises. Between 1660 and 1719 fifty-four major joint-stock companies received charters — twenty-three in mining and manufacturing, eleven in overseas trade, and twenty in banking, insurance, fishing, and other fields of endeavor. However, many of these later companies were fraudulent, set up by their organizers simply to fleece investors of their money. Finally, in 1720 fraud in the sale of stock in the South Sea Company led Parliament to pass the Bubble Act, legislation that placed severe restrictions upon the formation and operations of joint-stock companies. Already in decline, they became unimportant. The demise of joint-stock companies did not retard Great Britain's economic development, for merchants found other ways to raise the funds they needed and were sometimes able to protect themselves from personal liability for company debts through a variety of legal stratagems.

Many British merchants operated in partnership agreements, typically based on family ties; and, as markets expanded, many of these merchants specialized in the goods they handled and the services they offered. In contrast to Colonial American merchants, who usually handled a wide variety of goods, the British merchants were more apt to deal in only a handful of products.

The experiences of the Perrys of London illustrate well how British partnerships operated. From 1690 through 1720 the family firm — known first as Perry & Lane, later as Micajah Perry & Co.—was the leading importer of tobacco from the Chesapeake area of America to Great Britain. Micaiah Perry, founder of the merchant house, came from a family long interested in trade in the New World. He was himself born in New Haven in 1641, before moving to England at the age of ten. After receiving training at a leading merchant guild in London, Micaiah Perry began trading in a partnership with Thomas Lane, an arrangement that lasted until Lane's death in 1710. Like Perry, Lane had family connections in British America.

Beginning a limited trade in tobacco in the 1670s, Perry & Lane became the leading importer of the Chesapeake product to London by the late 1690s, a position maintained into the 1720s. By the time of Micaiah Perry's death in 1721, the firm was probably the largest private importer of tobacco in the world. In part, this success came through the firm's willingness to use a wide variety of methods to trade with all types of tobacco growers in the Chesapeake, from engaging in direct buying from very small growers to taking the output of large planters such as Robert "King" Carter on a consignment basis. This flexibility in buying methods served the firm well. So did flexibility in its shipping operations. Perry & Lane usually sent its tobacco to England in ships carrying the tobacco of other merchants as well; thus, the firm did not have to wait to fill an entire ship before sending tobacco to London. In part, success also came from being at the right place at the right time: demand for tobacco boomed in Europe, with tobacco imports to Great Britain rising from 350,000 pounds per year in the early 1630s to 28 million pounds annually by the late 1680s.

Upon Micaiah's death, control of the firm passed to his grandson (his son had died), Micajah Perry, then twenty-six years old. Trained as a clerk in a Philadelphia merchant house, Micajah proved unable to meet incursions of Scottish merchants into the Chesapeake tobacco trade. Under Micajah's leadership, the firm declined. Dealing more and more just with leading planters, the merchant house suffered from growing debt problems of the planters. In addition, Micajah came to prefer sending tobacco to London in his own ships, which proved an expensive mistake. Lacking full loads, the ships often sailed half-empty. Moreover, a decline in tobacco prices bit into the firm's profits. Noneconomic factors hurt the firm. Micajah diluted his energies by embarking on political careers. By the early 1730s the Perry house had slipped to fourth place as a London importer of tobacco, and two decades later Micajah died in poverty.

Changed market conditions, and an inability to adjust to them, were hardly unique to the Perry firm. Of the 177 firms or individuals importing tobacco into London in 1719, only 11 remained active in 1747. Ups and downs in economic standing characterized businesses in the preindustrial as well as industrial era. Risk was always present.

Important though it was, overseas trade was less vital than domestic commerce to the British economy. Domestic commerce was roughly three times greater in value than foreign trade in 1700. Domestic commerce was run by merchants operating on their own as single-owner proprietors or by merchants linked together as partners. These merchants were sedentary merchants. They lived in cities, where they had their offices, called countinghouses, the places where they kept their accounts. Some of the British merchants were general merchants engaged in all types of trade.

However, as their markets became larger and better integrated through transportation and financial improvements, more British merchants specialized in a manner similar to the Perrys. Merchants in Leeds, for instance, became famous for handling the cloth trade, building White Cloth Hall in 1755 to move their market indoors. It was in London that mercantile specialization went farthest. About two-thirds to three-quarters of Great Britain's empire and foreign trade passed through London in the early and mid-1700s, and this volume of trade allowed merchants to specialize by commodity and type of trade.

Some London merchants even left trade to specialize in providing services for businesses. Some went into banking; marine insurance grew up around Lloyd's coffeehouse; and stock brokers also first met in a coffeehouse, later setting up business in the London Stock Exchange in 1802. By the 1770s a London money market was developing, along with a group of specialist bill brokers. Here may be seen the origins of what became known as the City of London, an area of banks, insurance companies, and other businesses providing financial services located within the heart of London. Serving primarily firms involved in overseas trade, the City developed somewhat independently of British industry and in the twentieth century was accused by some for not providing enough financing for their country's manufacturers.

To handle their growing volume of business, English merchants refined techniques developed by Italian merchants in the Middle Ages. While some merchants continued to rely upon single-entry bookkeeping, an increasing number used double-entry, in which every transaction was recorded twice, in one place as a debit, in another as a credit. By periodically balancing their accounts, merchants could determine their financial situation. Merchants also used bills of exchange, written agreements between buyers and sellers of goods, as financial instruments by which they could handle transactions with each other. The seller drafted a bill for the goods telling when and how the goods would be paid for and sent the bill to the purchaser. The purchaser wrote on the bill that he accepted its terms, thus endorsing it. If endorsed by a reputable merchant, a bill of exchange might pass as currency through the hands of many different people before being redeemed and paid off. Promissory notes, written promises to pay a sum of money at a fixed time to a certain individual, were similar. Samples, as in wheat and woolen goods, helped rationalize trade by allowing merchants to know ahead of time the exact nature of goods they would receive in trade. All of these methods were important, not just in England, but in the New World as well, and they remain important to the present day.

English merchants did not have social status commensurate to their economic importance. Because of their feudal past, which associated power and prestige with the ownership of land, Englishmen held landed nobles and country squires in higher esteem than merchants. This carried over into politics. Landed wealth controlled Parliament until well into the nineteenth century. Trade and manufacturing were underrepresented. However, too much can be made of the division between land and trade, for the line blurred as the 1700s progressed. The landed gentry engaged in commercial activity, mining coal and iron on many of the great estates, and cutting forests for charcoal for use as a fuel. Moreover, by buying land and country homes, merchants could mingle with some of the gentry. It was a reasonably fluid situation, with a fair amount of intermarriage between the different groups. Only at the very top of British society did strict social divisions remain intact.

Colonial American Merchants

As in England, the merchant was the most important business leader in the North American colonies. The economies of the colonies were closely linked to those of Great Britain and Europe. The Atlantic Ocean acted as a bridge linking Europe, America, and Africa in a transatlantic economy, and the colonial merchants, together with their British counterparts, held this transatlantic economy together.

The Colonial American merchants were similar to English merchants in important ways. Most of the wealthiest merchants were sedentary merchants living in urban centers where they had their countinghouses. Most operated by themselves or more commonly as partners with each other. Joint-stock companies were not important in trade, although some did exist in other fields. Like their British counterparts, American merchants used bills of exchange, promissory notes, some double-entry bookkeeping (although most Colonial American merchants got by with single-entry bookkeeping), and samples in their work.

There was, however, a major difference between British and Colonial American merchants. Colonial American merchants, more than their British counterparts, were general merchants, not specialists. Colonial American merchants handled many different types of goods and took part in a wide range of commercial activities. Despite the growth of a commercial economy in North America, markets were still too small and too fragmented to allow much in the way of mercantile specialization. Only in the late 1700s and early 1800s, and even then only in the largest cities, did American merchants begin to specialize. In Philadelphia, for example, the most important merchants became increasingly specialized from the 1750s.

Most Colonial American merchants worked both as exporters and importers. In selling products in the colonies they acted as wholesalers and retailers; they imported goods from abroad and either resold them to smaller country merchants and peddlers or sold them directly to consumers through their own city stores. Colonial American merchants also engaged in many other business activities: owning ships (often as partners), loaning money to each other (Robert Morris, a Philadelphia merchant, started America's first bank in 1781), marine insurance (the merchant Thomas Willing formed America's first insurance company in 1757), real estate speculation, and, as in England, investing in mining and manufacturing.

Aaron Lopez was a leading general merchant. He came to the colonies in the early 1750s to escape the persecution of Jews then occurring in Portugal, settling in Newport, Rhode Island, where other family members were well established. From the outset, ties of family and friendship helped Lopez get ahead and allowed him to reduce his business risks. Using capital borrowed from other Jewish families, he sold soap to New York merchants and candles to Philadelphians, and he soon reached out by dealing in pewter, indigo, sugar, and tea. In the 1760s and 1770s Lopez added rum, textiles, naval stores, hardware, slaves, and many other goods to his list of exports and imports. As more of his trade went to England and the West Indies, rather than to Colonial America, Lopez came to rely on foreign agents, often family members, whom he sent abroad. While this approach to business, a trust in friends and family to overcome poor communications, usually worked well, it occasionally backfired. In 1767 Lopez sent his son-in-law to handle business in Jamaica, only to recall the man, who proved incompetent, two years later.

Most of Lopez's ventures prospered, leading him to diversify his interests further. His trading establishment at Newport came to include a privately owned wharf, a large warehouse, a retail store, and his business offices. Lopez owned thirty ships, either by himself or as a partner with other merchants, and controlled a large whaling fleet. He entered early forms of manufacturing—candle making, rum distilling, and shoemaking. At his death in 1782 he was a veritable merchant prince.

Colonial American merchants were among the most important social and political leaders of their day, in sharp contrast to the lower status of British merchants. Most colonists held the large sedentary merchants in high esteem and deferred to them as the natural leaders of society. Several factors accounted for the high social status of Colonial American merchants. America did not have a feudal tradition emphasizing landed wealth. Moreover, Puritanism, and more generally Protestantism, placed a high value upon hard work and, within reason, the acquisition of wealth. Many colonists viewed material success on earth as a sign of God's favor, an indication that a person was destined for heaven rather than hell in the afterlife. Finally, most colonists viewed the wilderness condition of the American continent as an obstacle to be conquered in wrenching a living from the earth. Colonists looked upon business activities and farming favorably, because they viewed them as tools by which nature might be subdued.

Building on the high esteem in which they were held, leading Colonial American merchants sought to set themselves apart as a social elite by wearing stylish clothing, living in luxurious homes, having their portraits painted by European artists, and wearing swords as a mark of gentility. Their high social status often involved the merchants in politics, for farmers and artisans (skilled workers) looked to them for leadership. Merchants were active in town and city politics as members of boards of selectmen (city councils), colonial assemblies (legislatures), and advisory bodies to colonial governors.

Tokugawa Merchants

Like Great Britain and North America, Japan possessed a commercial economy before industrialization; and, once again, it was largely merchants who knit this economy together. Tokugawa Japan had a wide variety of merchants: peddlers, rural merchants serving local trade, and big-city merchant-financiers in Kyoto, Edo, and Osaka handling interregional commerce.

Osaka had long been one of Japan's leading commercial centers, but in the Tokugawa period it emerged as the undisputed center of wholesale trades in the nation. By 1715 there were 5,655 wholesale merchants in Osaka. The *daimyo* sent rice collected as taxes for sale in Osaka and then for shipment to consumption centers like Edo. As trade routes became better established, the Osaka merchants began handling a wider variety of goods — salt, cotton, and tea. With large, better connected markets, the Osaka merchants were able to specialize. Merchants who had originally dealt in many different products at wholesale and retail concentrated on the wholesale trade in only one product. While specializing, the Osaka merchants also loaned money to the *daimyo*, first as advances on rice sales but soon as long-term loans. In conducting their businesses, the Osaka merchants were similar to their English and Colonial American counterparts in that they used bills of exchange and samples. However, few employed double-entry bookkeeping.

Even more than in Great Britain or Colonial America, business was organized around merchant houses in Japan. Japanese merchant houses were more than simply business arrangements. They were also kinship matters. Merchant houses included people related by family ties: the house head and his wife, the elder son and his wife, and any younger unmarried sons and daughters. Sons might also be adopted into the merchant house. Those working in the merchant house progressed up a ladder of promotions from apprentice to clerk. As merchant houses developed, the more successful ones came to consist of a main house in Osaka and branch houses throughout Japan, all woven together by family ties. As in the West, personal ties helped reduce risks in doing business. Blood relatives and close friends could be trusted, a necessity in a time of slow communications. Reinforcing the family nature of the merchant houses were rules and constitutions, which were commonly written down in the 1700s. These gave the houses an identity and sense of historical continuity beyond that of their individual members.

Today one of Japan's leading companies, Mitsui began as a merchant house in the Tokugawa period. Mitsui Sokubei, a samurai uprooted by the conflicts of the late 1500s and early 1600s, renounced his family's samurai status in 1616 to become a merchant and the founder of the House of Mitsui. Moving to a town just east of Kyoto, he and his family entered the brewing and money-lending businesses.

Expansion began when Sokubei's eldest son moved to Edo to open a clothing store called Echigoya. Hachirobei, Sokubei's third son, also moved to Edo with his own six sons in the 1670s and provided the impetus needed to turn the clothing business into a success. He did so by emphasizing a rapid turnover on his stock, for which he allowed only cash payments, a new concept in Japan. Hachirobei also broke new ground in his insistence upon selling at fixed prices and his willingness to sell in small quantities. The Echigoya store soon became the most fashionable and successful clothing store in Edo. Beginning his company's long-standing ties with the government, Hachirobei became a supplier of cloth to the shogun in 1687. He also soon opened prosperous shops in Kyoto and Osaka.

From these mercantile origins, Hachirobei took the Mitsuis into the business of money changing with the establishment of an exchange brokerage in Edo in 1683 and with similar exchanges in Kyoto and Osaka within another eight years. By 1691 the House of Mitsui had also become an official money changer to the Tokugawa government's treasury.

His successors built upon Hachirobei's foundations to expand Mitsui's operations. By 1740 the House of Mitsui had a well-developed structure. Members of the main, or headquarters, house, the eldest son's establishment, held regular meetings to set company policies and to distribute operating funds and capital to the branch houses and stores. The eleven branch houses, in turn, made regular payments to the headquarters house. A fifteen-step hierarchy of advancement from beginning apprentice to the highest levels of management provided a road to the top for members of the House of Mitsui. Promotion to the sixth rank depended on seniority, but beyond that level personal performance became important. Apprentices, who started at age twelve, severed all ties with the outside world and were brought up according to the rules of the house.

Diversified in its business interests and fortunate in possessing shrewd managers, Mitsui prospered. The government recognized Mitsui's success by allowing the company to establish a shop in Yokohama to trade with Western merchants in 1859, and the House of Mitsui successfully weathered the opening of Japan to the West and made the transition from preindustrial to industrial times. Not all merchant houses were so fortunate. Most, in fact, failed to make the transition to new ways of doing business in later times. Too inflexible, too specialized, and lacking the government ties the Mitsuis possessed, they failed.

Yet despite their business successes, the Mitsuis, once they had relinquished their samurai status, dropped in social esteem. Even more than was the case in Great Britain, merchants failed to participate fully in politics and society in Tokugawa Japan, for orthodox thinking relegated merchants to positions subordinate to other groups in society. Much the same was true of China. In Japan and China Confucianism dominated social thought and relations. It held that the physical world was based upon an inherently perfect order. Only when people lost sight of the order of things did disorder appear. Rulers, in particular, were supposed to prevent disorder. In Japan, in particular, social harmony was seen as depending on the maintenance of proper relations between four different groups—the samurai warrior-administrators, peasants, artisans, and merchants. Merchants were looked down upon, because, unlike the samurai, they sought private profits rather than the public good and because, unlike the peasants or artisans, they produced no tangible crops or products.

The Japanese view, compared to those in Great Britain and America, was a static conception of society. How did the merchants deal with it? There was a considerable amount of crossing of the line separating samurai from merchant, especially in the 1590s through the 1640s, much of the crossing being done by intermarriage. The Mitsuis voluntarily gave up samurai status to become merchants. On the other hand, Iwasaki Yataro, who began life as the son of a peasant, purchased samurai status and went on to found Mitsubishi. Nonetheless, there was not as much social mobility as in Colonial America or Great Britain.

In Japan, merchants, joined by samurai, developed their own distinctive urban culture. In certain districts in Japan's leading cities there developed centers of entertainment, "floating worlds," called *ukiyo*. These were places where merchants and samurai could temporarily mingle almost as equals, places where social distinctions based upon birth or status meant little. The most famous were Yoshiwara of Edo, Shinmachi of Osaka, and Shimabara of Kyoto. The floating worlds abounded in theaters, teahouses, public baths, restaurants, and brothels. New art forms and types of entertainment grew up for the merchants. The kabuki theater, which featured more action than the traditional Noh drama, developed in the 1600s. Puppetry that told stories was very popular in the 1700s. Woodblock prints pictured all sorts of scenes from daily life. One famous series of prints illustrated life along the Tokaido Road from Kyoto to Edo. A new type of poetry, the seventeen-syllable haiku, evolved from earlier forms of verse.

Additional Business People

While merchants were of prime importance in knitting together localities, regions, and nations in preindustrial times, other types of business people were also significant. Local storekeepers, often tied to the larger merchants by credit arrangements, sold goods at retail. They bought the goods displayed on the shelves of their shops from the merchants at wholesale, paying for them with agricultural products taken in trade from farmers, who lacked money with which to pay for the goods they wanted. Even the larger merchants found themselves accepting payment in kind. Thomas Hancock, the leading Boston merchant of the 1750s, accepted honey, wheat, whale oil, and lumber from shopkeepers with whom he did business. The shopkeepers, in turn, had accepted those goods from their customers in payment for their shop purchases. Nor was this situation limited to the West. In China, too, there were village peddlers, rural markets, big-city markets, and merchants controlling high finance (such as the merchants of Huizhou).

Whether making pottery in Burslem or cotton textiles in Izumi, artisans were important to the economies beginning to make the shift from preindustrial to industrial times. Upon their output depended a growing production of consumer goods, and from their beginnings fully developed industrialization soon arose. Artisans often became early-day manufacturers, especially in the United States, but in Great Britain and Japan as well (perhaps a bit less so in China). Artisans often worked long, hard hours, but the rhythm of that work differed from that of industrial work. Artisanal work was more episodic than industrial work. Artisans might labor twelve or more hours per day for four or five days and then take several days off work, what they called Saint Monday or Saint Tuesday. By contrast, industrial work was more uniform and disciplined, with the demands of machinery setting the pace.

Finally, there were the farmers. Except in frontier areas, where poor transportation limited their access to markets (as in northern Honshu or parts of the American West), most farmers were commercially minded. They were more and more acting as business people. Thus, one scholar wrote twenty-eight books advising Japanese farmers how to be more productive in the early and mid-1800s, stressing the advantages of higher yields, lower costs, and higher prices. In fact, the market-oriented farmers in all the nations we are considering in this book were ready for the demands of industrialization. Used to the discipline of time and consumer-oriented, they were well prepared to become industrial workers and the consumers of industrial products.

Salt Making in Zigong, China

Artisanal industries were, on occasion, large and complex. Such was the case of salt making in the Zigong area of China from the mid-1700s into the late 1800s. This salt making may rightly be classified as preindustrial because it did not use steam power until 1913. It has sometimes been argued that preindustrial Chinese lacked the entrepreneurial drive needed for economic modernization and that the heavy hand of the imperial government, as seen in many actions by Qing rulers, greatly retarded economic development. The positive experiences of the Zigong salt makers cast doubt on both of those assertions. Located just north of the Yangzi River in Sichuan Province, the Zigong area had the raw materials needed for salt making: subsurface brine (salt water), underground natural gas, and deposits of coal. Private enterprises held together the many steps in making salt and at their height in the late nineteenth century employed around 500,000 people. This employment made Zigong a leading nonagricultural area in China.

Developed without much in the way of Western influence prior to 1913, the salt companies are an example of successful artisanal indigenous businesses in China before industrialization. In this business growth, the state did not limit the movement of capital or workers, nor did it restrain the efforts of the business leaders. In fact, in the industry's early years, salt making developed in a time of relative political stability. While no national laws enforced property rights and contracts, national and local governments effectively enforced traditional practices in such matters. Then, too, taxes were usually reasonable, predictable, and sometimes negotiable. On the other hand, the government did little to provide an infrastructure, such as improved roads or water transportation, which would have benefited Zigong's salt trade — unlike the situations in Japan and America, where government aid to transportation was extensive.

New technologies using iron drills powered by as many as ten men apiece both deepened brine wells and allowed an expansion in the production of natural gas. Brine and gas wells soon reached depths of up to 3,000 feet. Systems of wooden pulleys, wheels, and containers suspended from derricks by bamboo cables and powered by teams of water buffalo lifted the brine from the wells to the surface. The brine and gas wells were found close together, but not always immediately adjacent to each other. So Chinese entrepreneurs found ways to transport the brine through bamboo pipes as much as six miles long, using pumps powered by water buffalo, to where the gas was located. Close to their wells the gas was used as a fuel, sometimes along with coal, to heat and evaporate the brine. Evaporation took place in large iron pans, which were continuously heated. Evaporation left salt, which was then packaged and sent to markets, most commonly by boat. As in other preindustrial economies, water transportation was the cheapest mode of transportation. The number of brine wells in Zigong rose from 298 in 1720 to 405 by the late nineteenth century, and the number of evaporation pans increased from 755 to 1,055 in the same period. The salt output of the Sichuan region more than tripled from 112 million pounds in 1850 to 390 million pounds annually by the 1890s, with over half of the salt coming from Zigong.

Many private companies arose to take advantage of opportunities and to limit the risks. Drilling companies leased land on which to drill for fixed terms, typically about twelve years. In these arrangements, the landowner contributed no funds for the drilling, which was the responsibility of the lessee(s), but did receive about one-quarter of the revenues from the sale of the brine. Lineage trusts, basically groups comprising extended families, provided most of the capital and expertise for the drilling. Through these trusts individuals and families pooled their resources to meet the capital expenses of salt making. As in so many preindustrial businesses worldwide, kinship and friendship lay at the heart of salt making in Zigong. However, in Zigong partnerships also sometimes brought together unrelated people to combine their capital. The partnerships had unlimited liability, a situation usually adhered to even when incorporation with the promise of limited liability became possible in 1904. In an unlimited liability partnership, each partner could be held liable for all of the partnership's debts. In an incorporated company or limited liability company, partners were not individually liable for the company's debts. If a company failed, investors could lose their investments in the company but could not be forced to pay the debts of the company. Salt making was originally a fragmented industry, with different groups drilling wells, operating wells, running and maintaining pipelines, owning evaporation operations, and selling salt—all linked together by a mix of customary agreements and written contracts.

However, over time concentration occurred. By the 1860s and 1870s four lineage groups controlled half of Zigong's salt production. Most groups had fortunes originally grounded in land ownership and gentry status in the region. Even more than for samurai in Tokugawa Japan, gentry standing was important for social status in Imperial China. It was gained by passing state-sponsored examinations on the classics. However, in Zigong the gentry, if not gentry elsewhere in China, increasingly got ahead through commerce, especially by vertically integrating the different steps in salt making. That is, each lineage trust came to own wells, pipelines, production facilities, and sales outlets. All profits were thus kept within the trust, and each part helped ensure stability of the others. The evaporating facilities of a trust could, for instance, be assured of their brine and gas from the trust's own wells and pipelines. This strategy was similar to vertical integration undertaken by many large American manufacturing businesses at about the same time, although there was no direct connection between the actions of the two groups of business leaders.

The lineage trusts also established new management structures. Just as British and Japanese merchant houses adopted written rules in the 1700s, the lineage trusts adopted sets of written management rules in the mid-1800s. Under the supervision of a general manager, the trust had a number of departments, such as countinghouses, procurement departments to buy supplies, and cash departments in charge of daily expenditures. At the level of individual wells and evaporating facilities there might be local counting-houses and departments. Sophisticated reporting and accounting helped hold the trusts together. In the absence of a governmental post office — very important for business development in the United States in early national times — the trusts had their own messenger services.

Political and technological changes eroded profits in salt making in Zigong in the twentieth century. The imperial government slapped new taxes on salt makers and took away the marketing of salt from the private companies, depriving them of a major source of profit, with both actions designed to help pay for mounting governmental expenses. When the Chinese replaced the imperial government with a republic in 1912, ending two thousand years of imperial rule, many of those taxes continued, as the Republic of China faced enormous debts requiring extensive revenues for their payment. More than that, when the Republic proved weak, regional warlords arose to exercise political power over much of China. Political disunity and internal conflict followed. Not until the 1930s was a new national government led by Chiang Kai-shek able to even partially extend its authority over Sichuan. Meanwhile, warlords placed large, often unpredictable taxes on salt makers. Two major technological innovations also changed the industry. One was the discovery of a new source of salt: underground rock salt, which could be dissolved in water pumped down into wells. Having a much higher salinity than the old-style brine, dissolved rock salt was easier to evaporate and less expensive to turn into salt. In addition, the use of steam-powered pumps to raise the rock-salt solution to the surface further lowered expenses. By the early 1930s salt rock accounted for 57 percent of Zigong's output of salt, with most of the salt-rock solution pumped from wells by steam power.

These changes gradually destroyed the power of the lineage trusts that had dominated salt making. Too complacent, the leaders of the lineage trusts were slow to move to rock salt and steam-powered pumps. New groups rose to power in Zigong salt making. For them, political networks (to help them try to avoid excessive taxation) and business networks were more important than vertical integration. Salt making once again became fragmented, with many different groups of partnerships and incorporated companies controlling its various steps. By the early 1930s only about 216,000 workers labored in Zigong's salt works, a decline by half in about fifty years. Except for the years of war with Japan (1937–45), when the Japanese occupied most of the other salt-making regions in China, making Zigong's salt especially valuable, salt making in Zigong never regained its late-nineteenth-century prominence.

In Zigong, then, lineage trusts and various types of networks long sufficed to raise capital for and manage companies engaged in the salt trade. However, in more capital-intensive industries arising from the mid-nineteenth century onward — railroads, steamship companies, cotton textile mills, and the like — these types of associations were not fully adequate and, arguably, may have hindered business development and economic growth.

Global Trade and Biotic Interchanges

If the development of merchant businesses was beginning to change the economic complexion of the world, the accompanying spread of trade fundamentally altered the globe's environmental makeup. European exploration, colonization, and trading activities brought innumerable changes to the world. Certainly one of the greatest consequences of global trade and exploration was the mixing of the world's biota — its flora and fauna, its plants and animals. Before the voyages of Columbus in the 1490s the biota of the Old and New Worlds had developed separately for millennia. From the 1490s, they became more and more intermixed, with very important consequences for people living in different regions.

The global interchange of plants and animals is best known with regard to Europe and the Americas. From the Americas, Europeans derived important new sources of food in the forms of vegetables and fruit, such as manioc, pumpkins, beans, tomatoes, and squash. Three new vegetables were of most importance. The white potato, native to the Andean highlands, went first to Europe and then from Europe was taken back to New England. It was this vegetable that, more than any other, allowed the population of Europe to increase in the 1700s and 1800s. Conversely, its failure could result in famine, as occurred in Ireland in the mid-1800s, resulting in massive immigration to the United States. Maize (corn) spread from the Americas to Europe and became an important new source of food. (However, when the

British referred to corn, as in the Corn Laws of the mid-1800s, they were actually talking about wheat.) Maize also spread to Africa, where it remains a staple crop today. Finally, tobacco, native to North America, became the major export of the Chesapeake colonies such as Virginia.

Even more in the way of flora and fauna traveled from Europe and the Canary Islands to the Americas. The list is long: wheat, sugar cane (used in making molasses and rum), chick peas, grapes, various types of melons, rice (originally from Asia), and bananas. The list also included Kentucky blue grass, daisies, and dandelions. Perhaps still more important was the movement of animals from Europe to America. Native Americans had few domesticated animals: the llama and alpaca, the guinea pig, the dog, and a few types of fowl. Europeans brought with them rats, horses, cattle, sheep and goats, chickens, and others. Perhaps most dramatic was the impact of the horse, which led to the creation of the mounted, nomadic Indian culture of the Great Plains in the 1600s, 1700s, and 1800s.

Most important, however, was the impact of disease. Native peoples in North and South America had no immunities to many European diseases, and their ranks were decimated by measles, mumps, and especially small pox. In Europe and Asia these diseases were associated with animal diseases. Thus, small pox was similar to chicken pox. People in Europe and Asia built up immunities to small pox by association with chickens, which carried chicken pox. Typically, well over half of a native population in the Americas was killed at its first exposure to small pox, often paving the way for their military defeat.

The mixture of flora and fauna was truly global, especially from the late 1700s onward, when Europeans and Americans fully explored the Pacific. European biota largely replaced the native biota of Australia and New Zealand in the 1800s and 1900s. One scholar has called this shift "ecological imperialism." Pacific Islanders were sickened and killed by the same European diseases as were Native Americans.

Changes in the Hawaiian Islands provide a good example of just how far-reaching such alterations were. The British explorer Captain James Cook "discovered" the islands in 1778, and soon diseases unintentionally brought in by westerners killed Hawaiians in large numbers. Small pox was, as elsewhere, most destructive. There were at least 300,000 Hawaiians in 1778. By 1900 just 90,000 remained. Captain Cook's men planted melons, onions, and pumpkins in 1778. Captain George Vancouver brought oranges, lemons, almonds, and grapes in 1792. Altogether, westerners introduced 111 plant species by 1840, including sixty-five fruits and vegetables.

By 1980 westerners had transplanted 5,000 species and varieties of plants. In addition, westerners brought in animals that multiplied to the point that they often became very destructive of Hawaiian plant life: goats, pigs, cattle, sheep, and horses. European rats came as well. Changes were great, with over 90 percent of the Hawaiian landscape transformed by the flora and fauna introduced by westerners. Most noticeable was the development of monoculture agriculture (farming dominated by one type of crop), the vast fields of sugar cane and pineapple that grew up in the nineteenth and early twentieth centuries. These were good cash crops, at least for a while, but they destroyed the subsistence economies of Hawaiians, led to their loss of land, and also, more recently, failed as parts of the Hawaiian economy, replaced by tourism.

Conclusions

This examination of preindustrial business systems must close with a word of caution. Even at the end of their preindustrial periods, no nation or region — much less the entire globe — possessed a fully integrated and developed economy. Regional specialization and domestic trade, while well under way, developed much more in later years. So, too, did urbanization and industrialization. Despite the development of commercial economies, the pace and volume of business were still slow and low when compared to what would soon come with industrialization. Thomas Hancock, the leading Boston merchant, ran his business with the aid of just a handful of clerks and sent out only about sixty-two letters each year.

For the preindustrial merchant, business was a very personal affair. Merchant firms were houses. Personal trust was more important than business organizations or managerial hierarchies in the conduct of economic affairs. This was a world of face-to-face personal contacts. Only through family and personal ties could the risks of doing business be limited. Communications and transportation, while improving, were still so primitive that merchants could not directly oversee ventures beyond their immediate locales. They had to trust others in distant markets and so relied on friends and family members to assist them in their business enterprises.

Similar economic situations led to similar business responses, but there were differences as well, resulting from the contrasts between the cultures and societies in which the business people operated. Many of the larger Japanese merchants, possessing fewer opportunities for the investment of their surplus funds — only the purchase of farm land and the making of loans — and having more routine businesses than their British or American counterparts, became conservative in their outlook, an attitude that left most of them ill-prepared to make the transition to industrialization. Lacking high social status, Japanese merchants did not take part in social or political affairs to the extent that Colonial American or British merchants did. Instead, Japanese merchants developed "floating worlds," to which there existed no real counterparts in Great Britain or North America.

Suggested Readings

Richard Grassby, *The Business Community of Seventeenth-Century England* (Cambridge, 1995), David Harris Sacks, *The Widening Gate: Bristol and the Atlantic Economy* (Berkeley, 1991), and Kenneth Morgan, *Bristol & the Atlantic Trade in the Eighteenth Century* (Cambridge, 1993), offer valuable insights into Great Britain's commercial and business practices. Edwin Perkins, *The Economy of Colonial America* (New York, 1988), Gary Walton and James Shepherd, *The Economic Rise of Early America* (Cambridge, 1979), and John J. McCusker and Russell R. Menard, *The Economy of British America, 1607–1789* (Chapel Hill, 1985), do the same for Colonial America. The essays comprising Marius Jansen and Gilbert Rozman, eds., *Japan in Transition: From Tokugawa to Meiji* (Princeton, 1986), and Chie Nakane and Shinzaburo Oishi, eds., *Tokugawa Japan: The Social and Economic Antecedents of Modern Japan* (Tokyo, 1990), examine alterations taking place in preindustrial Japan. Conrad Totman, *Early Modern Japan* (Berkeley, 1993), is a standard overview of Tokugawa history. For a case study of one domain, see Philip C. Brown, *Central Authority & Local Autonomy in the Formation of Early Modern Japan: The Case of Kaga Domain* (Stanford, 1993). On salt making in Zigong, see Madeleine Zelin, *The Merchants of Zigong: Industrial Entrepreneurship in Early Modern China* (New York, 2005). On earlier salt making, see Ping-Ti Ho, "The Salt Merchants of Yang-Chou: A Study of Commercial Capitalism in Eighteenth-Century China," *Harvard Journal of Asiatic Studies*, 17 (June 1954), 130–68. On economic matters during the Ming dynasty, see Ray Huang, *Taxation and Government Finance in Sixteenth-Century Ming China* (Cambridge, 1974). Also valuable is Helen Dunstan, *State or Merchant? Political Economy and Political Process in 1740s China* (Cambridge, Mass., 2006).

On the development of a transatlantic economy, see Jacob M. Price, *Perry of London: A Family and Firm on the Seaborne Frontier, 1615–1753* (Cambridge, Mass., 1992), Bernard Bailyn, *Atlantic History: Concept and Contours* (Cambridge, Mass., 2005), Carole Shammas and Elizabeth Mancke, eds., *The Creation of the Atlantic World* (Baltimore, 2005), and Peter A. Coclanis, ed., *The Atlantic Economy during the Seventeenth and Eighteenth Centuries: Organization, Practice, and Personnel* (Columbia, 2005).

On global ecological changes, see Jared Diamond, *Guns, Germs, and Steel: The Fates of Human Societies* (New York, 1998), Alfred D. Crosby Jr., *The Columbian Exchange: Biological and Cultural Consequences of 1492* (Westport, 1972), and Alfred D. Crosby Jr., *Ecological Imperialism: The Biological Expansion of Europe, 900–1900* (Cambridge, 1986).

The Many Paths
to Industrialization

A worldwide Industrial Revolution beginning in the 1600s and 1700s in Great Britain, and spreading to other nations in the 1800s and 1900s, reshaped business around the globe. Industrialization was a major divide in the history of the world, for a very important result was an acceleration of economic growth. Even in Western Europe before 1700 per capita income growth had been slow, about one-tenth of 1 percent per year, at which rate it doubled only every 630 years. Between 1820 and 1990 income per capita increased eightfold in Great Britain, fifteen times in Germany, seventeenfold in the United States, and twenty-five times in Japan. A broad-based change, industrialization affected numerous forms of production and distribution. In Great Britain the production of toys in Birmingham, everything from buttons to trinkets, was as affected as the making of cotton textiles in Lancashire. In Japan changes in silk reeling were as significant as those in steelmaking.

Industrialization so fundamentally altered key business practices that the history of business can be divided into two basic time periods: preindustrial business, dealt with in chapter 1, and industrial business, the topic of much of the remainder of this book. Still, business changes rarely occurred overnight, and new ways of doing things almost never completely replaced traditional production methods in just a few years. Older ways of conducting business long coexisted with the new, in some cases down to the present day. Industrialization was a complex process that worked itself out in different ways in different regions and nations. There was no single, uniform, or "correct" path to industrialization.

Nonetheless, over time certain changes occurred as industrialization took hold and spread, especially alterations in the nature of the work process and the ways by which laborers related to their jobs. Machines — tireless, regular, rapid, and precise — supplemented and replaced human labor in making products. Moreover, labor was often concentrated in central locations called factories, and in factories the tasks of workers became more and more specialized. As these alterations took place, workers lost some of their control over work processes to business people who owned the factories. Machines and factory owners came increasingly to set the pace of work and to determine how jobs would be performed. Yet, even so, considerable differences existed, and they continue to exist, from nation to nation and from industry to industry.

Political Frameworks

As we have already seen with regard to preindustrial economic growth, political and economic developments go hand in hand. So it was with industrialization. The governments of Great Britain, the United States, Japan, and China spurred industrialization to greater and lesser degrees. They did so by removing barriers to economic growth, what might be called a permissive or indirect role, and by taking actions to stimulate industrialization more directly, what can be labeled a direct role. The governments indirectly encouraged economic development and industrialization by providing stable political frameworks within which economic growth could occur. The political apparatus needed for the development of local, regional, and national markets was especially important. By contrast, political disunity and fragmented markets continued to hinder economic growth, including industrialization, in Germany. In terms of direct aid, the governments differed considerably, and the differences were related in a general way to the order in which each country industrialized. The British government provided the least amount of direct aid, the Japanese the most, with the United States and Chinese governments in the middle of this continuum.

Great Britain

Great Britain possessed a strong national government by the early 1700s, whose existence meant that Great Britain had a standard currency, legal system, and system of taxation. It also ensured that the country had no internal customs barriers or feudal tolls. Strong regional markets, and later a national market, developed, and these domestic markets were more important than foreign markets were for England's industrial growth. By way of comparison, France was still divided into three major areas by customs barriers. Germany was not even one nation. The Prussian monarchy tried to introduce free trade among its royal lands in 1797, but failed. Only in 1834 did three dozen states form the first German customs union, and only in 1871 did Germany become a unified nation.

Parliamentary action spurred economic growth and industrialization indirectly in Great Britain. Laws ensured that taxation fell mainly upon landed wealth, not capital which could be used to build up industry. The Bubble Act of 1720 outlawed many joint-stock companies, but capital accumulation remained possible through the formation of unincorporated joint-stock companies. Moreover, various types of trust agreements permitted stock to pass from one generation to the next. New limited liability laws that passed in 1856 and 1862 reversed the Bubble Act and made capital accumulation easier. Even so, most British companies remained partnerships, not limited companies or corporations. Family businesses remained very important in Great Britain into the twentieth century. The British government did much less in terms of direct aid. It did little to finance canals or railroads, for instance, activities in which the American and Japanese governments engaged. Nor did it set up model factories, as did the Japanese government.

The United States

The United States, of course, did not exist before the American Revolution. Each colony had been part of the British Empire, a situation that had economic as well as political repercussions. Until the 1750s and 1760s there had been relatively few economic or political ties between the colonies; stronger ties existed between the individual colonies and England. With the Declaration of Independence in 1776 and the American Revolution (ended by the Treaty of Paris in 1783) this situation changed abruptly. The colonies were no longer part of the British Empire. Now as states they had to devise a national government.

Americans set up their first national government under the Articles of Confederation in 1781. Under these Articles the national government was weak, reflecting the fear the colonists harbored against the strong British Parliament and king. There was no president or federal court system. The national legislature could not levy taxes, regulate trade, or deal with general welfare measures. However, some Americans, especially merchants and other business leaders, soon came to think that this type of government was too weak and that its weakness was retarding the development of their businesses. Merchants wanted a stronger national government to regulate trade between the states and to settle land disputes between the states. Merchants wanted help in expanding overseas trade, including a navy supported by taxes. Manufacturers wanted tariffs to limit the importation of foreign, especially British, goods.

As a result of these and other desires a convention was called to revise the Articles of Confederation in 1787, but instead of simply revising the Articles the delegates wrote the Constitution, which was adopted in 1789. The Constitution provided for a strong national government, broken only once during the Civil War of the 1860s. The Constitution created the presidency and a federal court system, which in the early 1800s became superior to the state courts. The Constitution increased greatly the powers of Congress. Perhaps most important for business was the commerce clause that empowered Congress to regulate interstate trade, commerce crossing state lines. This clause prevented state governments from setting up internal barriers to the movement of goods within the United States (such as tariffs on goods passing from New York to Pennsylvania), something very important for business people trying to develop more than local markets. For the first time, too, Congress had the power to tax. Congress used taxes to support, among other things, a navy; and the navy, in turn, defended American trade around the globe.

However, not all the legal changes affecting business occurred at the national level, for the United States possessed a federal system of government, with powers divided between the national and the state governments. Sometimes there was conflict between the two levels of government; but, for the most part, legal changes occurring at the state level also aided the development of business. State incorporation laws, like Britain's national limited liability laws, gave investors insulation from the debts of the corporations in which they invested, thus encouraging them to pool their capital for business ventures. The laws also gave corporations longevity, for unlike partnerships, corporations did not have to be dissolved if one investor left. New York passed the first general state incorporation law in 1811, and by 1860 all industrial states had some sort of general incorporation law. By 1904 corporations accounted for 75 percent of all industrial production in the United States.

Unlike in Great Britain, in the United States all governmental levels—federal, state, and local—offered direct aid to stimulate business growth. Most important was governmental financing of transportation improvements. Conflict between the North and South prevented the development of a truly national system of transportation, except the Post Office. Nonetheless, the federal government financed the building of the National Road across the Appalachian Mountains, funded the construction of several canals, and provided much of the financing for pathbreaking railroads—the Illinois Central in the 1850s and the Union Pacific-Central Pacific, America's first transcontinental, in the 1860s. Local and state governments provided even more aid, as they sought economic advantages over each other. New York financed the very important Erie Canal, completed in 1825, for example. The City of Baltimore provided much of the funding for the Baltimore & Ohio Railroad. Altogether, between 1815 and 1860 about 60 percent of the investment in transportation facilities in the United States came from governmental sources. All this support was needed for the growth of large regional markets and later a national market.

Japan and China

Tokugawa Japan possessed a decentralized military government. As the leader of his nation, the shogun, acting in theory on behalf of the emperor, provided Japan with some sense of unity. However, this was not a modern national government. It was based more upon personal bonds connecting the shogun, the *daimyo*, and the samurai than upon institutions. This situation changed with the Meiji Restoration of 1868 and with the formation of a new governmental system in following decades.

Much of the initial impetus for change came from outside forces. Americans and other foreigners had desired for years to trade with Japan, and in 1853 and 1854 Commodore Matthew Perry steamed into Tokyo Bay with his "black ships" of the American navy to force open Japanese ports. In 1854 two ports, and in later years additional ones, were opened to trade. Foreign merchants gained additional advantages. A 5 percent limit was placed on the tariffs the Japanese were allowed to charge on goods imported into Japan. Moreover, foreign nations demanded and received the right to extraterritoriality, according to which their citizens were governed by foreign, not Japanese, law while they lived in Japan.

The forced opening of their nation sorely troubled many Japanese, especially those in some of the domains on the fringes far from the shogun's seat of power in Edo — Tosa, Choshu, and Satsuma. It appeared that the shogun had failed to defend Japan in his military duties to the emperor. Samurai in these regions united against the shogun around the twin slogans of "honor the emperor" and "expel the barbarians." Shogunal forces failed to win military victories in battles in the mid-1860s. Then, in 1868 in the Meiji Restoration, the rebels deposed the shogun and, in theory at least, returned the emperor to power. Thus, the Meiji period in Japanese history, the years 1868 through 1912, is named after the Emperor Meiji who reigned during those years.

Once in power, the young, relatively economically humble samurai from

Choshu, Tosa, and Satsuma realized that the only practical way to achieve their goal of ridding their land of foreigners lay in building up the economic and military might of Japan. Their new slogan became "rich country, strong army." This aim, in turn, could, they thought, be accomplished only by borrowing from the West. Western naval bombardments of two Japanese ports in 1863 and 1864 showed that the West was too strong to be excluded immediately by force.

As part of their effort to transform Japan, the Meiji leaders set up a new system of government, step by step. In 1871 the old domains ruled by *daimyo* were abolished, and the country was instead divided into prefectures directly controlled by Tokyo (Edo became known as Tokyo in the early Meiji period). The *daimyo*, replaced by governors, were given lump sum payments in government bonds, and these payments became an important source of capital for new businesses. Universal military service began in 1873, and a national army based upon the German model was formed. In 1876 the stipends of the samurai were abolished, and, like the *daimyo*, the samurai were paid off in lump sums of government bonds. In 1885 a cabinet system of national government under a prime minister came into being, and in the same year a modernized civil service was put in place. Finally, in 1889 a constitution was promulgated as a gift to the people from the emperor. The constitution emphasized the prerogatives of the emperor and that the emperor was the source of authority in Japan, thus stressing the duties of Japanese subjects to their nation. The constitution created a two-house assembly called the Diet. The lower house, the House of Representatives, was elective; an upper house, the House of Peers, was appointed.

Japan's new national government gave indirect aid to industrialization and business growth. In contrast to the United States, where state and local governments were as important as the national government, in Japan most of the aid came from the new national government. In 1868 the Japanese government abolished road inspection stations and guardhouses separating the domains, thus ending political barriers to internal trade. The government provided for population mobility in ending the four-class system of samurai, peasant, artisan, and merchant in the same year and allowed peasants to grow whatever crops they desired in 1871. Certain laws stimulated business enterprise. In 1872 and 1876 the government made laws allowing the establishment of joint-stock banks, and by 1879 some 153 were in existence. The government also set up the Bank of Japan in 1882 with the sole privilege of issuing money and acting as a central bank. The passage of the General Incorporation Act of 1893, which was similar in its intent to the British limited liability laws of 1856 and 1862 and the American state incorporation laws, led to the formation of joint-stock companies worth 1 billion yen by 1916.

Direct aid, under the slogan of "develop industry and promote enterprise," took more forms than in Great Britain or the United States. In the 1870s the national government built the first railroads so necessary for internal trade, a Tokyo-Yokohama line and a line connecting Kyoto, Kobe, and Osaka. Most lines built in the 1880s and 1890s were constructed by private companies, but in 1906 much of Japan's railroad system was nationalized. The government also provided subsidies to ocean shipping companies and to shipbuilders. In 1896 state subsidies were given to Japanese shipyards to produce vessels for foreign trade. Then, too, the government encouraged Japanese to study abroad and brought foreigners into Japan, 500 by 1872, to help modernize the nation.

Most different from the situations in Great Britain or the United States, in the 1870s the Japanese government built and operated pilot or demonstration plants or factories in fields ranging from mining to shipbuilding to cotton spinning to cement making and to the production of glass. How important were these ventures? In silk reeling the government's model factory at Tomioka was a failure. In cotton spinning a large Osaka mill set up with private capital in 1883 was more important as a model than the smaller government plants. Financed by ninety-five shareholders, 60 percent of whom were Osaka and Tokyo merchants, the Osaka mill showed a profit from its first year of operations. Thus, while significant in some fields, such as iron and steel making, the importance of the government's pilot enterprises should not be overstressed.

In the pilot factories and other matters the Japanese government overreached itself, and in the 1880s the government entered a period of retrenchment in its economic activities, the "Matsukata Deflation," named after Finance Minister Matsukata Masayoshi. By 1896 the government had sold nearly all of its pilot plants, keeping only several arsenals, naval shipyards, a military woolen factory, and Yawata Iron and Steel.

The Meiji government's modernization efforts strengthened Japan in its dealings with other nations. In 1899 Great Britain relinquished the right to extraterritoriality for its citizens in Japan, and other nations soon followed suit. In 1911 Japan won back full control over its tariffs on imported goods. Japan also began building a commercial and territorial empire in Asia. In 1879 Japan gained what it considered clear recognition from China of its claims over Okinawa and the Ryukyu Islands and turned them into a prefecture. In 1876 the Japanese navy forced Korea to open its ports to trade, a move that brought Japan into conflict with China; and in 1894–95 Japan defeated China in the Sino-Japanese War. China ceded Taiwan to Japan, along with some other territories. Further expansion occurred in the twentieth century. Japan defeated Russia in the Russo-Japanese War of 1904–5 and as a result acquired control over Korea, the Liaodong Peninsula of China, Russian railroads in southern Manchuria, and the southern half of Sakhalin Island. In the First World War Japan took over many of Germany's territorial possessions and economic rights in China and the Pacific.

Like the Japanese government, the Chinese government sought at times to encourage economic modernization. The government sponsored a "self-strengthening" movement between 1861 and 1895 that aimed at providing China with the economic and military muscle to resist Western and Japanese imperialistic ventures. As we shall see in a later chapter, this nascent modernization plan had some notable successes, setting the stage for further economic advances in the twentieth century. It even foreshadowed, perhaps, Communist Party efforts at state control of business through state enterprises after 1949. However, when compared to the more wholehearted and longer-lasting Japanese government efforts to encourage industrialization, the Chinese government's actions were puny and less productive of change. Then, too, political disunity in China's early Republic years of the 1910s and 1920s hindered Chinese economic development.

Government, Business, and Industrialization

Strong national governments provided political frameworks conducive to economic and industrial growth, especially in Great Britain, the United States, and Japan. Either indirectly or directly the national governments stimulated industrial growth and business development. As latecomers to industrialization, when compared to Great Britain, the United States and Japan found it necessary to rely more on government to aid in economic growth. In Germany, another nation to industrialize later than Great Britain, organizations aided businesses as they industrialized. Large universal banks and trade associations or cartels were of special importance. Both America and Japan used government funding to build much of their infrastructures, especially mechanized transportation networks, needed for the creation of domestic markets. The Japanese government of early Meiji times tried to go further through its model factories, but the government's actual accomplishments should not be overemphasized. In terms of its achievements, the Japanese government was not much more important than the governments—federal, state, and local—in the United States. National governments were also active in opening overseas markets for industrial goods, especially in the cases of Great Britain and Japan (foreign markets became important for America's industrial goods only in the 1890s and later).

The Industrial Revolution

Often spurred by government aid, the Industrial Revolution was well under way across much of the globe by the late nineteenth century. The Industrial Revolution had begun much earlier in nations in which a confluence of factors—what might be called a "hot mix" of elements, ranging from the possession of raw materials to the availability of markets—favored its development. There was, in fact, more than one industrial revolution. The First Industrial Revolution, in which Great Britain led the world, involved making relatively technologically simple products such as cotton textiles, iron hardware, and the like. In the late nineteenth and early twentieth centuries a Second Industrial Revolution based on more scientifically and technologically complex industries such as alloyed steel, chemicals, electrical equipment, and automobiles developed. Even later in the twentieth century a Third Industrial Revolution and what is sometimes called a Fourth Industrial Revolution, both grounded in changes in communications and information handling, blossomed.

The Timing of Industrialization

There were signs of industrialization in Great Britain with regard to the use of new types of machinery and new sources of energy in the late 1600s and early 1700s. As early as 1705 primitive steam engines were pumping water out of coal mines, and four years later coking coal was being used to smelt iron. On the other hand, some forms of handicraft production continued with industrialization. The cotton textile industry was one of the first British industries to industrialize, but handloom weavers continued to be very important in this industry as late as the 1840s.

The consolidation of work in factories, which, along with the use of new types of machinery and sources of power, is often taken as one of the hallmarks of the First Industrial Revolution, took decades to accomplish. Factories appeared in some sectors of the economy well before they did in others, and even within a single field regional variations were substantial.

The centralization of work in factories offered employees and investors several advantages. Factories cut transportation costs associated with an earlier production method called the putting-out system. In the putting-out system merchants had distributed, or put out, raw materials to artisans (skilled workers), who made them into finished items in their homes. The merchants then collected the finished goods, such as shoes or cotton or woolen cloth, and found markets for them. Gathering workers in factories allowed business people to better supervise employees, thus permitting improvements in scheduling work processes and the quality of goods. Above all, from about the 1780s on factories allowed the use of new technologies — especially water-powered and steam-powered machinery — too big, too complex, and too expensive to be installed in a single cottage. Over time these advantages outweighed the disadvantages of factories — the expense of providing the fixed plant and its equipment, which increased fixed costs and correspondingly decreased manufacturers' abilities to respond quickly to market changes. Even so, large factories did not quickly sweep across Great Britain. Two-thirds of the nation's cotton textile mills of the mid-nineteenth century still employed fewer than fifty workers.

In other nations, too, industrialization was an uneven process, requiring many years to complete. Some industry existed in Colonial America, the production of pig iron, for example. By the 1820s and 1830s factory production was coming to dominate the making of cotton textiles in the United States, but not until the 1880s and later did mass production develop in many fields of manufacturing. In Japan, too, industrialization took many decades to mature. It is worth noting, as well, that for many years traditional industries such as silk reeling were among the mainstays of the Japanese economy. In China some industry, or at least proto-industry, existed as early as the Song dynasty (960–1126), as workshops in southern Chinese cities manufactured paper, ceramics, printed books, and metal articles.

In short, industrialization was a complex and lengthy process. No single, brief, five-year, ten-year, or even twenty-year period can be singled out as that time period in which any nation achieved sustained industrial growth. Nonetheless, industrialization was achieved over long periods of time, even as traditional methods of production lingered.

Nineteenth-century industrial advances were most pronounced in Great Britain, as that nation led the world in the First Industrial Revolution. By 1850 the British produced eight times as much iron, five times as much coal, and six times as much cloth as they had fifty years before. In 1830 the British mined 70 percent of the world's coal and produced 50 percent of its cotton and iron. Yet while industrialization was rapidly growing in importance, it was not fully developed even in Great Britain. In 1851 Britain's leading industry, cotton textiles, employed 292,000 people out of a population of 17 million, considerably less than the 390,000 employed in the traditional building trades.

The British made further industrial advances in the late nineteenth and early twentieth centuries. However, Great Britain fell behind the United States and Germany in the Second Industrial Revolution based on the production of technologically complex goods. By 1913, for example, 90 percent of the dyestuffs, 35 percent of the electro-technical goods, 30 percent of the pharmaceuticals, 29 percent of the machine tools, and 27 percent of the chemicals traded in world export markets were made in Germany.

Americans had made considerable industrial progress by 1860. Between 1810 and 1860 the value of manufactured goods produced in the United States rose from $200 million to $2 billion. Yet agriculture was still more important than industry to America's economy. It was in the late nineteenth and early twentieth centuries that the United States emerged as the world's leading industrial nation, especially in the products of the Second Industrial Revolution. Between 1869 and 1919 the value added by manufactures in the United States rose from $1.4 billion to $24 billion, a seventeenfold increase; and industry became more important than agriculture to the American economy.

Japan's industrial accomplishment was also marked. The proportion of Japan's workforce engaged in manufacturing rose from 4 percent in 1872 to 17 percent in 1920, and the capital invested in Japanese industries tripled in the same time period. By 1920 the manufacturing sector contributed nearly as much to Japan's economy as agriculture, and ten years later manufacturing contributed more. Yet for all the changes that had occurred in Japan, heavy industry was just really beginning to grow rapidly in 1920, fifty-two years after the Meiji Restoration. Japan was far from being the industrial superpower it would become after World War II.

Raw Materials

Many factors — including, as we have seen, government aid — contributed to economic growth and industrialization. The possession of raw materials, capital, labor, and markets all speeded the development of industry. It was the interaction of different elements, not one single factor, which led to the rise of industry in these nations. While all of the nations were similar in some of the elements favoring industrialization, there were significant differences as well; and those differences helped shape varied approaches to industrialization.

One reason Great Britain was the first nation in the world to industrialize was that it was endowed with or could easily trade for the raw materials upon which the First Industrial Revolution was based. England's cotton textile industry acquired raw cotton from America. Great Britain had iron ore and could purchase additional supplies from Scandinavia. Water power was used by the early cotton textile mills and charcoal in early ironmaking, but coal grew in importance as an energy source, due to the deforestation of large parts of Great Britain. The chemical industry was important for industrialization, for it supplied the detergents, bleaches, and dyes needed to finish cotton textiles; and England was fortunate in possessing the necessary chemicals. A final raw material the British had was food. Due to productivity gains in agriculture, Great Britain was self-sufficient in food production in the initial stages of industrialization.

An abundance of raw materials allowed the United States to catch up with and then, by 1900, surpass Great Britain as the world's leading industrial power. Cotton grown in the South; iron ore, first from eastern deposits and later from the Mesabi Range near Lake Superior; coal, especially Pennsylvania anthracite first put to use in the 1830s; and water power, which was more important than steam power into the 1850s, were among the most significant. Above all, the United States had wood, and wood was more important for initial industrialization in America than in England: it was used to make the frames and some parts of engines, as a fuel in ironmaking (more iron was made with charcoal than coking coal into the 1860s), and as a fuel for some steam engines. Like Great Britain, the United States had a climate that supported varied agriculture, and America was self-sufficient in food production.

The use of charcoal made from wood rather than coking coal as a fuel in smelting iron helps explain why America's iron industry was more dispersed than Britain's until the late nineteenth century. Charcoal was fragile and could not easily be transported long distances without breaking, thus rendering it useless as a fuel. Consequently, America's iron-smelting furnaces were for decades located across the Northeast and Midwest, where there were extensive hardwood forests. By comparison, Great Britain's iron industry, which used more easily transportable coal, more quickly became concentrated in just a few areas, especially in the Midlands.

Japan was not as well endowed with raw materials as Great Britain or the United States but possessed enough to start and sustain industrialization. Coal mines on Hokkaido and Kyushu were developed by the Meiji government and then sold to private enterprise. Japan also possessed iron mines, some of which the government sought to modernize and then sold to private companies. The government set up Yawata Iron and Steel in Kyushu in the 1890s. Japan possessed plenty of copper. The Sumitomo Besshi Copper mines had a long history, and Sumitomo modernized them with the help of French engineers in the Meiji period. A second source of copper lay in the Ani Copper mines, partially modernized by the Meiji government and then sold to a private entrepreneur. However, traditional industrial products were more important than coal, iron, and copper for industrial and economic growth in Meiji Japan. Silk made up 40 percent of Japan's exports in the years 1868 through 1893. Tea was another major export of the Meiji period. Like the United States, Japan depended heavily upon water power, readily available from many rivers, in the early stages of industrialization.

Capital

The availability of capital, the possession of funds to build the factories and machinery so necessary in putting raw materials to work, as much as its endowments of those materials, ensured Great Britain's early primacy as an industrial power. Initial industrialization did not require as much capital as might be imagined. Much of the machinery was simple in design, and Great Britain's capital supplies were adequate for these needs. Merchants often acted as partners to industrialists, as occasionally did commercial farmers with money to invest. Local banks were significant sources of capital, growing in importance from the 1840s by offering loans and extending overdrafts to nascent manufacturers. The number of such country banks rose from just a handful in 1750 to over 600 by 1810. Networks of kinship and friendship, often based on localities, were of prime importance in lending and investment. (By way of contrast, German industrialists depended more on a handful of large universal banks for their capital. These banks, in turn, played active managerial roles in the enterprises they funded. As a latecomer to industrialization, Germany simply did not have capital sources which were as fully developed and as diverse as Great Britain's.) Retained earnings, profits kept in a company and not paid out to investors as dividends, also became an important source of funds, especially for larger firms, as industrialization progressed.

Capital for American industry came from similar sources. Merchants in the northeastern cities who had made their way in foreign trade invested directly in manufacturing and railroads. Then, too, as in Great Britain, local networks of family and friends were important. Families and friends often invested through banks they controlled in industrial ventures they owned.

Entrepreneurial groups similar to investment clubs in modern-day America relied on funding from the sale of bank stocks from which they granted themselves generous loans, investing the proceeds in new plant and equipment. Retained earnings also fueled capital improvements, especially after the Civil War of the 1860s. For instance, by 1899 Carnegie Steel was making an annual net profit of $40 million, a very large sum then, most of which was reinvested in the business. In at least one respect America differed from Great Britain: by the mid-1800s foreign investors, especially the British, were important sources of capital. About 20 percent of American railroad securities were foreign-held.

Industrial capital in Japan came from varied sources. The government set up pilot plants and then sold them to private business at prices much lower than their costs of construction. Government revenues to pay for these industrial projects came from an agricultural land tax started in 1873, a tax that provided over half of the government's tax revenues into the 1890s. So, indirectly, some of the capital for industrialization derived from agriculture. However, it would be wrong to overestimate the role of government. Most of the capital came from private sources. Former *daimyo* and samurai invested funds granted them by the Meiji government in banking and other business enterprises. Wealthy landlords and merchants invested in banking, industry, and transportation projects. Leading merchants were, however, less important as a source of capital for industry in Japan than in Great Britain or the United States. Many of the major merchant houses of the Tokugawa period lacked the flexibility to survive the disruptions of the Meiji Restoration and make the transition from preindustrial to industrial times. It was lower-level, smaller-scale merchants, operating in rural areas and former castle towns, more than members of the great merchant houses, who invested most heavily in industry. A final source of revenue for Japan's economic modernization was China. Following its defeat by Japan in the Sino-Japanese War, China had to pay a large indemnity to Japan. The Japanese government then plowed much of that indemnity into government-owned industrial ventures, such as Yawata Iron and Steel. In effect, China paid for some of Japan's industrialization.

Labor

Workers were needed to man the new factories, and each nation was fortunate in possessing an adequate labor supply. A combination of a rising birthrate and a falling death rate more than doubled the population of England and Wales from 7 million in 1770 to about 18 million in 1851. This natural increase, plus immigration from Ireland, provided England's industrial labor force. Blessed with an ample supply of practically minded, skilled workers, many British businesses came to have factories in which workers controlled shop-floor activities. Management generally delegated to these workers decisions over how goods were to be made. This system worked reasonably well during the First Industrial Revolution, when industrial products were relatively technologically simple. However, as the products became more scientifically complex during the Second Industrial Revolution and later, the skills of the practically minded workers proved inadequate. More knowledge of science was needed in newer fields such as chemicals. When Great Britain's educational system failed to provide such knowledge to either workers or managers, parts of the nation's industrial establishment began falling behind those of some other nations.

Industrial labor came from several sources in the United States. There was a major farm-to-city movement from the 1820s on, with New England farmers' daughters providing much of the initial labor force for America's cotton textile mills. There was immigration from abroad: in the mid-1800s from northwestern Europe, and from the mid-1880s into the early 1900s from southeastern Europe. In the mid- and late nineteenth centuries immigration from China and Japan provided workers for the West Coast, until shut off by legislation and informal restrictions. Even with these varied sources, there was often a shortage of labor in America, especially of skilled workers. Faced with less-skilled workers than their British counterparts, American managers tended to impose more controls on them. There was, especially from the 1880s, less delegation over the work process to industrial workers in the United States than in Great Britain.

This control over labor, which most workers were willing to accept in return for relatively high wages, worked well as long as most of the goods being produced were standardized items turned out in long production runs; and that is exactly what the large domestic market in America demanded from the mid-nineteenth century well into the mid-twentieth century. (Unlike the case in Great Britain, research laboratories, controlled by management, provided American companies with the scientific knowledge necessary for the Second Industrial Revolution.) As global demand for more specialized industrial products made for niche markets mounted after World War II, and especially after 1970, better educated workers who could play more active roles in determining production processes for shorter and more flexible production runs were needed. An unwillingness of many American executives to utilize fully the capabilities of workers, for to do so would have meant relinquishing some control over work processes to them, came to hinder American businesses in global industrial competition.

In Japan, as in the United States and Great Britain, industrial labor came from varied sources. Initially, the daughters of samurai and farmers composed the workforce of the silk reeling and cotton textile mills, in manner similar to the importance of women in early textile establishments in England and America. Women made up 60 percent of Japan's industrial labor force as late as 1910. However, as heavy industry — metals, chemicals, shipbuilding, and the like — rose in significance, men entered the workforce in growing numbers. By 1920 men composed over half of the workforce in Japanese industry, a shift in composition that was paralleled in the United States and Great Britain. Increasingly well-educated and involved in determining how goods were made, skilled and knowledgeable workers, especially those employed by big businesses geared to export markets after World War II, proved to be one of the major strengths of Japan's industrial system. Suggestions and actions by Japanese workers were particularly important in improving the quality of Japanese goods.

Markets

On the supply side, raw materials (including power), capital, and labor were needed for industrialization. On the demand side, growing domestic and foreign markets sustained industrial expansion.

For Great Britain both domestic and foreign markets were significant. Most important, the same population increase that provided the workforce helped create a growing domestic market. Moreover, because income was fairly equitable in its distribution — at least more so than in France, for example — people had money to spend on industrial goods. As early as the 1600s, and certainly by the 1700s and 1800s, an increasing proportion of the British adopted a consumer outlook. Transportation improvements linked this nascent consumer market. In the 1780s and 1790s turnpikes began joining localities and regions, and at about the same time a mania for canal building swept Great Britain. By 1800 navigable water routes and good roads were connecting emerging industrial centers of the North to those of the Midlands, the Midlands to London, and London to the Atlantic. Still later came railroads. Railroad trackage increased from a few miles in 1825 to 6,300 miles twenty-five years later.

Even so, local and regional markets long remained of great importance for British merchants and manufacturers, certainly much longer than in America. Of the world's manufacturing nations, Great Britain alone industrialized substantially before completing the building of a national railroad network, a circumstance that encouraged regional rather than national developments. Then, too, regional preferences and tastes simply lingered longer in Great Britain than in some other nations.

Europe and the British colonies formed an overseas market, which, while less important than the domestic market, was significant. Most of Great Britain's exports came to consist of industrial goods, while they had earlier been agricultural products. Overseas markets were especially important outlets for cotton textiles, but not just for textiles; well into the twentieth century foreign markets took about a third of Great Britain's industrial output.

In the United States the development of domestic markets was of utmost importance. In the nineteenth century transportation improvements helped create regional markets and, from the 1850s, a national market that was the largest single free-trade area in the world. Turnpikes like the National Road were of minor significance. Of more importance were canals, 3,000 miles of which had been built by 1840. Still more important was the railroad: 30,000 miles by 1860, 166,000 by 1890, and 250,000 in 1916. Even more than in Great Britain, the United States possessed a market-oriented population of consumers eager to buy the industrial goods made available by the transportation improvements. America's population rose from 4 million people in 1790 to 31 million in 1860 to 106 million by 1920.

Both domestic and foreign markets took Japan's industrial products. Japan's population rose from roughly 36 million people in 1878 to 56 million by 1920, furthering the creation of regional markets and beginning to form a national market for industrial goods. As in the United States and Great Britain, transportation improvements began linking Japan's domestic markets. By 1906 6,000 miles of railroads had been constructed. However, a fully developed domestic market for a broad array of consumer goods did not fill out until after World War II. In addition to domestic markets, foreign markets were significant. In the early Meiji period Japan's exports amounted to a sum equal to about 7 percent of the nation's Gross National Product (GNP), but they rose to 15–20 percent in the late Meiji period, a level maintained into the 1930s. This importance of foreign markets contrasts with the experience of the United States. By the 1850s American exports came to a sum equal to only about 5 percent of the nation's GNP. Exports remained at about that proportion through World War II.

As we shall see, differing markets for industrial goods influenced the nature of industrial production in the different nations. Facing a wider variety of local, regional, and international markets than their American counterparts, British and Japanese industrialists less often emphasized long, standardized production runs of homogeneous products by unskilled or semi-skilled workers. Instead, they often stressed making a variety of goods by skilled workers for different market requirements. In this situation, the moving assembly line, which was introduced to America and the world by Henry Ford in the making of his Model T automobile in 1914, was less important in Great Britain and Japan than in the United States.

Industrialization in China

There were many paths to industrialization. Nations did not tread those paths in the same ways or at the same times. An observer in 1750 might well have concluded that China—or at least part of the nation, the Yangzi River delta, where the city of Shanghai was (is) located—was economically advanced and ready for industrialization. Home in the 1700s to 31–38 million people, more than in all of Great Britain, the Yangzi River delta might have been expected to industrialize then, especially since farmers there engaged in sideline activities (by-employment) and in proto-industry (handicraft production), such as spinning and weaving cotton textiles, similar to the types of activities that were also important in Japan. (There were, in fact, 1 million silk workers—cottage workers, not factory workers—in Suzhou in China by the mid-1600s.)

When China modernized, much of the industrialization occurred in the Shanghai area, but that was not until the late 1800s and early 1900s. Several factors explain why China industrialized a bit later than most European nations. The Qing Dynasty was weak and divided by the mid-nineteenth century. Thus, Great Britain was able through warfare to force open Chinese ports to trade in the 1840s and later. Then, too, a major religious conflict, the Taiping Rebellion, raged through much of China in the mid-1800s, almost bringing down imperial rule. Moreover, Chinese business people did not develop the financial institutions, laws, and instruments needed for full-fledged industrialization until the twentieth century. China went quite far with artisanal industries, as in the Zigong salt trade. Financing via lineage trusts, like family-business financing in Great Britain, was effective up to a point. Then, too, some long-distance banking existed in China, based on merchants and financiers in Shanxi Province.

However, for decades China lacked the commercial laws (such as incorporation laws) needed to develop large capital-intensive businesses independent of the state. Only in 1904 did the first nationwide incorporation law come into existence in China (there was an earlier one in the British colony of Hong Kong), allowing fuller mobilization of capital for industrial ventures. Earlier imperial laws basically ignored small businesses and reserved for the state the right to claim essential businesses as its monopolies. It was also at about the same time that Chinese began forming modern banks (mostly state banks), which in turn loaned some of their funds to nascent industrialists.

Deficiencies in some raw materials may have also mattered. For instance, according to a historian who has compared industrialization in China to that in northwest Europe, a lack of coal when and where it was most needed may have retarded industrialization in China. Large-scale industrialization required new sources of inanimate energy (that is, non-human and non-animal energy). That meant water power and steam power. Water power was very important in early industrialization, especially in America and Great Britain; but it was not by itself sufficient. Water power was not flexible enough, due to low water in late summer and to freeze-ups in the winter. Steam power could come from two major sources, the burning of wood and the burning of coal. However, wood burning no longer sufficed in the Yangzi River delta, which was mainly deforested. That circumstance left coal as the option for fuel. Only a few areas, such as Zigong in Sichuan, had usable natural gas; and oil would be commonly used only in the twentieth century. China had a fair amount of coal, but most of it was in the North. There was relatively little coal farther south in the Yangzi River Valley.

The Process of Industrialization
How, exactly, did industrialization proceed? By the mid-1700s Great Britain possessed an environment conducive to industrialization, but the mere existence of a favorable environment does not explain why and how industrialization occurred.

Two phenomena merit stress in explaining the course of industrialization in Great Britain. First, industrialization evolved as a challenge and response process, that is, as an innovation in one stage of manufacturing brought forth an innovation in another stage as a way of removing a production bottleneck. Second, industrial advances were interrelated, as can be seen in the development of innovations in metallurgy and steam power, for example.

The cotton textile industry provided a classic example of how innovations occurred in a sequence of challenge and response. In the mid-1700s the problem lay in supplying cotton cloth weavers with enough cotton yarn. Inventions removed this bottleneck in production: carding machines to prepare the cotton fiber for spinning and, most important, a host of spinning machines that replaced the spinning wheel in making thread — Hargreave's spinning jenny in 1765, Arkwright's water frame in 1769, and Crompton's spinning mule in 1779. These spinning machines produced better yarn and much more of it than the spinning wheel. The water frame could, for instance, do the work of several hundred spinning wheels. These advances in spinning thread created a bottleneck in weaving, as handloom weavers failed to keep up with the outpouring of thread. The power loom, invented in 1787, removed this bottleneck, and by the mid-1820s a power loom could perform the work of seven and one-half handlooms. Andrew Carnegie, who founded the largest steel company in nineteenth-century America, immigrated to the United States from Scotland with his family in 1848 after his father failed as a handloom weaver. The development of a chemicals industry removed bottlenecks in the bleaching and dyeing of cottons.

Something of the same process occurred in the iron industry. The switch from charcoal to coking coal in smelting iron created pressures for innovation in the refining of iron, a bottleneck removed with the development of puddling in 1784 and the hot blast in 1829. The expansion of the iron industry also demonstrated well the interrelatedness of Great Britain's industrial advances; iron was used in making steam engines, many of these steam engines powered pumps that emptied water out of coal mines, and the coal was used to power the pumps and to make iron.

Even more than their British counterparts, American manufacturers sought to achieve high-volume, low-cost production. They took steps in this direction before the Civil War. As in Great Britain, industrialization meant using machinery to produce manufactured goods. High-volume, low-cost production could not be attained through hand labor and craftsmanship. Faced with a shortage of skilled workers, American industrialists aimed at the standardization or interchangeability of parts in such industries as clock making, small arms, and farm machinery — a goal partially achieved in the 1830s, 1840s, and 1850s. Standardization was favored as a way of cutting labor costs and controlling workers. America's industrial progress caught the British by surprise. In the 1850s the British government sent commissions to the United States to study the secrets of America's industrial success, which the British called the American System. Even so, much remained undone. High-volume, low-cost production had been achieved in just a handful of fields before the Civil War.

It was with technological breakthroughs in three major fields of industrial production that the United States fully achieved high-volume, low-cost production in the 1880s. In liquids and semi-liquids—oil, distilled liquors, and drugs—new processes using heat greatly increased the speed and volume of production. Catalytic cracking speeded the refining of oil, for example. In the processing of agricultural or semi-agricultural goods into consumer products—flour, soap, matches, and cigarettes—new pieces of machinery came into use. The Bonsack machine, adopted in the mid-1880s, produced over 100,000 cigarettes in one day, the same time in which a team of ten men could roll at most only 20,000 by hand. In the steelmaking and metal-working industries two types of changes were important. Technological breakthroughs, the Bessemer and open hearth processes, combined with new, more efficient plant layouts to greatly increase America's iron and steel production.

As a latecomer to industrialization, Japan was able to benefit from the earlier experiences of both Great Britain and the United States. Just as Americans borrowed from the British, as in the cotton textile industry, the Japanese borrowed from other nations—Germany, as well as Great Britain and the United States. Technological transfer or borrowing was especially important in the establishment of Japan's cotton textile industry. Technology, technicians, and machinery all came mainly from Great Britain, but the Japanese soon adapted the technology to their own uses. The adaptation was so complete that Japanese mills using British machinery were soon outproducing British and Chinese mills similarly equipped in China. In 1929 the Japanese company Toyoda Automatic Loom was so technologically advanced that it leased rights to manufacture and sell a new type of power loom to Platt Brothers, a leading British loom maker. Soon thereafter, Toyoda went into making its first automobiles.

One circumstance that set Japanese industrialization and economic growth apart from that of Great Britain or the United States was the importance of war as a stimulatory factor. The Sino-Japanese War of 1894–95 was especially important: the number of factories in Japan rose from 2,746 in 1892 to 7,640 four years later; and the number of industrial workers climbed from 396,000 in 1894 to 454,000 in 1896. Japan's wars spurred the development of heavy industry, such as Yawata Iron and Steel and shipbuilding firms like Mitsubishi. In 1906 a Japanese shipyard launched a 10,000-ton warship that was technologically on par with those of Western nations.

Industrialization and the "Tragedy of the Commons"
Industrialization in all nations affected far-flung aspects of life. It brought even frontier areas into the commercial economy. This integration can be

seen in the rapid exploitation of natural resources to produce goods for national and international markets — timber, minerals, oil, and so on. Two lesser-known examples of this accelerated use of natural resources, the hunting of buffalo in the American West to near extinction during the 1870s and 1880s and the similar near extinction of many species of oceanic fish by over-fishing about a century later, illustrate the past nature and the continuing importance of this trend. Both these examples illuminate well a phenomenon called the "tragedy of the commons." Most of the industrialization and, more generally, economic modernization that we examine in this volume was based on the private ownership of resources. Tragedy of the commons means that when no one owns a resource, when it is common property or common ground, it is in the interests of everyone to exploit it as quickly as possible. To do otherwise — for instance, to follow conservation practices — would be to simply give competitors an unwarranted advantage. However, in situations involving a tragedy of the commons everyone usually suffers in the end as that resource is overused, sometimes to the brink of extinction. The basic question is how to have conservation measures cover resources that no one group or nation completely owns or controls. How can intergroup agreements be made to work?

Buffalo had long roamed across much of what is now the United States, as far east as the Carolinas and Georgia, and as far west as Oregon. They were prized by Indians and Euro-Americans for their robes and were hunted to extinction east of the Mississippi by 1833. However, there were still about 30 million buffalo west of the Mississippi River in the 1850s. Those buffalo became central to the lives of many tribes on the Great Plains. Indians there hunted them on foot and on horseback. Wastage, as defined by environmentalists today, occurred. Indians killed more buffalo than they needed for their own use, surrounding herds by fire, driving them over cliffs, and killing them on horseback. Even so, the taking of buffalo by Indians for their own consumption was not what led to their near extermination.

Rather, it was growing demand in eastern and midwestern cities for buffalo hides (the buffalo skin with the hair scraped off) that condemned the buffalo. A cluster of technological innovations, the products of the industrial revolution, was especially important. By the 1850s and 1860s railroads were entering the Great Plains, and the first transcontinental line was completed in 1869. Railroads made it possible to ship the buffalo hides from where the buffalo were killed to their markets, a good example of the importance of markets in business development. In the same period, new types of rifles, almost like small cannon, using standard parts were mass produced.

Finally, in 1871–72 new tanning methods allowed buffalo hides to be substituted for cowhides in numerous items, most importantly in shoes and industrial belting. Industrial belting connected steam engines to individual pieces of machinery in factories. Industry itself, then, provided much of the market for the hides. Thus, industrialization linked a natural resource, the buffalo, to new production methods and to new market uses.

What followed has been called the Great Buffalo Hunt from 1867 to 1884. White (and, occasionally, black) commercial hide hunters moving west from the Mississippi River after the Civil War slaughtered buffalo by the millions. The hunters acted as small-scale businessmen. A buffalo outfit usually consisted of one or two hunters, along with six or seven skinners, a cook, and perhaps a wagoneer. Since none of them had any ownership rights over the wild buffalo, none had any reason to conserve the buffalo. Moreover, the military encouraged them to kill the buffalo as a way of destroying the food supply of plains Indians. The hunters sought the buffalo hides for their leather. Only rarely was the meat systematically taken. Most was left to rot on the plains. By 1874 the great Kansas-Nebraska herds were fast disappearing, and hide hunters shifted their attention south into Texas and north into the Dakotas and Montana. By 1878–79 the southern herds were virtually gone and the northern plains came under intensified hunting pressure. By the winter of 1883 even the northern herds were eliminated. Only a few remnant bands of buffalo remained, such as the one in Yellowstone National Park, created in 1872.

Much of the same story took place globally with regard to fish after World War II. Fishing became industrialized. Large fleets of catcher boats and factory ships plied the high seas using long lines, trawls, and purse-seine and drift nets to catch everything in sight. Since no one owned the fish in the wild, there was initially little incentive to conserve them. Conservation efforts at first dealt with two different but related matters: who owned oil, minerals, and fish under or on the sea beds of continental shelves and who owned fish in water above the continental shelves. (Continental shelves underlie shallow, off-shore waters.) In the late 1940s President Harry S Truman made two important proclamations. First, he said that all resources on or underneath the United States' continental shelves belonged to the United States. He was mainly concerned about undersea oil in places like the Gulf of Mexico. Second, Truman reserved for the United States the right to proclaim conservation zones for fish above America's continental shelves but did not actually do so. Other nations soon followed the American lead. Iceland claimed the right to control fisheries above its continental shelves to a depth of 200 meters. Argentina, Panama, Mexico, Peru, and Chile claimed jurisdiction over all fisheries 200 miles out to sea, regardless of the depth.

Next came United Nations' actions. In 1958 and 1960 the UN sponsored Law of the Sea Conferences that adopted a convention giving coastal nations almost exclusive control over the exploitation of their continental shelves — oil, minerals, and some fish (at least sedentary creatures on the bottom, like crabs and lobsters) to a depth of 200 meters. By 1963 enough countries, including the United States and the Soviet Union, had ratified the convention to put it into effect. In 1964 the U.S. Congress gave the convention bite by passing legislation confirming the United States' ownership of resources and creatures on the nation's continental shelf.

An even more thoroughgoing change in the world's commercial ocean fisheries occurred with the adoption of 200-mile exclusive economic zones (EEZs) by a growing number of nations in the 1970s. The United States proclaimed such a zone in 1976 with the passage by Congress of the Federal Fishery Conservation and Management Act, renewed with some changes in 1996. This legislation extended the federal government's control over fishing and the exploitation of undersea resources 200 miles out to sea from American shores regardless of ocean depths. Eight regional management councils set Total Allowable Catches (TACs), designed to be sustainable, for different types of fish in their areas. Foreign vessels could fish within the 200-mile zones only if American ships did not take all of the TACs. A 1982 UN Law of the Sea Conference resulted in a global affirmation of 200-mile EEZs and was implemented in 1994. However, not all was progress toward conservation. UN Law of the Sea Conferences in the mid-1990s failed to put in place regulatory schemes for fishing on the high seas beyond the 200-mile limits.

None of the agreements of the UN or individual national governments fully ensured that fishery resources would be used in a sustainable manner, and many world fisheries were over fished. Too often nations controlling the 200-mile EEZs permitted more fishing than fish stocks could sustain, and beyond the 200-mile limits just about anything went. New England's cod fishery, which in the mid-1970s accounted for 23 percent of the entire global fish catch, crashed a few years later and did not recover. The global over fishing crisis continued into the twenty-first century. A thorough scientific investigation revealed in 2006 that 29 percent of the world's fish species being taken commercially had totally collapsed by 2003; that is, catches amounted to less than 10 percent of what had earlier been taken. Moreover, the report showed that the global fish catch had peaked in 1994 and then declined by 13 percent over the following decade, despite a substantial increase in worldwide fishing efforts. As a result, Americans and other people around the globe found their favorite types of fish disappearing from their dinner tables: North Atlantic cod, swordfish, blue-fin tuna, and wild Atlantic salmon, to name a few.

Conclusions

As already suggested, there was no single path to industrialization. The role of the state differed from nation to nation, as did the ways in which raw materials, capital, and labor were combined. Differing markets could also lead to different approaches to economic growth and industrial development. Even within a single nation there were often marked regional variations, as a glance at the initial industrialization of the United States illustrates.

In America four major regional variations to industrialization developed. In the Northeast, from Maine south through Pennsylvania, mill villages using water power sprang up, some 400 by 1820, to produce textiles, milled lumber, ground grain, and sometimes iron and paper. Entrepreneurs founding the villages provided living quarters for families to try to hold onto a stable supply of workers in a time of labor shortage, and industrial work was often done by entire families. Bigger one-industry cities and towns—such as Lowell, Massachusetts, for large cotton-textile factories funded by merchants, and Lynn, Connecticut, for centralized and mechanized shoemaking—also grew up. Here increasingly deskilled workers made longer and longer production runs of homogeneous products. More diversified industrialized cities, such as New York and Philadelphia, were a third variant. In these cities many smaller and medium-size businesses employing mainly skilled workers made a wide range of goods, including cotton textiles, in successful competition with larger counterparts in the one-industry towns such as Lowell. Frequently started by artisans and usually family-owned or owned by just a few partners, many of these smaller firms proved successful well into the twentieth century. Finally, in the South industrial slavery developed. By the 1850s about 5 percent of the region's slaves, some 150,000 to 200,000 people, labored in textile mills, iron works, sugar refineries, and other industrial enterprises.

However gradual and varied in its onset and development at times, industrialization altered forever parts of the world's business systems, as seen most dramatically in the tragedy of the commons. By vastly increasing the speed of production and the volume of output—what business historian Alfred D. Chandler Jr. has called the "throughput" of business—industrialization created new challenges for business leaders. In some nations, most notably the United States, business people formed larger firms as they sought to control and channel this growing throughput. However, the impact of the economic and technological forces of industrialization upon the business firm varied considerably from place to place and nation to nation. Social, cultural, and political factors also affected the timing of the development of new business methods and helped determine the shapes new industrial companies assumed. Even within nations differences appeared, leading to the formation of varied sorts of companies. Thus, in the United States, which pioneered in the development of big business, and even more so in Great Britain, Japan, and China, smaller firms remained very important in manufacturing, as well as in other fields of endeavor. The story of industrial business was one of complexity, diversity, and unevenness.

Suggested Readings

David Landes, *The Unbound Prometheus: Technological Change and Industrial Development in Western Europe from 1750 to the Present* (Cambridge, 1969), Sidney Pollard, *Peaceful Conquest: The Industrialization of Europe, 1760–1970* (Oxford, 1981), Maxine Berg, *The Age of Manufactures, 1700–1820* (Oxford, 1994), and Pat Hudson, *The Industrial Revolution* (London, 1992), examine industrialization in Great Britain and Europe from various perspectives. Thomas Cochran, *Frontiers of Change: Early Industrialism in America* (Oxford, 1981), David Hounshell, *From the American System to Mass Production, 1800–1932* (Baltimore, 1984), and Walter Licht, *Industrializing America: The Nineteenth Century* (Baltimore, 1995), investigate industrialism and economic growth in nineteenth-century America. Nakamura Takafusa, *Economic Growth in Prewar Japan* (New Haven, 1983), and Thomas C. Smith, *Native Sources of Japanese Industrialization, 1750–1920* (Berkeley, 1988), are valuable introductions to economic and industrial changes in Japan. Kenneth Pomeranz, *The Great Divergence: China, Europe, and the Making of the Modern World Economy* (Princeton, 2000), is provocative and controversial.

On the destruction of the buffalo, see Andrew C. Isenberg, *The Destruction of the Bison* (Cambridge, 2000). On the global over fishing crisis, see James R. McGoodwin, *Crisis in the World's Fisheries: People, Problems, and Policies* (Stanford, 1990), and Carl Safina, *Song for a Blue Ocean* (New York, 1997).

British and German Businesses during Industrialization

Industrialization affected the nature and structure of British firms less than it did companies in some other nations. Nearly all British manufacturing ventures remained small family firms organized as single-owner proprietorships or partnerships, and kinship connections continued to be of utmost importance in their operation. Like Britain's preindustrial merchants, most British manufacturers specialized in what they did; few sought to control all steps in making and selling goods. Instead, they devised alternatives to direct controls, ranging from regional groupings of smaller, specialized firms to the extensive use of subcontracting. These methods of business management and organization succeeded, and as a result Great Britain was the workshop of the world well into the nineteenth century. By way of contrast, in Germany big businesses were more important during industrialization and later. Turning out producer goods — in comparison to British firms, which focused more on consumer goods — German industrial companies were generally larger and more likely to be vertically integrated. However, even in Germany, small and medium-size companies that linked together in various sorts of networks, often regional in scope, remained significant.

The Continuing Dominance of Small Businesses in Great Britain

Small family firms, usually organized as single-owner proprietorships or partnerships, accounted for most of Great Britain's industrial and economic growth during the eighteenth and nineteenth centuries. Their development took place in a volatile business environment, with many firms failing each year, only to be replaced by new ventures. In the eighteenth century some 33,000 businesses declared bankruptcy in Great Britain (and still others failed without legally becoming bankrupt). Britain's national income rose 0.87 percent annually, but the number of bankrupt firms climbed 1.15 percent per year. Moreover, rates of bankruptcy rose considerably in the mid- and late 1700s, as industrialization sped up.

The Family Firm

In Great Britain's unstable economic situation, partnerships based on ties of family and friendship made sense. British industrial companies often developed, as had their preindustrial antecedents, as parts of local and regional networks. Despite the existence of laws protecting bankrupts, most of these smaller family enterprises had unlimited liability, meaning that their owners were personally responsible for any debts the companies incurred. Far from being seen as a hindrance, unlimited liability was often viewed as an ingredient essential in instilling trust in those who might be interested in new manufacturing ventures, for it showed that the owners would stand behind their firms. Beyond providing networks of trust that could be tapped for capital, families and friends were valuable to nascent enterprises as sources of labor and business information. Extended families, including cousins and in-laws, were especially important in providing businesses with knowledge of markets.

Reinforcing the tendency toward smaller family firms was the nature of those markets. The contrast to the United States was marked. Despite its continuing growth, the domestic British market was smaller and less prosperous than America's. By 1880 the United States possessed a population of 50 million people with a national income of $7.2 million. In the same year Great Britain's population stood at 35 million with a national income of only $5.2 million. By 1920 the United States had a population and national income nearly triple that of Great Britain's. Moreover, because of its longer history, Great Britain's national market was more divided by regional tastes and preferences than was America's. Foreign markets were more important for British business than for America's. The ratio of British foreign trade to national income was about 27–30 percent in 1860 through 1913, while for the United States the ratio was only about 5 percent. Throughout much of the twentieth century, overseas markets took about a third of Great Britain's industrial output.

Britain also possessed a better established system of wholesalers and retailers than did the United States, a legacy of Britain's long existence as a commercial nation. These marketers were able to sell successfully the expanding output of Great Britain's factories. Because Great Britain is much smaller than America (in terms of geographic size Britain is smaller than the three contiguous states of New York, Pennsylvania, and Ohio), markets were more geographically concentrated in large cities.

In short, when compared to many of their American counterparts, Brit-

Great Britain, around 1800

ish industrialists faced segmented markets, not one large homogeneous market. This circumstance meant that British manufacturers tended not to turn out long production runs of identical goods, something for which big businesses with large factories were particularly well suited. Each regional and overseas market demanded variants. That British industrialists could dispose of their goods through a well-articulated system of independent marketers meant that they did not have to own or control directly their sales outlets, thus also allowing them to keep their firms relatively small.

Political factors also encouraged reliance on small firms. Again, the comparison to the United States is striking. As we shall see in the next chapter, in the United States the Sherman Act of 1890 outlawed cartels; that is, the law forbade industrialists or other companies to get together to divide up markets or set prices for their goods. Ironically, this legislation encouraged formerly independent companies to merge and form big businesses in a quest to stabilize their business environment. However, no such legal prohibition against cartels existed in Great Britain. Small British firms could gain many of the benefits available to American companies only through merger by simply joining cartels, and those cartels helped preserve small industrial businesses in Great Britain.

As a result, regionally oriented small family firms spurred much of British industrialization. Even after the passage of the Joint Stock Acts of 1856 and 1862 permitted the formation of limited companies, the equivalent of incorporated businesses in America, most British enterprises remained partnerships. As late as 1885 limited companies accounted for only 5 to 10 percent of the total number of important business organizations in England. Only in the 1880s was there a significant decline in the use of partnership, and even with the rise of publicly held companies family influence on British business remained important.

In these typically small industrial firms there was little separation of ownership from management. Throughout the nineteenth century and into the twentieth, ownership and management remained united, with business long remaining a personal, not a bureaucratic, affair. Business bureaucracies with divisions between top and middle management, sophisticated accounting systems and the like, were slow to spread in Great Britain, for they simply were not urgently needed.

Britain's business system worked, certainly into the late nineteenth century. As late as 1880 British manufacturers accounted for 41 percent of the world's trade in industrial goods, and in 1913 they still controlled 30 percent. The system succeeded because many British firms found effective ways to cooperate. Sometimes small manufacturers worked in relative isolation, selling their products through manufacturers' representatives. More commonly, however, two other methods emerged, both of which were also used extensively in Japan when that nation industrialized.

First of all, small firms acted as subcontractors for larger companies. In the eighteenth century, coal mines subcontracted work to gangs of men, a practice that spread to some iron foundries and textile mills. In the nineteenth century, subcontracting sometimes extended beyond labor. The building and operation of canals was often managed on a subcontracted basis, as was that of some early railroads. Chartered in 1821, the Stockton & Darlington Railroad was constructed by subcontractors. Moreover, through the 1840s subcontractors maintained the railroad's right of way, repaired its locomotives, and even wound its clocks. However, as their lines grew longer and became more complex in their operations, railroads found it necessary to take over subcontractor functions, thus internalizing actions previously undertaken by independent small businesses.

Industrial Districts

Second, small companies often complemented the work of each other by locating in a particular region and then sharing the stages in making and selling a product, with no single company controlling all the steps. For example, Great Britain possessed 1,200 cotton textile factories by 1834, most comprising independent companies, nearly all of which were single-owner proprietorships or partnerships. These companies performed just one step of the manufacturing process. In 1884 about 41 percent of the firms engaged in spinning only, 33 percent took part in weaving only, and a mere 27 percent integrated spinning with weaving. Financial services, market exchanges, and transportation networks were well enough developed to handle the growing output of cotton textiles. Spinning became localized in south Lancashire towns, and weaving became specialized in northwest Lancashire towns. The spinning and weaving companies were linked by merchants in the well-developed Manchester Exchange and by their geographical closeness to each other. Few textile makers had their own marketing outlets. Great Britain had a well-established system of marketers fully able to sell the finished products of their mills. As late as 1930 only twenty-six of Britain's 2,000 yarn and cloth producers possessed their own marketing facilities.

Beyond cotton textiles, one of the best-known British industrial districts was the Sheffield steel district in the Midlands. Small quantities of iron and steel had been made in Sheffield from the 1400s, but in the 1700s and 1800s the Sheffield district emerged as a center for the production of crucible steel in Europe. In crucible steel making, clay pots contained the iron bars and alloys melted by charcoal (and later by coking coal) to become steel. Long an art more than a science, these melts were small, often less than 100 pounds per crucible.

Several factors led to Sheffield's emergence as a crucible-steel center. The region possessed a skilled, intelligent workforce, a legacy of its centuries in making iron and steel. A tremendous diversity of skills was present; using even scant funds from family and friends, many skilled workers became "little masters" who ran their own crucible steel firms. In addition, Sheffield had rivers to provide waterpower for the forging, grinding, and rolling operations needed to produce cutlery (knives) and other finished products. Charcoal, clay, and bar iron were also available. Finally, there was rising demand for the crucible steel, which was very hard and which could, thus, be used for the cutting edges of cutlery and all sorts of tools. By 1856 Sheffield had 124 crucible steel makers. Most of these were small, specialized family firms engaged in only one or two types of operations, such as grinding or hardening steel. The many firms competed with but also complemented each other. That is, they depended on each other to make finished goods; few of the companies performed all the steps needed to turn out a final product. They composed a definite cluster or district several miles long, and this clustering fostered innovation, adaptability, and a quest for quality, as people and ideas moved fairly freely from firm to firm. Altogether, the Sheffield district made 90 percent of Britain's steel and 50 percent of the world's steel in the mid-nineteenth century.

Sheffield continued to develop as a steel district between 1850 and 1920. Eschewing mass-production methods, most of Sheffield's steel makers stayed with the crucible process. They turned out specialty-steel products for niche markets: steel projectiles for cannons and steel plating for ships, for example. They produced ever more sophisticated cutting tools, and they used chemical processes to make more alloyed steels (such as manganese and tungsten steel), which went into bicycles, automobiles, machine tools, and the like. Many of the firms contributed to funding for the Sheffield Technical School (later part of Sheffield University), established in 1884. Research from the school, in turn, helped the companies in their quest for new processes and products. One breakthrough was stainless steel. Most of Sheffield's steel companies remained small or medium-size enterprises. There were about 150 steel makers in the Sheffield district at the time of World War I, along with hundreds of toolmakers. Most were run as family-owned, personally managed firms.

Industrial districts, often composed of small and medium-size manufacturers, were common in Great Britain and Europe. By the 1890s, for instance, the British engineering industry (that is, producers of machine tools) had become congeries of distinct smaller businesses linked by a common set of metalworking processes and the manual skills associated with them. Companies in Lancashire, Yorkshire, and the East Midlands made textile machinery; firms in Clydeside, the Northeast Coast, and on the Thames produced marine engines; companies in Lincolnshire and East Anglia made agricultural equipment; and firms in the West Midlands turned out hardware and (slightly later) automobiles. The characteristic unit was a small-to-medium-size family firm with fewer than 500 employees. Even the larger companies often operated more as collections of workshops than as integrated factories. In the Oyonnax valley of France, to relate another example of the growth of an industrial district, small producers made early-day plastics, first from the natural material of animal horn, later from celluloid. For decades in the late nineteenth and early twentieth centuries, small artisanal production and larger factory production coexisted side by side. A mechanics workshop opened in 1904 helped supply well-trained workers and gave some unity to plastics production in the valley. Ship making in Norway, metalworking, cotton textiles, and silk production in parts of Italy, and ribbon making in France also attest to the importance of industrial districts.

Thus, networks of firms, whether joined together in industrial districts or linked in subcontracting arrangements, remained important in industrial times. Certainly, fully independent, stand-alone firms existed, but most companies were bound up in some types of network arrangement or arrangements. In a sense, company boundaries were often ambiguous and permeable, as firms interacted with each other in a myriad of ways.

Big Business Begins in Great Britain

When compared to the situations in the United States and some other nations during industrialization, big businesses were slower to develop in Great Britain. Still, some firms grew large by the international standards of their day. As early as the mid-1700s the ironworks of Ambrose Crowley consisted of rolling, plating, and slitting mills, four steel furnaces, and two large forges. The company also owned ten warehouses and four ships. The ironworks employed about 800 men, with another 150 engaged in transport, and an additional 150 handling the company's affairs in London. As one of Great Britain's largest business enterprises, the ironworks began replacing personal with bureaucratic management methods. Frustrated in his attempts to run his large enterprise by himself, Crowley drew up a constitution, a set of written orders, to govern the work of his laborers, foremen, and middle managers.

Companies and Industries

Nor was Crowley's ironworks alone as a good-sized industrial enterprise. By 1813 one coal mine employed 600 people and possessed twenty miles of underground railroads upon which 1,000 horses pulled carts. Sixteen years later forty-one Tyneside coal mines employed an average of 300 people apiece. By 1790 the four largest copper and tin mines employed over 1,000 people each and were using a total of seventeen steam engines. Forty-six years later thirty-six mines had an average employment of about 200. By the 1790s most British ironworks were giving work to about 300 hands, while those in Shropshire employed an average of 700. By 1830 some employed over 5,000 workers. Even the cotton textile industry, which was a stronghold of small businesses, saw the development of some large firms. As early as 1795 Peels had twenty-three mills, William Douglas and Partners nine, and Robinsons five. By 1815 New Lanark employed 1,600 workers, James Finlay & Company 1,500, and Strutts 1,500. In the early 1830s the Manchester mills were employing an average of 300 to 400 workers, while seven firms employed over 1,000 apiece.

Great Britain experienced a wave of mergers in the late nineteenth century, and this merger movement led to the further development of big business. For example, in 1902 Dudley Docker, a Birmingham industrialist, merged five of England's largest rolling-stock companies to create the Metropolitan Amalgamated Carriage and Wagon Company. Between 1888 and 1914 an average of 67 companies disappeared via mergers every year, and in 1898 through 1900 the average soared to 650. Many of these mergers were designed simply to limit competition and to preserve the status quo rather than to reduce costs of production in the interests of increasing their international competitiveness.

With these mergers, big businesses developed in many of the same fields in which they arose in the United States. In 1919, 177 of Britain's 200 largest industrial ventures operated in just a few fields: food processing, textiles, chemicals, metals, and machinery. In these fields, more than in others, there were advantages to be gained by joining all or most of the stages of production and sales in single firms, and there existed markets large enough to support such linkages. There were economies of scale. That is, by building larger factories business leaders were able to reduce the cost of production per unit of their goods, and these cost reductions (often passed on, at least in part, to consumers in the form of lower prices) broadened the markets for those goods. Then, too, there existed economies of scope. That is, business owners could often use factories to produce a range of related goods and, more important, could use marketing networks set up for one product to push additional products.

In the fields mentioned above it often made sense to handle all the production and marketing functions in individual firms, what is called vertical integration. To ensure stability in their operations and to keep all the profits for themselves, executives sought to control all the steps of making and selling their goods. When their output in a given period of time — their throughput — reached a high level, manufacturers found it valuable to own their own supplies of raw materials and their own sales outlets. In this way they could be sure of protecting their firms from shortages of raw materials in times of peak demand, and they could also be reasonably certain of selling the growing throughput of their factories.

Still, when compared to what was taking place in the United States, British industrialists were less likely to fully integrate their operations. Britain's smaller, more compact, and more segmented markets, along with the existence of a well-established network of wholesalers and retailers, militated against vertical integration. Even the largest British firms tended to be smaller than their American counterparts. In 1930 only the largest fifty British industrial companies were big enough to have made the list of the top 200 manufacturing ventures in the United States.

Beer and Cigarettes

While large firms arose in many of the same industries in Britain as in America, there was a major difference: in almost every one of those industries British enterprises tended to produce consumer rather than industrial goods. British entrepreneurs proved most successful in making branded, packaged goods: cigarettes, soap, sugar, flour, jams, and the like. Most began — as did, for instance, Cadbury Brothers in chocolates — in producing for regional markets. They then expanded to serve the national market later by exploiting economies of scale and scope.

The British brewing industry, especially that part located in London, witnessed the beginnings of big business at an early date. The experiences of breweries reveal a great deal about the development of Britain's early industrial ventures, their growth, and their limitations. The experiences also illustrate that industrialization was a broad-based development, extending beyond such well-known industries as cotton textiles and steel making.

Industrialization in brewing involved the use of machinery. By the early 1800s London breweries were using machinery to grind grain, mash the ground malt in vats, and pump and move liquids. An increasing number of the machines were steam powered, until by 1805 steam power had nearly replaced horse power, being more economical and more reliable. The growing use of machinery led to more efficient factory designs. The sizes of vats and utensils increased dramatically. Malt and water were lifted by steam-powered machinery to the top floors of the breweries; then gravity carried them down through the various processes involved in brewing beer. Lying behind these alterations was the unquenchable London market. At a time when beer was a perishable good — for this was before refrigeration or preservatives — only a large local market could support big breweries.

As they came to use steam-powered machinery and to be housed in larger buildings, the breweries became capital intensive (that is, they required growing amounts of money for their expansion and operations) and grew in size. By the late 1700s the largest London breweries were giving work to 100 men apiece and were capitalized at £200,000 each. By the 1830s firm capitalization had quadrupled.

More than most other early industrialists, London brewers began linking in single companies the different steps involved in making and selling beer. In the 1780s some sought to control their sources of raw materials by entering into long-term contracts with farmers for their grain; and in the next decade some began setting up their own retail outlets, pubs (public houses) that exclusively served their beer in London and nearby areas. As yet, the perishable nature of beer precluded the development of national chains of pubs. Some brewers also kept pigs and cattle to eat the waste materials resulting from the brewing process, selling their meat and milk on the London market.

Even as they expanded, most breweries remained partnerships whose members continued to raise capital from family and friends. Many of the brewers also had personal friendships with leading London bankers and received loans from their institutions. The partners ran their breweries directly, with little in the way of managerial organizations. The brewers made all the key decisions on buying the raw materials, setting up production processes, and selling the beer. They walked the brewery floors to engage in hands-on management. While considerably larger than their preindustrial antecedents, the London breweries were not so large or complex as to need intricate management staffs or managerial techniques. Indeed, many brewers found time to become involved in other forms of trade and in local politics.

A somewhat similar story unfolded in Britain's tobacco industry at a later date. When it was formed in 1901, the Imperial Tobacco Company was capitalized at nearly £12 million (then about $60 million), making it the largest manufacturer in Great Britain. Imperial Tobacco was a combination of thirteen formerly independent British firms joined together to oppose the entrance of James Duke's American Tobacco Company, the largest American tobacco firm, into the British market.

Of the companies coming together to form Imperial Tobacco, the largest was W. D. & H. O. Wills of Bristol, England's leading maker of cigarettes, which was capitalized at almost £7 million. Wills began its history in a competitive business environment. The linking of different regions in Great Britain by the railroad began breaking down local monopolies in the 1840s, though regional tastes remained more important than in the United States. In 1846 Wills began giving special brand names to some of its smoking tobaccos as a way of differentiating them from their competitors, and in the 1860s Wills led other tobacco companies in setting up a national selling network. The use of packing machines for loose tobacco and the adoption of airtight tins in the 1880s also moved Wills ahead of other British companies.

However, it was Wills's movement into cigarette making that gave the company dominance over the British market. Wills brought out its first handmade cigarette in 1871. In 1884 Wills purchased exclusive British rights to an American-designed cigarette-making machine called the Bonsack machine. The Bonsack machine replaced hand labor with machine work, thus greatly speeding up cigarette making. A team of ten cigarette makers working by hand could produce 20,000 cigarettes per day; one person supervising a single Bonsack machine could turn out 100,000. In 1888 the company started making cheap cigarettes for the mass market with Bonsack machines. Within two years, Wills had captured 59 percent of the British cigarette market, and, despite the acquisition of the Bonsack machine by other British companies, still held 55 percent of the market in 1901. As in the United States, the control of technology essential in increasing the throughput of business allowed some British firms to move ahead of their competitors and become big businesses. The Bonsack machine helped Wills, as it did Duke's American Tobacco, defeat rivals in the cigarette industry.

Management

Even within the largest big businesses in Great Britain, family ownership and management long remained more common than in the United States. As late as 1930, 70 percent of Great Britain's 200 largest companies had family members sitting on their boards of directors. Nonetheless, some changes occurred in the structure of the management of Britain's newly emerging big businesses. Departmentalized central offices developed in embryo form, as proprietors and partners began delegating responsibility in a few companies. That is, in some firms there was a division of authority between the different partners so that each became, in effect, a department head (such as the head of sales) with several paid managers under him. In other cases there was a single managing director, financed by sleeping (inactive) partners, with a number of managers below him. However, even after the British merger movement most of the resulting big businesses were loosely organized. Typically, the central offices of the British firms consisted of a large number of the executives from the former partnerships who met only a few times each year to set prices, review the activities of the different parts of the company, and allocate funds for expansion.

Below the level of top management, some alterations also took place. The nature of the manager of a large works — that person below the active proprietor or partners, but above the foremen or clerks — was changing. Managers became better educated, and their salaries and social status rose. The differences in income and status separating works managers from the managing partners, which had been considerable in the mid-1700s, nearly vanished by the 1830s. As their companies became larger and more complex, some proprietors and managers devised new accounting methods to help them run their enterprises. Building upon the efforts of estate keepers, merchants, and very early industrialists, nineteenth-century manufacturers began developing financial, cost, and capital accounting. None, however, went as far in developing new accounting methods as did executives in the United States.

As would happen in the United States and Japan, some British railroads became big businesses for their day. As they grew in size and complexity, they began developing new management methods. The London and North Western Railroad (LNWR), formed in 1846 and capitalized at £29 million, employed 12,000 workers on 800 miles of track by the early 1850s. As it expanded the scope of its operations, the LNWR devised a new system of management. The LNWR was composed of three regional divisions, each of which had its own secretary, superintendent, locomotive manager, and goods manager (purchasing manager). Each of these people reported to a general manager who coordinated their work and oversaw all the operations of the line. New accounting methods that allowed for depreciation (something very important in capital-intensive businesses) and more precise record keeping of all sorts — with middle managers in charge of gathering and analyzing the statistics and figures — developed well beyond what was being done in other British businesses.

Unlike what was occurring in America at about the same time, there was little spillover of new managerial techniques from British railroads to British industrial firms. Few British railroad executives were involved in other types of business ventures. Moreover, the smaller size of most British industrial ventures meant that extensive changes were not required. In the United States, to get ahead of the story just a bit, Andrew Carnegie applied management methods he learned from the Pennsylvania Railroad in running a gigantic steel empire he built in the 1870s through the 1890s.

Industrial Leaders

Who were Great Britain's business leaders? The pioneer industrialists were a diverse lot coming from many backgrounds, but men with mercantile links predominated. Most early industrialists came from middle-class origins, not from working-class families. Most successful industrial entrepreneurs used networks of families and friends to get ahead. As in so much in Britain, access to local and regional family networks often proved a crucial determinant of business success.

By the late nineteenth century patterns of business success, while varied, showed more commonality. Cultural homogeneity among members of Britain's middle class, including many business people, increased as regional identities lessened. In the years 1870 through 1889, 57 percent of the British business leaders were the sons of businessmen, 19 percent were the sons of public officials, 13 percent were the sons of farmers, and 11 percent were the sons of clerical workers and laborers. British business leaders were motivated by a desire to enrich themselves and move up socially. As in earlier times, entrepreneurs often moved from one venture to another, prepared to save what could be salvaged from business disappointments while moving on to new enterprises.

Management and Labor

Relationships between management and labor took several forms in Britain's industrial establishments. Much of the conflict and accommodation revolved around the question of who would control the work process. Laborers, especially skilled ones, often sought to remain in control by subcontracting their labor as a group to business owners and factory managers. Workers usually got what they wanted, successfully negotiating with the managers of Britain's many small firms on a piecemeal basis. By way of contrast, workers would have a much more difficult time trying to get what they wanted from the much larger, more powerful industrial firms that grew up in the United States. Only through direct state intervention, with the passage of laws by Congress in the 1930s, did American workers succeed. Such direct governmental intervention to help workers was less necessary and less common in Great Britain.

Subcontracting relieved a firm's managers of the need to supervise directly all of their company's activities. It was this situation that gave skilled workers in many fields considerable control over work processes. Workers decided how and at what speed they would labor in return for a set amount of pay for a certain amount of completed work — tons of coal mined, yards of cloth produced, and so forth. These practically minded workers proved to be one of the strengths of Britain's early industrialization. Improvements they made on the job, usually of an incremental, not breakthrough, nature, helped Britain stay competitive for decades.

Nonetheless, as time passed, employers sometimes sought to erode this control in bargaining sessions with workers joined together in trade unions. Employers tried to impose new forms of industrial discipline by gaining control of the pace, price, and organization of work. New agreements between employers and workers often favored the former. An 1898 agreement between employers and machinery makers (engineers in British parlance), for example, gave employers the right to determine the manning and operation of machinery, including the employment of apprentices. Few agreements went this far in extending employer control over shop-floor activities. Even in the area of engineering, workers retained considerable control over the details of their shop-floor activities. In fact, before World War I national collective bargaining was really just beginning. Regional collective bargaining was important in such industries as steel, shipbuilding, and textiles; but even there it often collapsed because of disagreements among the many small manufacturers. Most of the agreements that were reached were sliding-scale ones, in which wages fluctuated with the price of the product.

The introduction of what was called scientific management failed to give British industrialists much control over workers. Begun in America in the late nineteenth century, scientific management or Taylorism (named after its founder Frederick Taylor) sought to make factory work more efficient by taking control of work processes from workers and giving it to factory foremen. Workers were instructed in the most efficient ways of fulfilling their tasks and paid when they met factory norms or quotas for those tasks. This approach met stiff opposition from British trade unions and from many factory owners. Less interested than their American counterparts in long runs of homogeneous products, British industrialists were less concerned with scientific management as a way to make their businesses more efficient and profitable.

Instead, some British manufacturers turned to welfare capitalism or welfare work, especially in fields in which big businesses sought to stabilize their operations. Industrial welfare work encompassed a broad range of company-supplied benefits for workers: the provision of sick pay, old-age pensions, safer working conditions, sports facilities, and (occasionally) housing. The goal was to keep workers loyal to their companies without changing relations of power. Industrial welfare work was most common in those industries that were capital intensive, in those fields in which the main costs of doing business lay in the capital tied up in the plant and equipment, not in workers' salaries. Managers wanted to avoid conflict that might interfere with the throughput of their plants: railroads, gas works, iron and steel factories, breweries, and chemical plants. Smaller, less capital-intensive firms tended to rely more on informal arrangements than on systematic welfare plans.

British Businesses in Sales and Services

Businesses in sales and services grew up along with those in manufacturing and were essential to the development of industrial firms. Far from being afterthoughts, marketing and service businesses were important for the growth of the British economy, both in their own right and in terms of the roles they played in their nation's industrialization. Banks helped finance industrial concerns, and shopkeepers sold the new factory products. As in so much of British business, small firms predominated in sales and services; but there was a trend, especially in banking, toward bigness.

Retailing

If the country was long the "workshop of the world," Great Britain was also often called "a nation of shopkeepers." Fixed-place shops coexisted throughout the eighteenth century with itinerant trading and open-air markets. From the mid-nineteenth century, however, small shops took over most retailing from peddlers and public markets, especially in the larger cities. Already rising in numbers in southern England in the late 1700s, family shops increased dramatically in numbers throughout the Midlands and northern England in the 1800s.

In the nineteenth and early twentieth centuries new types of outlets challenged family retailers. Department stores, which developed in the United States at about the same time, served urban customers. William Whitley opened what is often called the first department store in Great Britain in 1863, bringing under one roof departments selling many different goods, thus offering convenience to his customers. More than convenience was involved, however. Possessing, by around 1900, tearooms, restaurants, club rooms, and hair-dressing salons, the department stores brought glamour into the lives of middle-class consumers. Being consumers, not just producers, became a major part of their lives for growing numbers of people. By emphasizing stock turn, the rapid, high-volume sale of goods at fixed prices, department stores made considerable sums on low profit margins.

Still other forms of retailing developed. Multiples (chain stores) appeared in nearly all types of British retailing by World War I, but especially in areas dealing with mass-produced, standardized consumer goods, just as was occurring in the United States. Most were regional in scope, but some grew to become national federations: Lipton, Maypole (in groceries), Jesse Boot (pharmacy), and Marks and Spencer (variety goods). Cooperative stores owned by consumers also came to sell commodities such as tea, margarine, and flour. They expanded through vertical integration to form, as early as 1863, the Co-operative Society, through which local cooperatives could make bulk purchases of consumer goods. The Society also came to own factories to manufacture and process household and branded goods. For those in the countryside, stores selling through mail-order catalogues grew up—as did Sears and Montgomery, Ward in the United States.

The Development of Banking

The trend toward concentration was more pronounced in some service industries, most notably banking, than in retailing. The rate of growth in the number of retail banks peaked in the third quarter of the nineteenth century and then slowed down. The deposits of commercial banks in England and Wales rose eightfold between 1848 and 1913, to £800 million. As this expansion occurred, the nature of bank ownership changed dramatically. In 1850, 327 private banks with 518 offices (branches) greatly outnumbered the ninety-nine joint-stock banks controlling 576 offices. By 1913, however, forty-one joint-stock banks had 6,426 offices, while twenty-nine private banks possessed just 147 offices. Banking had been transformed as a relatively small group of joint-stock banks, mainly with headquarters in London, dominated British banking nationwide by the time of World War I.

Corporate capitalism replaced personal capitalism in British banking; here was an area where larger firms flourished. Banking legislation passed by Parliament in 1825 and 1833, together with the more general measures allowing the formation of joint-stock companies in 1856 and 1862, encouraged the formation of joint-stock banks. By the time of World War I the "Big Five" banks — Barclay, Lloyds, the Midland, the National Provincial, and the Westminster — had about 80 percent of the domestic deposits in England and were among the largest banks in the world. It was banks like these that came to make up the City of London financial establishment.

The banking situation in Britain differed from that in the United States. Possessing more concentrated urban-industrial markets than the United States, Britain came to have a banking system dominated by a handful of large city banks. Into the 1980s America's banking system was much more atomized and decentralized than that of Britain. American laws, in contrast to those of many other nations, made it difficult for banks to own branches across state lines or, in many cases, even within single states. The desire of Americans to have a federal system of government (and state government regulation of business) contributed to the spread of a decentralized banking system. As a consequence, tens of thousands of smaller institutions dominated commercial banking in the United States well into the twentieth century.

Banking and Industry

Britain's banking system proved responsive to the capital needs of nineteenth-century industry. Hundreds of smaller country banks developed in the late 1700s and early 1800s, and many of these institutions made loans (often called overdrafts) to nascent manufacturers. Local networks of family and friends were important in arranging these transactions. In Sheffield, for example, close ties of kinship and ownership linked bank directors to steel making firms, creating an effective regional network of information and credit.

While often involved in financing foreign trade and in making investments overseas, the large City of London banks also helped finance British industry. While small and medium-size manufacturing ventures continued to rely on local sources of capital, including local banks, larger manufacturers found in the City banks an important source of funding. Domestic manufacturers were not ignored by City banks seeking to invest funds elsewhere. The extension of City bank branch networks throughout England may even have increased the availability of capital to industry. There was enough bank funding to meet the demand for it. If any weakness existed in the financing of Great Britain's industrial system, it was on the part of the manufacturers. Eager to maintain family control over their enterprises, they may not have asked for all the funding they might have been able to use. Rapid expansion was not, perhaps, a key priority for them.

Businesses in Industrializing Germany

Germany was a latecomer to industrialization, coming to the process after Great Britain; and a brief look at how industrialization affected business development in Germany is revealing. While there were certainly similarities in the German and British experiences, there was no single path of development.

Big Business and Industrial Development

Germany became a politically unified nation in 1871, paving the way for the development of a national market. Even earlier a customs union formed among some German states in 1834, and railroad growth from the 1850s spurred economic development. Much of Germany's industrial strength of the late nineteenth and early twentieth centuries lay in heavy industries — older ones, such as coal and iron and steel, and newer ones such as chemicals, electrical equipment, and heavy industrial equipment. It was in these fields that Germany's largest and most vertically integrated firms arose; at the outbreak of World War I all of Germany's twenty largest companies were in these realms. German industrialization stressed heavy industries rather than light industries (such as cotton textiles and silk reeling) and emphasized producer rather than consumer goods.

Two institutions were of particular significance for German business development. While their roles should not be overstressed, large universal banks, such as the Deutsche Bank (formed in 1870) and the Dresdner Bank (started in 1872), were of importance for businesses in some industries. Combining the functions of investment, commercial, and savings banks, these institutions provided both capital and managerial advice for some of Germany's big businesses, especially in the years before World War I. After changes were made in Germany's Company Law in 1884, bankers often sat on the supervisory boards of companies in heavy industry. The universal banks were deeply engaged in the affairs of businesses in the coal and the iron and steel industries, but were much less involved in the work of chemical or mechanical engineering companies. Cartels were also especially important in Germany. The German government allowed, and at times

Modern Germany

promoted, the development of cartels as a way of encouraging the nation's newly industrializing firms to cooperate in their competition with better established companies abroad. Cartels numbered 500–600 by 1911, with further cartelization occurring in the 1920s and 1930s.

Smaller Firms in German Industrialization

However, the picture of German industrialization and business development is more complex than simply a story of big businesses, universal banks, and cartels. As in all of the other nations we are examining, smaller firms were of considerable significance. Small and medium-size companies in Germany — collectively called the *Mittelstand* — were a mix of businesses in handicraft trades, small craft shops, industrial firms, businesses associated with agriculture, and retailers and wholesalers. They often identified closely with their regions. Many were linked through local and regional chambers of commerce, and were integrated only slowly and unevenly into Germany's national market in the twentieth century. The adoption of electricity, which was a more flexible power source than steam power, encouraged the decentralization of some industrialization, allowing, for example, the development of Württemberg as an industrial region. As in Great Britain, regional business networks remained important even as national big businesses arose. And, beyond manufacturing, small firms were the norm in sales. Between 1895 and 1907 the number of retail outlets with fewer than five employees rose from 560,000 to 800,000.

The small and medium-size firms in manufacturing were usually strongly controlled by families, with little input from universal banks, which concentrated on the larger national manufacturers. Municipal savings banks and cooperative credit unions, in addition to families, provided the financing for the small and medium-size firms. The companies employed skilled craftsmen to produce manufactured products for niche markets: watches and clocks, cameras, optical and musical instruments, and engines of various sorts, to list a few.

Labor and Industrialization

A craft tradition, combined with the availability of an excellent polytechnic education, well served German industrial companies, large and small. Skilled, well-educated workers took considerable pride in their labor, and were generally more receptive to the introduction of new technologies than their counterparts in other industrializing nations, making technological transfers reasonably easy. Perhaps German workers were more open to technological change because they did not have to fear that management would deploy technology in ways that undermined their control of work processes, as management often did in Great Britain and the United States. Skilled workers in Germany seldom used their collective power to thwart the introduction of new ways of doing things.

Conclusions

Big businesses like Imperial Tobacco were the exception, not the rule, in prewar Great Britain; small and medium-size companies, not large firms, led Britain's industrial advance. Even Imperial Tobacco, Great Britain's largest industrial enterprise, which was capitalized at $60 million, was a pygmy when compared to America's biggest business, United States Steel, which was formed in the same year, 1901, and was capitalized at $1.4 billion. In only a handful of manufacturing and service fields did large companies dominate Britain's business scene. Instead, smaller firms employing practical, skilled workers ruled the day. The nature of Britain's markets, along with the nation's geography, laws, and other factors, militated against the extensive development of big business. Britain's thousands of independent firms, often woven together in various sorts of arrangements short of their merger into large, vertically integrated firms, made the nation the world leader in manufacturing for most of the 1800s. Only during the closing decades of the nineteenth century did the United States overtake Britain as an industrial power. In Germany, big businesses were more important from the start of industrialization, aided by large banks and cartels; and by around 1900 Germany, like the United States, surpassed Great Britain in important measures of industrialization, such as steel production. However, in Germany, like Great Britain, small firms, the *Mittelstand*, remained important well into the twentieth century.

Suggested Readings

The essays composing Geoffrey Jones and Mary Rose, eds., *Family Capitalism* (Brookfield, 1993), examine the importance of family firms in Great Britain and beyond from the eighteenth through the twentieth centuries. Katrina Honeyman, *Origins of Enterprise: Business Leadership in the Industrial Revolution* (Manchester, 1983), and Francois Crouzet, *The First Industrialists: The Problem of Origins* (Cambridge, 1985), investigate business leadership during industrialization. Julian Hoppit, *Risk and Failure in English Business, 1700–1800* (Cambridge, 1987), examines bankruptcy and the growing risks in British business.

Much has been written about the British cotton textile industry. S. D. Chapman, *The Cotton Textile Industry in the Industrial Revolution* (London, 1972), D. A. Farnie, *The English Cotton Industry in the World Market, 1815–1896* (Oxford, 1979), and Mary Rose, *Firms, Networks and Business Values: The British and American Cotton Industries since 1750* (Cambridge, 2000), examine the industry from different viewpoints. On the Sheffield steel industry, see Geoffrey Tweedale, *Steel City: Entrepreneurship, Strategy, and Technology in Sheffield, 1743–1993* (Oxford, 1995). On the importance of industrial districts in Europe, see Charles F. Sabel and Jonathan Zeitlin, eds., *World of Possibilities: Flexibility and Mass Production in Western Industrialization* (Cambridge, 1997). John Wilson and Andrew Popp, eds., *Industrial Clusters and Regional Business Networks in England, 1750–1970* (Aldershot, 2003), points out the limitations as well as the successes of industrial districts in Great Britain.

B. W. E. Alford, *W. D. & H. O. Wills and the Development of the U.K. Tobacco Industry, 1786–1965* (London, 1973), Maurice Kirby, *The Origins of Railway Enterprise: The Stockton and Darlington Railway, 1821–1863* (New York, 1993), and T. R. Gourvish and R. G. Wilson, *The British Brewing Industry, 1830–1980* (New York, 1994), are solid company or industry histories. H. L. Malchow, *Gentlemen Capitalists: The Social and Political World of the Victorian Businessman* (Stanford, 1992), presents four finely drawn business biographies. R. P. T. Davenport-Hines, *Dudley Docker: the Life and Times of a Trade Warrior* (Cambridge, 1984), is an excellent business biography of an industrialist who sought to rationalize British business in the early twentieth century.

Less has been written on marketing and services than on manufacturing. For an introduction to the development of marketing see the essays, mainly about the British experience, in Richard Tedlow and Geoffrey Jones, eds., *The Rise and Fall of Mass Marketing* (London, 1994). Stanley Chapman, "British Marketing Enterprise: The Changing Roles of Merchants, Manufacturers, and Financiers, 1700–1860," *Business History Review* 53 (Summer 1979): 205–34, and R. P. T. Davenport-Hines, ed., *Markets and Bagmen: Studies in the History of Marketing and British Industrial Performance, 1830–1939* (Brookfield, 1986), are also valuable. Youssef Cassis, *City Bankers, 1890–1914* (Cambridge, 1994), offers a close look at the banking community composing the City of London. For a comparative study of the impact of anti-trust laws on industry, see Tony Freyer, *Regulating Big Business: Antitrust in Great Britain and America 1880–1990* (Cambridge, 1992). Robert Fitzgerald, *British Labour Management & Industrial Welfare* (London, 1988), and Isaac Cohen, *American Management and British Labor* (Westport, 1990), place British labor practices in the context of industry structures. Larry G. Gerber, *The Irony of State Intervention: American Industrial Relations Policy in Comparative Perspectives* (DeKalb, 2005) is a valuable comparison of American and British labor policies.

On the development of German business, see Wilfried Feldenkirchen, "Concentration in Germany Industry, 1870–1939," in Hans Pohl, ed., *The*

Concentration Process in the Entrepreneurial Economy Since the late 19th Century (Wiesbaden, 1988), and Jeffrey Fear, "German Capitalism," Harvard Business School Case N1-796-004 (14 December 1995). For an excellent history of one important firm, see Wilfried Feldenkirchen, *Werner Von Siemens: Inventor and International Entrepreneur* (Columbus, 1994). For an overview of business development in France, see Michael S. Smith, *The Emergence of Modern Business Enterprise in France, 1800–1930* (Cambridge, Mass., 2006).

Big and Small Businesses in Industrializing America

After the Civil War, U.S. industrialists were the world leaders in achieving high-volume, low-cost production in manufacturing—in the processing of liquids, agricultural goods, metals, and some other products. This approach to mass production, encouraged by the existence of a large national market and made possible by technological breakthroughs, led to the rise of big business in the United States. Only later did big business develop in as major a way in other nations. However, the growth of big business in America did not cause the demise of small and medium-size firms, even in manufacturing. Manufacturers of all sizes coexisted in a sometimes uneasy mix that changed over time and continues to change to the present day. Beyond manufacturing, most types of sales and services remained the realm of smaller firms, where most Americans continued to work.

Large Business Firms

The new big businesses that developed in the United States differed from their smaller counterparts in fundamental ways. Many big businesses were organized as corporations, rather than as partnerships, and many developed managerial hierarchies as time progressed. Bureaucratic management began replacing personal management. Most fundamentally, many big businesses, especially large industrial firms, sought to internalize within their operations all the steps involved in making and selling goods. Their managers did not want to rely on other firms, and so tried to do everything in their own companies. To some extent, large British companies were moving in the same directions—as we saw in chapter 3—but large American firms went much farther.

Incorporation and Firm Size

As the nineteenth century progressed, more and more American industrial companies were corporations, as permitted by the general incorporation laws of most states. A shrinking proportion was single-owner proprietorships or partnerships. Many manufacturing concerns were capital intensive and needed to raise vast sums of money to build factories. The corporate form of organization, with its promise of limited liability for investors (investors were not held personally responsible for the debts of the corporations in which they invested), proved especially attractive to would-be industrialists. Another advantage of the corporation was that, unlike a partnership, it did not have to be reorganized every time an investor left the business. More than in Great Britain, business leaders in the United States embraced incorporation; by 1904 corporations accounted for three-quarters of the United States' industrial output.

As executives formed corporations, big businesses arose in America. The size of business firms increased dramatically. In the 1850s the largest industrial enterprises were cotton textile mills. However, only a few were capitalized at over $1 million or employed more than 500 workers. In 1860 no single American company was valued at as much as $10 million, but by 1904 over 300 were. In 1901 the newly formed United States Steel Corporation was capitalized at $1.4 billion to become America's and the world's first billion-dollar company and employed over 100,000 workers. By 1929 the corporation employed 440,000.

Firm Structure

The new big businesses developed structures different from those of earlier enterprises. These structures evolved in response to the opportunities of the national market and in response to the growing complexity of manufacturing processes. The national market offered pleasing possibilities to American businessmen, a market of continental size for their products. Larger, richer, and more homogeneous than that of any other nation, the U.S. domestic market stimulated business executives to develop firms that could produce and sell long runs of standardized goods; thus economies of scale could be exploited well in the American context. So could economies of scope, by which industrial firms could use their factories to turn out a growing variety of goods and by which they could employ their marketing networks to sell those goods. However, the national market also created virulent competition. The railroad and the telegraph brought businesses across the nation into competition with each other by destroying local monopolies that had been based upon the high cost of inland transportation. Technological breakthroughs in production were also a double-edged sword. The innovations increased production, but this vast increase proved difficult to sell by conventional means.

Vertical integration was the common American response to the challenges of market and technological change. Much more than was true in other nations, vertically integrated companies came to dominate the industrial landscape of the United States. In vertical integration a company that initially engages in only one stage of the production and sale of a good may integrate backward to control its sources of raw materials and may integrate forward to control the making and selling of its finished goods. Through vertical integration, big businesses in America combined mass production with mass distribution. (See Figure 1.)

Vertical integration offered several advantages to executives operating on a large scale in the national market. Through vertical integration business leaders could partially insulate their firms from the buffets of the national market. By controlling raw materials, they could assure themselves of adequate supplies during times of peak demand, and by controlling all stages of manufacturing they could keep all of the profits within their own firms. There were also advantages in controlling marketing networks, and in some fields big businesses arose when industrialists set up marketing systems to handle their goods. Business executives using new types of machinery to turn out high volumes of matches, cigarettes, flour, and canned goods found America's wholesalers overwhelmed by the increased output — the throughput of their firms — and set up their own national marketing systems. Similarly, producers making or growing perishables such as beer, meat, and citrus fruits found marketers unable to guarantee the needed speed of delivery to market and also established their own national systems. Finally, manufacturers of technologically complex goods such as reapers, sewing machines, typewriters, and elevators set up their own systems, because established marketers could not adequately demonstrate such complex products to prospective customers, finance their purchase by customers, or service and repair the products after sales.

Andrew Carnegie vertically integrated his large steel company in the 1880s and 1890s by controlling his sources of raw materials: iron ore, coking coal, limestone, and so forth. His company also owned the ore ships and railroads needed to transport them to Pittsburgh, where the smelters and steel plants were located. Finally, Carnegie's firm set up sales outlets to market its goods. An efficient set-up designed to serve the country's rapidly growing national market, Carnegie Steel (the forerunner of United States Steel) made large standardized runs of homogeneous products such as railroad rails and structural beams for skyscrapers. This strategy was very different from that of the hundreds of small steel makers in Great Britain's

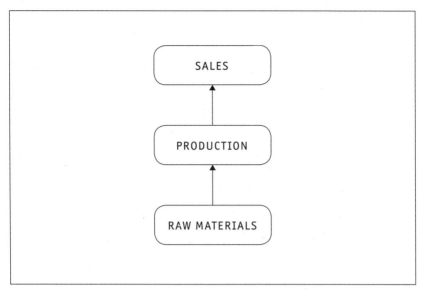

FIGURE 1 *Vertical integration in U.S. business*

Sheffield district, who aimed mainly at producing specialized products for niche markets.

Horizontal integration provided a second strategy by which American industrialists structured their big businesses. In horizontal integration a number of companies joined together to control one step in the production and sale of goods. As in vertical integration, the aim was to decrease competition and control the vicissitudes of the national market. Thus, forty-one companies came together in 1882 to form the Standard Oil Trust to control much of the refining of petroleum in America. To be successful, horizontal integration was usually soon accompanied by vertical integration, as businesses sought to control their raw materials and markets, as well as production. Standard Oil, for example, acquired its own crude oil fields, built its own long-distance pipelines, and set up its own sales outlets in the late nineteenth and early twentieth centuries.

Business integration, both vertical and horizontal, took place more through mergers of formerly independent companies than by internally generated growth. Mergers became increasingly common from the 1880s on, culminating in America's first major merger movement. Between 1894 and 1905 over 3,000 individual firms capitalized at over $6 billion merged in the United States, at about the same time that Great Britain experienced its first merger movement.

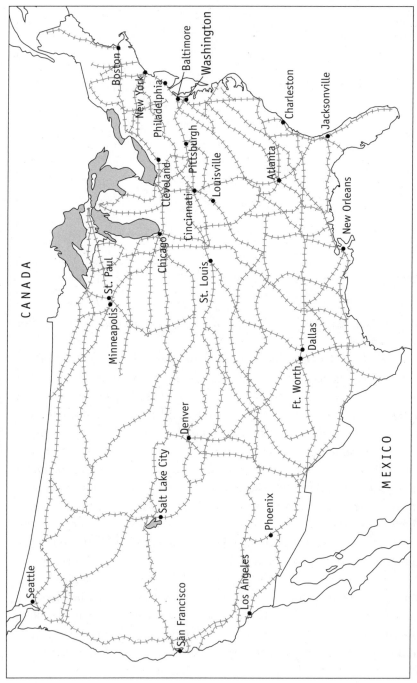

Major railroads in the United States, around 1910

Bureaucratic Management

In those industrial firms which grew in size and complexity, personal management gave way to bureaucratic management. Companies became too large and too complex to be run as one-man shows. With plants spread across the United States, many industrial companies became multi-unit enterprises, and in them four interrelated managerial changes occurred.

Executives established strong central (corporate) offices for their companies. Staffed by top management, these offices took charge of making the big strategic decisions for the company, planning for the future, and coordinating the work of the different parts of the company. The central offices soon became functionally departmentalized, with different committees of executives in charge of different functions of the company—production, sales, transportation, and so on. By 1886 Standard Oil possessed a functionally departmentalized head office consisting of different committees for domestic commerce, foreign trade, manufacturing, and transportation. An executive committee of Standard's top officers was supposed to oversee and coordinate the work of these committees.

Middle management, which had not existed earlier, developed to run the many daily operations of the new big businesses, to staff the various production facilities and sales outlets. In the late nineteenth century the Burlington, Chicago & Quincy Railroad had 191 middle-level managers, and in the early 1900s Singer Sewing Machine had 1,700 branch offices across America run by middle managers.

To control their growing industrial empires industrialists went beyond the preindustrial merchant's simple accounting methods based on double-entry bookkeeping. They developed new accounting methods to help plan for the future of their companies as well as to keep track of past and current operations. Big business leaders began developing financial accounting, including the use of operating ratios, as a way to judge the performances of their firms. They started using capital accounting, with its provisions for depreciation, as a way to plan for the future. True cost accounting was developed as a way to keep track of and to compare the internal workings of various parts of their plants.

There was also the beginning of the separation of ownership from management in big businesses. A growing proportion of corporate officers became men (rarely women in this time period) working on salary for their companies' stockholders. While far from disappearing, family firms became rarer in the realm of big business.

The replacement of personal by bureaucratic management took place first on America's largest railroads, some of which had become big businesses by the 1850s, and then spread to the mammoth industrial enterprises arising in the 1880s and later. Four railroads — the Pennsylvania, the Baltimore & Ohio, the New York Central, and the New York & Erie — controlled trackage from the East Coast to the Midwest by the mid-1850s. As they grew from small local carriers to substantial interregional lines, these railroads faced unprecedented operating difficulties, such as how to schedule large numbers of trains and run them safely on time, and strategic problems, such as how to meet the moves of their competitors and how to raise the enormous amounts of capital needed for their expansion. All responded by establishing bureaucratic management systems.

Large industrial firms operating on a national scale encountered the same types of challenges and made a similar response — again, the adoption of bureaucratic management — a generation or two later. Andrew Carnegie, who served as the superintendent of the western division of the Pennsylvania Railroad, applied the lessons he learned on that line in running the steel company he put together in the late nineteenth century. While always in control of strategic decision making, Carnegie delegated authority over operations to his steel mill managers, rarely interfering with their decisions. From his work on the railroad Carnegie also took an abiding concern for controlling costs and promoting high-volume production to his steel mills.

James Duke and the American Tobacco Company

The evolution of the American Tobacco Company presents a classic case study in the development of big business in American industry. James Buchanan Duke, known by most nineteenth-century Americans as "Buck Duke," transformed the American tobacco industry through the development of American Tobacco, the firm which brought the mass production of cigarettes to the American public. Moreover, Duke's character was typical, in many important respects, of those of America's business leaders of the late nineteenth and early twentieth centuries.

By 1880 Duke had taken over a family business in pipe tobacco in North Carolina, and it was from this base that he soon built the largest tobacco-processing company in the world. Realizing that other well-established companies already controlled the plug (chewing) and pipe tobacco fields, Duke looked elsewhere for expansion possibilities. He found his chance in cigarettes, a relatively new field of tobacco processing whose market was rapidly increasing — 1.8 million cigarettes were sold in America in 1869, but 500 million in 1880. As we saw in chapter 3, in those days cigarettes were made by hand, with a supervisor and team of ten turning out about 20,000 cigarettes a day. In 1881 Duke hired a team of eleven men to begin his production. In this labor-intensive business there were no economies of scale, and Duke was, at first, simply one of many cigarette makers.

Duke surged ahead of the other cigarette producers with the purchase of rights to use automatic cigarette-rolling machines patented by James Bonsack of Virginia. Perfected in 1884, a Bonsack machine could turn out over 100,000 cigarettes a day. Use of the Bonsack machines gave Duke a cost advantage over his rivals, just as such machines helped W. D. & H. O. Wills move ahead of its competitors in Great Britain. By 1885 Duke controlled 10 percent of America's cigarette market. He then engaged in horizontal integration, taking over his competitors — Allen and Ginter of Richmond, Kinney Tobacco of New York, Goodwin and Company of Rochester, and others — to form one gigantic company, the American Tobacco Company, in 1890.

Duke next sought to move beyond cigarettes to acquire companies in chewing and pipe tobacco making both in and beyond the United States. By 1910 American Tobacco possessed 86 percent of the cigarette market, 85 percent of the plug market, 79 percent of the pipe tobacco market, and 14 percent of the cigar market in the United States. Duke went abroad by taking on British cigarette makers in 1901. After a fierce battle, American Tobacco and Imperial Tobacco agreed to a truce. American Tobacco agreed to get out of the British market, and Imperial Tobacco said it would leave the American market. Together they formed a new company, two-thirds owned by American Tobacco, to sell cigarettes to the rest of the world. Vertical integration followed American Tobacco's horizontal integration, as Duke acquired companies making licorice, cotton bags to hold tobacco, boxes, and tin foil. American Tobacco also purchased the United Cigar Stores, which had 392 retail outlets.

Eventually, American Tobacco's control over the American market led to its dissolution at the hands of the Justice Department of the federal government. In 1908 the department brought suit against the company under the terms of the Sherman Act of 1890, and three years later the U.S. Supreme Court ordered that the company be split up. From the dissolution of American Tobacco came new firms that long dominated the American tobacco market: the (new) American Tobacco Company, the Liggett and Myers Tobacco Company, the R. J. Reynolds Tobacco Company, and the P. Lorillard Company. Duke left American Tobacco a few months after its breakup and died in 1925.

Shortly before his death, Duke told a friend why he thought he had been successful in business. "I resolved from the time I was a mere boy to do a big business," Duke observed. "I loved business better than anything else. I worked from early morning until late at night. I was sorry to have to leave off at night and glad when morning came so I could get at it again." Business was Duke's life. He loved the thrill of the game and was an empire builder.

However, Duke was not a good administrator. He failed to establish a rational management system for his company. Nor did Duke really provide American Tobacco with a goal beyond growth for growth's sake. Perhaps not surprisingly, American Tobacco's earnings, as a percentage of sales, fell from 29 percent in 1891 to 22 percent in 1908. Duke left American Tobacco a few months after its dissolution. His later life was not a happy one. Disturbed by the death of his father, dismayed by marital difficulties, and upset by the breakup of his company, Duke tended to drift and turn to drink. However, he believed in the value of education and endowed Duke University as his memorial.

The Visible Hand of Management

Big business was clearly established in America by the time of the First World War. By 1917 the United States possessed 278 companies capitalized at $20 million or more. Of these companies 236 were in manufacturing. Some 171 were in only six fields: food processing, chemicals, oil, metals, machine-making, and transportation equipment. Even more than in Great Britain, it was in these capital-intensive industrial areas that there were the greatest opportunities for American executives to exploit economies of scale and scope through the formation of large vertically integrated firms. Parts of American industry came to be characterized by oligopoly; in these fields a handful of large companies dominated their markets. As early as 1904 just a few major companies controlled at least half of the output of 78 different industries in the United States.

As their companies became big businesses, the decisions of the corporate executives replaced market forces in determining the production and distribution of products in some industrial fields. Decisions made in earlier times by the free interplay of market forces, what the British economist Adam Smith called "the invisible hand" of the market in his famous book *The Wealth of Nations* in 1776, were now made by the visible hand of business management. Nearly all of the 236 big businesses in manufacturing were vertically integrated, and 85 percent of them were organized around some sort of centralized, functionally departmentalized management structure.

The Continuing Importance of Small Businesses

With the development of big businesses like American Tobacco, Carnegie Steel, and Standard Oil, smaller businesses found themselves in an ambiguous position. The proportion of America's industrial output coming from small businesses dropped as large manufacturing ventures rose to prominence. Even so, opportunities in the nation's expanding industrial economy beckoned to small business owners, and small businesses increased in absolute numbers. Moreover, small firms remained mainstays in sales and services.

Small Business in Manufacturing

While not as important as in Great Britain, small businesses remained significant in American manufacturing. In 1914 nearly a third of America's industrial workers found employment in plants with 500 or more in their labor forces, and another third in those with 100 to 499. Even so, a third was still employed by firms with 100 or fewer workers. Some 54 percent worked in companies employing no more than 250 people. Altogether, about 54,000 manufacturing businesses had six to twenty workers.

Most small businesses that succeeded in manufacturing did so as flexible firms producing specialty products for niche markets, either on their own or as members of regional business networks — much like the Sheffield steel makers. Rather than competing head-to-head with large mass-production industrialists, they coexisted with big businesses by differentiating their products from those of their larger competitors. Thus, the exploitation of economies of scale and scope were much less important for small businesses than for their larger counterparts. Small businesses used instead their flexibility to produce goods, often in small batches and short production runs, for rapidly changing regional and seasonal markets. Part of the ability to accomplish this task lay in the employment of intelligent, innovative workforces. Another part lay in the flexible use of the most advanced technologies of the day. This strategy has remained at the core of much small business success in manufacturing to the present day.

Large and Small Firms in Textiles and Steel

America's textile industry provides a good example of how large and small firms could coexist — and a real contrast to the situation in Great Britain, where the industry was composed mainly of smaller companies. As the nineteenth century progressed, America's textile industry divided into two segments. At Waltham and Lowell in New England, large factories employed unskilled workers to turn out standardized textiles for the mass market. By 1850 twelve corporations employed 12,000 textile workers in Lowell. However, a very different pattern unfolded in Philadelphia. There, in 1850 some 326 firms employed 12,400 textile workers. Two-thirds of these firms possessed twenty-five or fewer workers. Though employing as many workers in the aggregate as their counterparts in Lowell, the Philadelphia firms were capitalized at much less, $4.7 million, about a third of the amount invested in the Lowell companies.

The Philadelphia firms competed successfully throughout the nineteenth century by stressing specialization and flexibility in production and marketing. Like most of their British counterparts, few Philadelphia firms tried to master all aspects of textile production. Most specialized in one or two steps which they then did very well indeed, using the most up-to-date machinery and employing skilled workers, often men, at high wages. Productivity levels were high. With skilled workforces and modern machinery, the Philadelphia mills could rapidly switch to various types of cotton, wool, and other fabrics as needed. Small size and versatility continued to be hallmarks of Philadelphia textile firms into the mid-twentieth century. Only when national economic problems joined particular local problems of the Philadelphia mills during the Great Depression of the 1930s did the Philadelphia textile businesses decline.

A similar story developed in America's iron and steel industries. Much of Pittsburgh's iron and steel industries took form as collections of relatively small specialized businesses. Not even the formation of United States Steel in 1901 radically altered this situation. Only a few of the small firms became part of United States Steel, and this development was more than offset by the formation of sixteen new iron and steel firms in Pittsburgh between 1898 and 1901. In 1901 the forty small independent producers in Pittsburgh had a production capacity of 3.8 million tons of iron and steel, compared to the 2.6 million ton capacity of United States Steel. In 1920 fully 78 percent of the independents in existence two decades before were still doing business, and even after America's second major merger movement, which occurred in the 1920s, about 50 percent were active. The Great Depression put many of these firms out of business, but on the eve of World War II 28 percent of the original independents remained operative.

The success of small firms in the iron and steel industries was not limited to the Pittsburgh region or to firms that developed as part of regional groupings. The growth of the Buckeye Steel Castings Company of Columbus, Ohio, suggests the continuing importance of stand-alone small businesses in manufacturing.

Formed as a partnership in 1881, Buckeye Steel initially produced a variety of cast iron goods for the local market. Buckeye lacked a specialty product or any other advantage over its competitors and came very close to failing during the mid-1880s. At that time a new president, Wilbur Goodspeed, changed the direction of the company. Coming to Columbus from Cleveland in 1886, Goodspeed had Buckeye Steel develop a specialty product for a niche market, an automatic railroad car coupler. This technologically sophisticated product gave Buckeye an edge over its competitors and allowed the company to break into the national market.

In entering this market, Buckeye Steel's executives relied heavily upon their personal connections with other business people. While in business in Cleveland, Goodspeed had come to know high-ranking executives at the Standard Oil Company, which was headquartered in that city. (Goodspeed and some of the Standard Oil executives set up the Cleveland Gatling Gun Regiment, a private paramilitary outfit, in the wake of nationwide railroad strike in 1877.) Soon after he took over at Buckeye Steel, Goodspeed negotiated an arrangement favorable to both parties. In return for receiving a large block of common stock in Buckeye Steel for free, the Standard Oil executives agreed to use their influence to persuade all the railroads that shipped Standard's petroleum products to market (few long-distance pipelines existed then) to purchase their couplers solely from Buckeye Steel. Railroad orders soared, and Buckeye Steel emerged as a very successful business, becoming a medium-size firm by national standards at the time of World War I.

Common attitudes and circumstances ran behind the success of those small companies that proved capable of coexisting with large manufacturing concerns. The smaller firms developed specialty products which they then sold in niche markets, thereby avoiding direct competition with their larger counterparts. To make this strategy work, small companies adopted or developed themselves the most advanced production technologies available. These small companies were not backward workshops using obsolete equipment, but rather forward-looking companies run by managers deeply committed to their success. Most of the firms continued to be operated as family enterprises similar to their British counterparts, devoid for the most part of managerial hierarchies. A sense of personal satisfaction, almost a sense of craftsmanship, remained an important motivating factor for both executives and workers. Factors external to their companies also prepared the way to success. In some instances government aid helped. Such was the case with Buckeye Steel. In 1893 Congress passed legislation requiring that all railroad cars be equipped with automatic couplers within five years. This act was a piece of safety legislation designed to protect trainmen who were often injured while joining cars together with the old-style manual couplers. This law helped create a national market for Buckeye Steel's main product. In other cases, especially where regional networks developed, favorable local environments proved valuable. In Philadelphia the textile companies benefited from various sorts of local government aid and were also able to join together to support for many years a trade school to ensure the availability of a steady supply of skilled workers.

Sales and Services: Realms of Small Firms

The rise of big business led to significant changes in distribution and sales. Big business in marketing took several forms. As in Great Britain, department stores like Macy's, Bloomingdale's, and Lazarus grew up to serve large concentrated urban markets. Catalogue stores such as Montgomery Ward and Sears, Roebuck served rural and small-town America. Chain stores got their start. The Great Atlantic and Pacific Tea Company (A&P) began operations in 1859 and had about 200 stores selling tea, coffee, and groceries by 1900. Beginning in 1879, F. W. Woolworth set up Five and Ten Cent Stores, which had a sales volume of more than $15 million by 1905.

However, most sales, especially at the retail level, continued to be made by small neighborhood stores in cities or by small general stores in the countryside. In 1929, 168,000 wholesalers employed 1.6 million people, for an average employment per establishment of just under ten people. Retailing remained even more the province of small businesses. In the same year, 1.5 million retail establishments employed 5.7 million people, for an average employment of just over three people per store. As late as 1890 just ten chains (each composed of at least two stores) existed in America, and even in 1915 there were only 515. Scale economies proved more elusive in selling than in making products and were often offset by a small marketer's knowledge of local conditions. As in Great Britain, the new market outlets such as department stores and chain stores cut into, but did not displace, the sales made by more traditional retail establishments.

In the service sector, commercial banking remained a home for small businesses in the United States. Unlike many industrialized or industrializing nations, the United States possessed no central bank. Nothing resembling the "Big Five" banks of Great Britain or the large universal banks of Germany developed. Instead, Americans depended upon a mixture of thousands of nationally or state chartered banks to meet their commercial needs. In 1896 there were about 11,500 commercial banks with assets of roughly $6.2 billion in the United States, by 1920 some 30,300 possessing assets of $47.5 billion.

Most of these institutions remained small and independently owned, a situation that possessed both positive and negative aspects. Bankers serving local areas could rely on their personal knowledge in making loans to farmers and business people. They could thereby serve their localities well. Still, there were weaknesses too. Banks operated almost in isolation from each other, which contributed to the development of financial panics and depressions of varying intensity in 1873, 1884, 1893, 1903, and 1907. Branch banking might have provided some stability, but federal and state laws resulting from Americans' fears about economic concentration severely limited branching.

Business, Society, and Politics

America's business practices mirrored social and cultural norms in the United States. The fears which Americans had about concentrated power prevented the development of a centralized banking system. Even so, the rise of big business led to innovations in social thought, law, and government activities. After a lag time, legal decisions and governmental actions caught up with changes occurring in the economic realm. In particular, the federal government began monitoring and regulating the actions of some big businesses through the creation of independent regulatory commissions. Taking this step required time. When compared to Great Britain, and in some ways Japan, the United States developed big businesses before it possessed big government.

Nonetheless, reform did take place. As Americans reformed both city and rural life in the wake of industrialization, urbanization, and business changes, they did so as part of a transatlantic effort at social and political modernization. While certainly responding directly to what was occurring in their own nation, American reformers were also well versed in what was taking place in Europe, especially in Great Britain. As in earlier times, the Atlantic Ocean served as a bridge, not a barrier, to the flow of people and ideas.

A Business Elite

Large and small firms differed in the types of people they attracted as owners and managers. American business leaders formed something of an elite in the late 1800s and early 1900s. There was clearly social mobility in America. A penniless immigrant like Andrew Carnegie, the founder of Carnegie Steel, America's largest nineteenth-century industrial enterprise, could rise from rags to riches in a single generation; but Carnegie was the exception, not the rule. Most big businesses were run by well-educated men who came from middle-class or upper-class backgrounds and who were native-born.

While an elite, America's business elite was a relatively open one, at least for white males. No women or minorities and very few immigrants rose to the top of large firms. Money was the common denominator that provided access to the upper reaches of American society for the newly rich railroad barons and industrialists. Titles of nobility and the possession of old family names counted for less in the United States than in Europe. Through what the American economist Thorstein Veblen labeled "conspicuous consumption" — using their wealth to build mansions, acquire art, buy private railroad cars, and host lavish parties (at one, the tongues of peacocks were served) — America's business leaders could buy their way into society.

Business, Public Attitudes, and Politics

Americans loved the material abundance, the outpouring of goods, and the rising standard of living they associated with big business. Americans were well on their way to becoming the leading consumers of the world. However, there was considerable ambivalence in attitudes toward the rise of big business. In the late nineteenth century industrial development was sudden, new, and disruptive of traditional ways of doing things. The general response to the rise of big business in the United States was to try to control it through regulation by the government.

Federal government regulation of business began during the Progressive period, roughly the years 1900 through 1920. The Interstate Commerce Commission (ICC), a federal government agency set up by the Interstate Commerce Act of 1887, had its power to regulate railroads enhanced by new legislation, especially in 1906 and 1910. The Meat Inspection Act and the Pure Foods and Drug Act, both passed by Congress in 1906, gave the federal government responsibility for the regulation of America's food and drug industries, and the Food and Drug Administration was set up in that year. In addition, the Federal Reserve Act of 1913 established the Federal Reserve System to regulate banking practices and the money supply in the United States.

However, the federal government was far from the powerful organization that it would later become. In America's federal system much governmental authority, including the power to regulate many businesses, lay with state and local governments. In fact, much of the most effective regulation of business occurred at the state, not the federal, level. Then, too, there existed an anti-state tinge to American thought that limited the power of the federal government. This strain of thought was sometimes expressed in Supreme Court decisions, including several which for some years limited the power of the ICC over railroads.

While the main thrust of American public policy at both the federal and state levels was to regulate rather than destroy big business, law makers passed far-reaching antitrust measures. These measures grew out of America's common law tradition, which reflected a sense of distrust toward big business. Common law fell short of outlawing big business, but it did place restrictions upon how large companies could act. The common law protected small firms from some, but not all, of the depredations of their larger competitors. A new level of action began with the passage of the Sherman Act by Congress in 1890. Its supporters intended that the act encompass the common law tradition. The Sherman Act outlawed restraints of trade, but the law's sponsors intended that "reasonable" restraints, those not injurious to the public and not preventing new firms from entering business fields, be allowed to continue.

As interpreted by the U.S. Supreme Court from 1911, the Sherman Act permitted large firms to exist, as long as they grew big through reasonable means. The Sherman Act was used to break up American Tobacco and Standard Oil in 1911, but only because these two companies were perceived as having become large by unreasonable methods. Ironically, the Supreme Court's "rule of reason" stimulated combination, not competition. The Sherman Act was used most commonly to break up loose combinations among businesses, especially cartels. Tight combinations, such as vertically integrated companies, were not attacked as often or as effectively, and as a consequence business leaders continued to form them. Of the 127 actions taken under the terms of the Sherman Act between 1905 and 1915, seventy-two were filed against loose combinations of smaller firms, thirty-two against tight combinations, twelve each against labor unions and agricultural produce dealers, and ten against miscellaneous others. Thus were laws, public attitudes, and economics reconciled, in a manner significantly different from that which prevailed elsewhere. By way of contrast, in Great Britain cartels of smaller firms were tolerated, and in Germany cartels were encouraged by law, a situation that contributed to their greater significance, especially in manufacturing.

Labor in an Industrializing Society

Conflict between labor and management accompanied industrialization and the rise of big business in the United States. As large companies moved toward mass production in some fields, they produced goods in settings much larger than the plants in which British or German workers labored. This shift to large-scale factory production occurred so rapidly that it upset workers accustomed to traditional ways of making products. Industrial change was also often accompanied by more dangerous working conditions, longer hours of work, and low wages. Throughout these years, managers and workers in the United States, as in Great Britain, vied with each other over the issue of who would control the work process — that is, how industrial work was performed, at what speed, and with what reward system.

In this struggle for control of the workplace, superintendents of large American factories increasingly employed the "drive" system of managing labor. Managers sought to extract as much work as possible in a given period of time, usually ten- or twelve-hour working days. Their goal was to operate their capital-intensive plants, in which the cost of labor was a relatively minor expense, at full bore. To do so, they wrested more and more power from foremen — men charged with hiring and firing workers, and who had considerable say, along with skilled workers, in determining just how tasks were performed. By the turn of the century foremen found their authority circumscribed.

In the effort to seize control of the work floor, managers were aided by the spread of scientific management, managerial practices that aimed at making tasks and the flow of work in factories more efficient. Scientific management stressed the need for better record keeping and accounting methods to keep track of work being done in manufacturing plants, but, above all, it emphasized the value of undermining labor's power in the workplace. Managers wanted to establish uniform and, presumably, more efficient work processes, allowing their plants to run at peak capacity, with no production bottlenecks hindering the transformation of raw materials into finished goods for America's voracious consumers. While no factory adopted all aspects of scientific management, many large ones put some of them into practice. The adoption of scientific management was more common in the large American factories than in the smaller British ones, where workers had more say.

Workers, especially skilled ones, opposed efforts to reduce their control over the labor process. Workers wanted higher wages, shorter working hours, and better working conditions, not diminished power and privileges. In order to accomplish their goals, workers formed nationwide unions designed to bargain with the large industrial firms. Established in 1869, the Knights of Labor sought to group all workers, skilled and unskilled, into local "assemblies" across the United States. The Knights rejected the wage system, wanting, instead, for workers to own their own factories and to buy and sell goods through cooperatives. The Knights achieved some success in the 1870s, but they became less important in the mid-1880s, after losing a nationwide railroad strike. Longer-lived was the American Federation of Labor (AFL), formed in the 1880s as a group of trade unions composed mainly of skilled workers. The AFL accepted the wage system and sought to secure higher wages, shorter working hours, and better working conditions by bargaining collectively with management. Relatively unimportant in the nineteenth century, the AFL became America's leading labor organization in the early twentieth century.

The opposing interests of managers and workers led to industrial conflict and violence. Between 1876 and 1896 the United States experienced more strikes, with more people killed and injured in them, than did any other industrial nation. The list of conflicts was long. Nationwide railroad strikes in 1877 and 1885–86 featured pitched battles between workers and private police in the pay of the railroads. So, too, did a strike against Carnegie Steel in 1894 in Homestead, Pennsylvania.

Over time, managers and workers partially reconciled their divergent interests. By World War I some big business, like their British counterparts, had adopted welfare capitalism. To decrease labor turnover and to try to keep unions out of their plants, many large firms had improved working and living conditions for their employees. While significant, these efforts did not go as far as many workers wanted. Most worrisome to workers, welfare capitalism left control of the work process in the hands of the managers. When compared to their counterparts in Great Britain, America's skilled workers had less control over shop-floor activities by the twentieth century. Instead, in the United States managers seized control of the work process in many industrial firms, especially large ones.

The control exerted by American managers helps explain the relative ease with which mass-production techniques, especially those that deskilled workers (that is, those that replaced craftsmanship with machine production), were introduced and diffused in the United States. In return for a higher material standard of living, many American workers gradually yielded control over their working lives to managers. In short, output soared in mass-production industries, but at the price of a loss of independence in the workplace.

In smaller manufacturing firms, the labor situation varied. Small businesses have a reputation for operating under sweatshop conditions, and many did—small firms in the garment trades, for example. However, there is another side to the story. Operating less-capital-intensive plants and depending more on skilled workers, the heads of some smaller manufacturing plants were more likely to leave control of the shop floor in the hands of their workers, approximating more closely the British practice. Buckeye Steel was one such company, for example.

Labor-management conflict was certainly less obvious in small manufacturing firms than in large ones. Particularly in textiles, the small Philadelphia industrialists relied heavily upon highly skilled workers, who were, like the owner-managers of the companies, flexible in their approaches to their tasks. Willing and able to perform a wide variety of tasks, the workers were well paid and rarely went on strike. Perhaps because they were both close to their workers in relatively small plants and because they cared for the welfare of the city, Pittsburgh's independent iron and steel leaders tended toward a grudging acceptance of unions and a pragmatic willingness to try to work with them. More than the operators of the much larger Carnegie mills, the owner-operators of the small independent facilities sought to achieve a harmonious relationship with their workers, especially in the 1870s and 1880s. In the 1890s and later, however, following the lead of the larger firms, the independent mill owners became less tolerant of labor. As they adopted more capital-intensive equipment and were influenced by the examples of violence against labor at Carnegie Steel, they turned more of their attention to breaking unions. Nonetheless, small business, at least in these two cases, continued to be receptive to the needs of workers.

Conclusions

As the United States industrialized, complex relationships developed between large and small firms. There was conflict between businesses as well as between workers and managers. The development of specialty products for niche markets did not shield all small manufacturers from the onslaughts of their larger counterparts. However, the evolving situation was a mixed one. In some fields large and small firms grew up symbiotically. While many large industrial businesses became vertically integrated to some degree, few were totally integrated. Small firms frequently acted as subcontractors for their larger brethren. Buckeye Steel, for example, supplied the automatic couplers that large railroad car manufacturers used in their production efforts. Production networks were important. A similar example of mutually beneficial arrangements lay in sales. As they expanded their output to meet the demand of America's domestic market, some manufacturers relied on franchised agents. Rather than own their sales outlets, a very costly proposition, manufacturers depended upon agents closely tied to but still legally independent from their firms to make the sales. For example, the Singer Sewing Machine Company and the McCormick Harvester Company employed franchise sales systems in the nineteenth century, a practice that would be refined and become widespread in the twentieth century.

Suggested Readings

Alfred D. Chandler Jr., *The Visible Hand: The Managerial Revolution in American Business* (Cambridge, 1977) is a masterly survey of the rise of big business in America. Harold Livesay, *American Made* (Boston, 2006), looks at the contributions of individuals to the development of America's business system. For a different appraisal, see Richard Bensel, *The Political Economy of American Industrialization, 1877–1900* (Cambridge, 2000). On the history of small businesses, see Stuart Bruchey, ed., *Small Business in American Life* (New York, 1980), and Mansel G. Blackford, *A History of Small Business in America* (Chapel Hill, 2003). On the importance of industrial districts in the United States, see Philip Scranton, *Endless Novelty: Specialty Production and American Industrialization, 1865–1925* (Princeton, 1997). Thomas Dicke, *Franchising in America* (Chapel Hill, 1992), looks at the history of franchising in America's business system.

Business and economic historians have been reevaluating the nature of the business firm, with ramifications that go beyond the history of American business. See especially Naomi R. Lamoreaux, Daniel M. G. Raff, and Peter Temin, "Beyond Markets and Hierarchies: Toward a New Synthesis of American Business History," *American Historical Review* 108 (April 2003), 404–33. See also the many articles on this topic in *Enterprise and Society* 5 (Sept. 2004).

On the changing nature of management and ownership in American business, see Oliver Zunz, *Making America Corporate, 1870–1920* (Chicago, 1990), and Pamela W. Laird, *Pull: Networking and Success since Benjamin Franklin* (Cambridge, Mass., 2006). On women in American business, see Angel Kwolek-Folland, *Incorporating Women: A History of Women and Business in the United States* (New York, 1998). On African Americans in business, see Juliet E. K. Walker, *The History of Black Business in America: Capitalism, Race, Entrepreneurship* (New York, 1998).

Thomas McCraw, *The Prophets of Regulation* (Cambridge, Mass., 1984), examines government-business relations in modern America. Martin Sklar, *The Corporate Reconstruction of American Capitalism, 1890–1916* (Cambridge, 1988), connects changes in America's corporate, legal, and business systems. Daniel Nelson, *Managers and Workers: Origins of the New Factory System in the United States, 1880–1920* (Madison, 1975), is an excellent place to start in understanding changing shop-floor relationships in the United States. Daniel T. Rodgers, *Atlantic Crossings: Social Politics in a Progressive Age* (Cambridge, Mass., 1998), stresses linkages in reform developments in Europe and the United States.

Japanese and Chinese Businesses during Industrialization

From a merchant house in Tokugawa times, Mitsui emerged as a large, diversified, nationwide company in the late Meiji period. Called a zaibatsu, Mitsui had extensive interests in banking, manufacturing, mining, and trading. As the transformation of Mitsui demonstrated, in Japan, no less than in the United States, industrialization changed business firms and business practices. New companies grew up. As new firms and forms of business arose in Japan, types of business management, the status of business leaders, and the nature of labor relations underwent alterations. However, as in the United States and Great Britain, there was continuity as well as change in Japan's business system. Family networks lay at the heart of zaibatsu; and far from all of Japan's businesses, even in manufacturing, became zaibatsu. Smaller companies in manufacturing, sales, and services played significant roles in Japan's development. In China, too, a mixture of large, medium-size, and small firms was important as that nation industrialized in the late nineteenth and early twentieth centuries. Family connections and ties to localities were of great importance, regardless of company size, much as they had been for the preindustrial salt makers in Zigong.

The Rise of the Zaibatsu in Japan

Few of the large merchant houses of the Tokugawa period made successful transitions into the new industrial times of Meiji Japan. As we have seen, there was much economic activity in the late Tokugawa and early Meiji periods. However, much of this action took place outside of the realms of the large merchant houses. Mitsui and Sumitomo adjusted to new economic circumstances and flourished in them, but those companies were exceptional. More commonly, new types of companies and company groupings developed, as Japanese business people sought to deal with rapid economic change.

Merchant Houses and Industrialization

Most of the large merchant houses failed to make the shift and declined in significance. The political changes that accompanied the Meiji Restoration hurt many of them. They lost their ability to make loans to the *daimyo* and samurai, a major source of their income. Currency reforms, especially the adoption of a national currency based on the yen, decreased their importance as money-changers. Then, too, many Japanese merchants had become more conservative than their British or American counterparts because of the restrictions placed on their activities in the Tokugawa period. Most lacked the daring to enter industrial enterprises.

Business leaders taking advantage of new opportunities to go into shipbuilding, railroads, manufacturing, and banking did so increasingly through the formation of joint-stock companies. Some joint-stock companies existed in an informal way as early as the 1870s and 1880s. Legal recognition through a General Incorporation Act of 1893 and a Commercial Code that went into effect six years later spurred their development. The code, especially, inspired budding business people to think about businesses in new ways. Japan possessed 3,336 joint-stock companies in 1882 and 8,612 twenty years later. Several factors accounted for the popularity of joint-stock companies: the ease with which they could mobilize capital, their association with the greatly admired technology of the West, and the fact that ex-samurai preferred not to work in more traditional family businesses.

While few merchant houses made the transition into the industrial era, they may have helped pave the way for the joint-stock companies. Both the merchant houses and the joint-stock companies emphasized the perpetual existence of business enterprises and stressed the amassing of assets. However, in other ways merchant houses may have hampered the development of joint-stock companies. The stress the merchant houses placed on the family made it psychologically difficult for members of different merchant houses to cooperate in the formation of new business ventures.

Zaibatsu Development

While large, vertically integrated, single-industry corporations were particularly important in the United States' industrialization, in Japan big diversified companies called zaibatsu became powerful in industry and some other business fields in the opening decades of the twentieth century. Zaibatsu provided a way for Japan to compete effectively with other nations. They were more diversified than big businesses in Great Britain or the United States. Zaibatsu were composed of manufacturing ventures (typi-

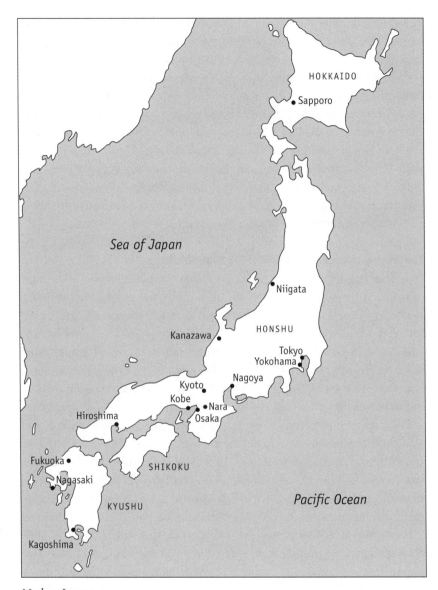

Modern Japan

cally in both light industries such as silk reeling and cotton spinning and emerging heavy industries such as shipbuilding, chemicals, and iron and steel making), mining ventures, a bank to finance these concerns, and a trading company to sell the products overseas.

Zaibatsu developed in several ways. A few, such as Mitsui, evolved from

Tokugawa merchant houses. More, such as Mitsubishi, grew out of enterprises closely connected to the fortunes of the new Japanese government and, like the government itself, were organizations founded in the Meiji period. Still other zaibatsu, such as Nissan, called "new zaibatsu," were formed in the 1920s and 1930s and were closely associated with the Japanese government's efforts to build up heavy industry for military purposes. In the years before the First World War eight major zaibatsu emerged — Mitsui, Mitsubishi, Sumitomo, Yasuda, Asano, Okura, Furukawa, and Kawasaki — the first four of which were known as the "Big Four." By the early 1920s zaibatsu controlled much of the mining, shipbuilding, banking, foreign trade, and industry of Japan. Altogether, zaibatsu accounted for about one-quarter to one-third of Japan's GNP by the close of the 1920s.

The Growth of Trading Companies: The Sogo Shosha

Of special importance in the rise of the zaibatsu and the growth of the Japanese economy was the development of trading companies called *sogo shosha*. The trading companies often grew up to handle the foreign trade of the zaibatsu. Thus, Mitsui Bussan and Mitsubishi Shoji took care of the exports and imports of their zaibatsu. The trading companies were important not just to their zaibatsu, but to the overall development of the Japanese economy, especially its industrial sector. The trading companies did more than trade. Possessing overseas offices, they provided much of the knowledge of foreign technologies and business practices, managerial expertise, and some of the capital needed by Japanese firms. Between 1868 and 1913 *sogo shosha* were formed to compete with Western merchant houses that initially handled Japan's foreign trade, and by the end of this period they were operating throughout Asia, Europe, and the United States. Some were even beginning to handle transactions that did not involve Japan. Even at the start of World War I, however, most *sogo shosha* were specialty traders, not fully developed general trading companies. Then, between 1914 and 1930 *sogo shosha* greatly expanded the scope of their activities to become fully developed general trading companies.

Mitsui Bussan and Mitsubishi Shoji were the largest and most important trading companies. Mitsui Bussan was particularly significant in spurring the growth of Japan's cotton textile industry by importing textile-making machinery and raw cotton for cotton textile companies, which lacked the knowledge to do so. Mitsui Bussan also opened up foreign markets, especially in Asia, for the finished cotton cloth and in the years 1907 through 1910 handled about half of Japan's fabric exports. Mitsui Bussan invested in new industrial companies; by 1940 it held investments totaling 275 million yen in 253 companies in fourteen industries ranging from rayon to sugar refining to the making of elevators. Set up in 1918, Mitsubishi Shoji began with 900 employees and a capitalization of 15 million yen. By the 1930s Mitsubishi Shoji had grown to include six commodity divisions trading in metals, machinery, fuel (mainly petroleum), agricultural products, fishery products, and fertilizers. By the time of World War II, Mitsubishi Shoji had 6,500 employees, possessed 100 million yen in capital, and had offices around the world.

Mitsui and Mitsubishi

The development of Mitsui and Mitsubishi typified common trends in the evolution of zaibatsu in Japan. As we have seen, Mitsui began as a merchant house in the Tokugawa period. Mitsubishi, on the other hand, was one of the many new companies of the Meiji years. However, despite the differences in their origins, both companies became zaibatsu in the Meiji period and, in altered form, both continue as leading businesses in Japan today.

The House of Mitsui had the foresight to back the new Japanese government during the Meiji Restoration and for its support was rewarded with the handling of government funds in the 1870s and 1880s. This major source of revenue lasted until 1887 and helped Mitsui make the transition into the new period of industrialization. New business leadership was also important in Mitsui's success.

Nakamigawa Hikojiro, an entrepreneur who had been involved in newspapers and railroads in the 1880s, was brought in from outside of the Mitsui family as the vice-president of Mitsui Bank in 1891. Nakamigawa soon became the head of the bank and then the head of the entire Mitsui combine. Nakamigawa imposed centralized management over the Mitsui enterprises. He reorganized Mitsui Bank, Mitsui Bussan, Mitsui Mining, and Mitsui Wearing Apparel as partnership companies, all of which were owned by the Mitsui family. At about the same time, what had previously been a temporary council of the Mitsui family emerged as a powerful board of directors that made all the important decisions for the different partnerships. Nakamigawa followed two other policies designed to bring Mitsui to a new stage of development. He purchased industrial and mining companies, especially those in silk reeling, cotton spinning, engineering, paper making, and coal mining. He also brought in new men, particularly from Keio University, where he had studied and taught, to run the Mitsui enterprises.

Nakamigawa died in 1901, and after his death Mitsui underwent further alterations in the opening years of the twentieth century. In 1909 the central managing organ, the board of directors, was reorganized as the Mitsui Gomei Company, a general partnership owned by the Mitsui family, and some authority was delegated to the various Mitsui enterprises. Nonetheless, Mitsui's management remained centralized. For example, as late as 1922 Mitsui Bussan had to secure permission from Mitsui Gomei to lend money or enter into certain types of contracts. This centralization of authority may have stifled innovation and growth at Mitsui. Mitsui Gomei was composed of the heads of the different Mitsui operating companies. As a result, no one took a long-range attitude toward the future of the entire Mitsui enterprise. Planning and strategic decision making suffered as a consequence. Mitsui proved slower than many of its rivals to enter the new fields of heavy industry that developed in Japan in the 1920s and 1930s.

In the interests of economic democracy, the United States, as the major power occupying Japan after World War II, broke up zaibatsu in the years 1946 through 1949. However, this move was short-lived, for Cold War concerns soon overcame American desires for industrial democracy in Japan. To rebuild Japan as a pro-Western bastion in Asia, especially after China became a Communist nation in 1949, the United States encouraged economic growth in the nation. As part of this policy, zaibatsu were allowed to reorganize.

Mitsui was among those zaibatsu dismantled, only to reorganize in a new form called a *keiretsu* in the 1950s and 1960s. By 1971 Mitsui consisted of Mitsui Bank, Mitsui Bussan, and seventy-one other major enterprises. The postwar Mitsui differed from the prewar Mitsui. Mitsui was no longer held together by a head office that operated as a holding company owning stock in other companies. No such head office existed. Nor was Mitsui dominated by a single family. Instead, Mitsui came to consist of many companies loosely held together by meetings of the companies' executives every Monday, what became known as the Monday Club. Stock interchanges among the Mitsui companies and borrowing from the Mitsui Bank also provided some sense of unity.

Iwasaki Yataro founded Mitsubishi. Born the son of a peasant, he purchased samurai status in the Tosa domain and rose in the domain's bureaucracy as a procurer of arms and ships. (Some scholars argue that Iwasaki captured control of his domain government.) After the Meiji Restoration, the domain was abolished and its ships became the basis for an independent shipping company with Iwasaki as its manager. In 1873 Iwasaki took over this company as his own and renamed it Mitsubishi. He rallied support for his nascent venture by cloaking it in the mantle of nationalism, saying that the firm would help make Japan strong in shipping. Iwasaki's approach appealed to his employees, many of whom were former samurai from Tosa.

Mitsubishi began business with ten ships. With them the company entered the coastal trade, edging out competitors by cutting rates. Mitsubishi benefited from government contracts, carrying troops and supplies for several military expeditions in the 1870s, and by the late 1870s controlled 73 percent of Japanese shipping. Mitsubishi's rapid rise attracted the attention of other Japanese business leaders who formed the Kyodo Unyu Shipping Company to compete with Mitsubishi in the early 1880s. Out of this competition came the formation of a new shipping company in 1885, the Nippon Yusen Company (the N.Y.K.), with Mitsubishi as the largest stockholder. However, Mitsubishi's owners sold most of their holdings in N.Y.K. between 1887 and 1892 to enter fields that promised larger profits than shipping.

Mitsubishi's diversification began even before the shipping competition of the 1880s. Iwasaki Yataro led Mitsubishi into warehousing, insurance, coal mining, and the ownership of a shipyard in Nagasaki. Under his guidance, Mitsubishi also entered banking in a tentative way with the formation of a foreign exchange and discount bank to serve merchants using its ships. Yataro ran Mitsubishi with force and determination. There was little separation of ownership from management and almost no delegation of authority under his rule.

Iwasaki Yataro died in 1885, and Mitsubishi's management structure changed under the leadership of his successors. After making some preliminary alterations in the late 1880s, Iwasaki Yanosuke, Yataro's younger brother, and Iwasaki Hisaya, Yataro's eldest son, took advantage of Japan's new General Incorporation Law to reorganize Mitsubishi in 1893. Mitsubishi became a company with limited liability, consisting of a head office and departments in banking, mining, coal sales, and general affairs. The head office continued to run the company with an iron hand. As president, Iwasaki Hisaya delegated little in the way of responsibilities to the departments.

Major alterations occurred about a decade later. In 1906 Iwasaki Koyata, Yanosuke's eldest son, who had been receiving an education at Cambridge University, returned home and became a vice-president in Mitsubishi. When Yanosuke died in 1908, Koyata assumed his father's share in Mitsubishi and used his power to reorganize the company. The mining, shipbuilding, and banking departments became divisions in the company, and by

1913 the company had grown to include six divisions: banking, metal mining, coal mining, trading (a forerunner of Mitsubishi Shoji), shipbuilding, and real estate. Each division possessed a considerable degree of autonomy. The divisions determined their own investments, managed their own personnel affairs, established their own business procedures, and maintained communications with other operating units. The head office concerned itself with coordinating the work of the divisions and planning for the future of the zaibatsu as a whole. Control was exercised by having thrice-weekly meetings of all of the division managers (who were hired from outside the Iwasaki family) presided over by the vice-president of the head office.

In this manner, decentralized management replaced centralized management at Mitsubishi to some extent, as the functions of the head office and the divisions were separated and as the divisions assumed authority over their own affairs. The changes also marked the spread of bureaucratic management in general at Mitsubishi, as rules and regulations became increasingly important in running the firm.

Further changes occurred when Iwasaki Koyata took over as president of Mitsubishi in 1916. Over the next three years, he reorganized the six divisions as joint-stock companies. The head office became a holding company, owning a controlling share of the stock in each of the joint-stock companies. By selling some of the shares in the new joint-stock companies to the public, Koyata was able to raise funds for Mitsubishi's continuing diversification drive. Finally, in 1919 and 1920 a board of directors was set up as the top authority within Mitsubishi's management. With this reorganization, Mitsubishi moved away from decentralized management, and the joint-stock companies lost some of the power they had possessed over their affairs when they had been divisions.

With new management structures in place, Mitsubishi continued to diversify during the first four decades of the twentieth century. Iwasaki Koyata proved to be aggressive, much like his uncle Yataro, and his personality dominated Mitsubishi until his death in 1945. Mitsubishi's interests in shipbuilding at its yards in Nagasaki and, from 1905 on, in Kobe led the company into a broad range of heavy industries in the 1920s and 1930s: iron and steel, chemicals, mining, aircraft (including the famous Japanese Zero of the Second World War), and electrical equipment. Heavy industry became much more important for Mitsubishi than for Mitsui. Mitsubishi also came to consist of a major bank to finance its concerns and the trading company Mitsubishi Shoji, which had branches around the world.

While the Iwasaki family, especially Koyata, remained important in running Mitsubishi, nonfamily, bureaucratic management rose in significance. People from outside the Iwasaki family headed the joint-stock companies that evolved from the divisions, and standard procedures were developed to coordinate the work of the various components of the Mitsubishi empire. Yet family ownership and management remained more important than in the United States. The Iwasaki family maintained their overall control of Mitsubishi through their grip on the head office, which in turn owned a controlling share in each of the joint-stock companies until after World War II.

The same American efforts that broke up Mitsui right after World War II led to the dissolution of the Mitsubishi holding company and some of Mitsubishi's joint-stock companies. Mitsubishi Shoji was, for example, split into 123 independent firms. However, once again American-sponsored antitrust work was short-lived. In 1954 Mitsubishi Shoji was reunited, and in the 1950s and 1960s the component companies of the Mitsubishi zaibatsu began working together again, soon forming, like Mitsui, a *keiretsu*. Mitsubishi Bank provided leadership for the group and gave it some cohesion by loaning money mainly to the Mitsubishi members; and, as at Mitsui, stock ownership among member companies also lent unity to the Mitsubishi group of companies. Finally, Mitsubishi executives met every Friday, in what became known as the Friday Club, informal get-togethers similar to Mitsui's Monday Club, to coordinate activities. By 1971 Mitsubishi consisted of Mitsubishi Bank, Mitsubishi Shoji, and eighty-six major companies in manufacturing and many other fields.

Managing Zaibatsu

Zaibatsu operated as loose confederations of companies owned by family groups in the 1890s and early 1900s. Then, in the 1910s and 1920s a considerable degree of centralization of managerial control over the different enterprises composing the zaibatsu occurred. Most zaibatsu came to consist of a center company organized as a family partnership and other companies, called "core companies"—the bank, trading company, mining ventures, and manufacturing enterprises—which were often joint-stock companies, a majority of whose shares were owned by the center company. The core companies, in turn, often owned many smaller companies as their subsidiaries. (See Figure 2.) Mitsui Bussan controlled wholly or partly over 200 manufacturing businesses.

In a typical zaibatsu, officers in the center company, who were usually family members, also held presidencies and directorships in the core companies and helped coordinate the activities of the zaibatsu as a whole.

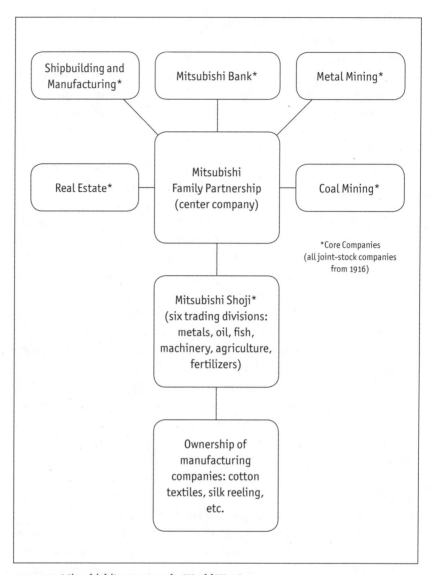

FIGURE 2 *Mitsubishi's structure by World War I*

Despite this tendency toward centralization of authority, there existed a tension into the 1940s between decentralizing and centralizing forces in the management of zaibatsu, as the center companies often sought to increase their power and the core companies tried to retain or increase their autonomy.

In many of the zaibatsu, professional managers selected from outside the founding families came to hold much of the real power as managing directors of the various core companies. With the employment of these outsiders as managing directors, ownership and management began to become divorced in Japanese business, though not to nearly the degree as in the United States. As in Great Britain, personal management, despite some bureaucratization of business, remained strong. Families continued to control the center companies of most zaibatsu until after the Second World War.

The Significance of the Zaibatsu

Japan's zaibatsu offered a viable alternative to the districts of small firms in Great Britain and the large, vertically integrated manufacturers in the United States. With their *sogo shosha* and their banks, the zaibatsu were able to compete effectively with leading Western companies. Especially up to about 1920, the zaibatsu succeeded more through the exercise of economies of scope than those of scale. Most of their individual manufacturing plants remained relatively small, and were often more labor intensive than capital intensive. It was by bringing together in family-controlled enterprises a wide range of financial, insurance, shipping, and marketing services that the zaibatsu moved ahead. Economies of scale in finance were especially significant.

The Continuing Importance of Non-Zaibatsu Firms in Japan

Not all of Japan's largest businesses were zaibatsu. Especially in the early and mid-Meiji years, many were single-industry businesses. Relatively large independent firms existed, for instance, in cotton textiles (these Japanese cotton textile makers were, however, generally smaller than their American counterparts in Lowell and Waltham). Then, too, small firms were significant in many types of manufacturing, much as they were in Great Britain. In sales and services a range of large and small non-zaibatsu companies jockeyed for position.

Cotton Textile Companies

Of Japan's fifty largest manufacturing and mining companies in 1896, twenty-eight were cotton-textile companies. These firms became even larger as a result of a merger movement, influenced by the models of mergers in the United States and Great Britain. Between 1900 and 1903 the number of companies engaged in cotton spinning decreased from seventy-eight to forty-six. These and most other Japanese industrial companies were not as highly integrated as large American manufacturers. The Japanese firms were more like the British ones, or like smaller firms in American manufacturing, such as the Philadelphia textile companies. While many Japanese cotton textile companies had integrated spinning and weaving by World War I, the firms depended on other companies, often the trading companies, to buy their raw cotton and sell their finished cloth.

Several reasons account for this relative lack of vertical integration, factors similar to those explaining its rareness in Great Britain. Japan had a well-developed marketing system from the Tokugawa years, elaborated still more by the *sogo shosha* in the Meiji period; and so manufacturers did not have to set up their own marketing networks. Then, too, Japan's national market was smaller than America's, allowing established marketers to handle the goods bound for that market adequately. For ideological reasons as well, manufacturers did not want to enter marketing, which they viewed as less virtuous than manufacturing. As a result of these various reasons, fully vertically integrated companies were not the norm in Japanese manufacturing.

Trading Companies

Large non-zaibatsu companies arose outside of manufacturing. Not all *sogo shosha*, for example, were parts of zaibatsu. Marubeni was an independent trading company that became a major force in Japan's woolen and rayon cloth industries. Marubeni, and other trading companies such as C. Itoh, bought woolen yarn and rayon from spinning companies, sold them to weavers, and bought the output of the weavers for sale inside Japan or for export.

Ataka and Company's history illustrates another way trading companies were important to Japan's industrial growth. Formed in 1904, Ataka and Company was soon trading in steel, machinery, textiles, fertilizers, chemicals, and wood products around the globe. The company acquired agency rights from Western machinery makers such as the Gleason Company in the United States and was an important source of new technologies for Japan.

Smaller Businesses in Manufacturing

While zaibatsu and some other large businesses, such as those in cotton textiles, were very important in Japan's industrial development, smaller firms were also significant. Most of Japan's growing number of industrial workers labored in small or medium-size enterprises. In 1909 businesses employing 5–49 workers accounted for 46 percent of Japan's manufacturing employment, those with 50–499 workers 37 percent, and establishments employing 500 or more workers 21 percent. Ten years later the corresponding proportions were 34 percent, 35 percent, and 32 percent. In the United States about one-third of all industrial workers labored in companies with fewer than 100 employees in 1914.

Thus, the proportion of Japanese workers laboring in large establishments grew, but even in what were boom years during World War I large establishments accounted for less than one-third of the nation's industrial workforce. Some of the smaller manufacturers were subcontractors for larger firms; they made semi-finished goods, for instance, for core companies of zaibatsu. However, most were not. The importance of subcontracting for small firms really developed only in the 1920s, the 1930s, and later.

Up to World War I most of the small manufacturers were independent of their larger counterparts, with most operating as family enterprises or small workshops. These businesses were often composed of a factory owner employing family members and a few hired workers. Smaller industrialists processed food products or worked in traditional fields such as silk reeling and ceramics. Others ran small textile mills (not all textile mills were large-scale affairs). Only Japan's nascent heavy industry sector — chemicals, metals, machinery, and equipment — was dominated by big businesses. Heavy industry did not lead Japan's industrial development. It was only in the 1930s and later that heavy industries became more important than light industries such as cotton textiles and silk reeling as the engine of Japan's economic advance.

Many of the small-scale industrial facilities were located in the countryside rather than in urban areas, a continuation of a trend from Tokugawa years. Farmers had long depended on by-employment in making tatami mats and similar items to supplement their incomes from the sale of crops, a situation that continued into the twentieth century. However, by the early 1900s some Western-inspired goods, as well as traditional items, were being made, including new types of farming implements, wire brushes, and kerosene lamps, for example.

Businesses in Sales

In selling their products, early manufacturers sometimes set up their own sales outlets, a form of vertical integration similar to that which was common in America in the late nineteenth and early twentieth centuries. Some manufacturers of nontraditional goods — makers of beer, confectionaries, cosmetics, chemical seasonings, electrical appliances, Western-style paper, wheat flour, and sugar—found distribution systems inherited from Tokugawa times inadequate and created their own marketing channels. A few—some makers of confectionaries and cosmetics, for example—went even further, setting up retail outlets as well.

However, vertical integration into sales was uncommon in Japan until after World War II, and even then less so than in America. Japan resembled Great Britain more than the United States in terms of marketing. Japan's major urban markets were relatively close together on one island, Honshu, and were well-linked by traditional marketers. Small retailers, who bought their goods from larger wholesalers—often, in fact, from several levels of wholesalers—were the channels through which manufacturers reached the vast majority of Japanese consumers. In 1885 there were over 1 million retailers in Japan, which then had a population of about 38 million people. From the 1880s on Japan's retailers became increasingly specialized, particularly those serving the nation's growing urban markets. General stores came to deal in just a single line of goods. These specialty stores sometimes grouped together in planned shopping streets, such as the famous Ginza in Tokyo, which opened in 1878.

Large-scale retailing in the form of department stores represented something of a new departure in marketing. In the first two decades of the twentieth century dry goods stores converted themselves into department stores, which, like their counterparts in America and Great Britain, served urban markets. By 1898, 18 percent of the Japanese lived in cities of at least 10,000 people, and by 1918, 32 percent did. Mitsui's Echigoya in Edo became the Mitsukoshi Department Store in Tokyo. Created by a graduate of the new Keio University, one of the college graduates recruited by Nakamigawa for Mitsui, Mitsukoshi was modeled on Harrods of London. By the time of World War I Mitsukoshi's five-story building sold a wide range of consumer goods, ranging from Western umbrellas to children's clothing. The store also contained a restaurant, a tailor's shop, and a photographic studio.

Department stores grew in importance as the twentieth century unfolded. Small businesses composed 98 percent of the retail outlets in Tokyo in 1931, but accounted for only slightly more than one-half of all sales. By way of contrast, the city's eight department stores made one-third of the sales. Still, Tokyo was not typical of all of Japan. In smaller towns and cities department stores were less significant. Moreover, even in Tokyo an important variant held sway for several decades in the Meiji period. Called *kan koba*, this type of retail outlet consisted of a department store leased by the building's owner to various independent retailers. Originating in Tokyo in the late 1870s, *kan koba* spread to many Japanese cities in the 1880s, but declined in significance during the 1890s due to poor managerial practices and fierce retail competition.

By around 1910 Japan possessed a complex marketing system composed of several tiers and types of wholesalers and retailers. Well into the years after World War II foreign businesses had a difficult time breaking into this complex, many-layered marketing network, and this difficulty helps explain why foreign firms had trouble getting started in Japan. As a result, many foreign companies, such as Starbuck's Coffee in the mid-1990s, entered Japan with the help of a Japanese company in a joint-venture project. The Japanese partners aided in opening markets, arranging financing, and smoothing the way with government officials for the non-Japanese firms.

Banking

Like sales, banking developed along several lines. The new government promulgated laws enabling the establishment of joint-stock banks in 1872 and ten years later set up the Bank of Japan as a national bank headquartered in Tokyo. With government promotion, Japan's banking system grew rapidly, especially after 1876, when the government stopped requiring the convertibility of bank notes into gold. Through World War I local traditional industries were the most important customers of Japan's financial institutions. Much as occurred in Great Britain and America, local banks, often operating as parts of kinship networks, provided some of the financing for business development. Compared with what would develop later in Japan, this was a decentralized banking system. Large city banks and the Bank of Japan were important, as were banks that were parts of zaibatsu; but so, too, were many other banks in smaller urban centers. Of Japan's 1,345 commercial banks in 1919, some 1,155 had authorized capital of less than 1 million yen apiece.

Only with financial crises of the 1920s and the resulting failures of many small and medium-size banks did banking really begin to become concentrated. The passage of a new bank law in 1927 further promoted the concentration of banking. By 1931 only 310 of Japan's 683 commercial banks had an authorized capital of less than 1 million yen each. Concentration developed still more during the worldwide depression of the 1930s, as smaller banks continued to fail and be taken over by their larger brethren. By 1941 Japan possessed only 186 banks, of which just seventy-eight had authorized capital of less than 1 million yen.

The increasing concentration of the banking business in Japan reflects a common trend in capitalistic economies. As we have seen, the Big Five city banks in Great Britain came to dominate that nation's financial activities in the early 1900s. In Germany, too, a handful of large universal banks were of most importance. Only in the United States, where a fear of concentrated economic power led to the passage of laws making branch banking difficult, was the banking system truly decentralized.

Business Leaders, Society, and Labor in Japan

As Japan's business system changed, so did the nature of its business leaders, public attitudes toward business, and the nature of labor relations. The management of big businesses in general, not just zaibatsu, became more bureaucratic; and managers became something of a business elite. Many Japanese adopted a more favorable attitude toward business leaders than they had held in Tokugawa times. With industrialization there also occurred changes in labor-management relations. Even so, important elements of continuity underlay relationships between business and society. It proved especially difficult for many Japanese to change their ideas about the social status of business leaders, who had ranked behind all other groups in social standing during Tokugawa times.

Japan's Business Elite

By 1903 Japan had 388 nonbanking businesses with capital assets of 10,000 yen or more, mostly joint-stock companies, which could be considered big businesses. These companies, like zaibatsu, began developing bureaucratic management. Of these companies, 141 possessed managerial structures consisting of only a president and directors, but 152 had structures made up of a president, senior executive director (or managing director), and some other directors. Only ninety companies had neither a president nor a senior executive director. By the early 1920s company management had expanded to include typically a president, senior executive director, several other executive directors, and a junior executive director, each with fairly distinct responsibilities within their companies.

As in Great Britain and the United States, Japan's big business leaders formed something of an elite. In the 1880s about 19 percent of Japan's business leaders were the sons of merchants, 31 percent were the sons of small businessmen, another 23 percent were the sons of samurai, and 22 percent were the sons of farmers. By the 1920s some 35 percent were the sons of businessmen, 37 percent the sons of samurai, and 21 percent the sons of farmers. (No women made it to the top ranks of Japanese business.) Few farmers or laborers rose from rags to riches by going into business in Meiji or Taisho Japan. Education played a greater role in helping define Japan's business elite than it did in most other nations. More and more top managers of large companies were college graduates. In 1924 some 244 of the top 384 business managers in the nation had earned the equivalent of a college degree. Most of these managers graduated from just three institutions of higher learning: 103 from Tokyo University, forty-nine from the Tokyo Higher Commercial School, and forty-eight from Keio Academy (later Keio University).

Changing Attitudes toward Business

Merchants in Tokugawa Japan ranked behind samurai, peasants, and artisans in the nation's social order. This situation changed in Meiji Japan. The public image of business leaders rose, and their new heightened image was partially reconciled to the older Confucian ideals. However, this shift in how business leaders were viewed was neither easy nor complete by the 1920s and 1930s. The creation of new industries came to be seen by some Japanese as a service to the state, because they would, it was hoped, make Japan strong. Some Japanese political and economic leaders came to view business people as the new samurai of their nation. When conducted for the right reasons, for public as well as private gains, business enterprise could, they reasoned, be virtuous.

Shibusawa Eiichi did much to spread this new attitude. Fourteen years old when Perry opened Japan to the West, Shibusawa was a member of the group seeking to overthrow the Tokugawa government. After the Meiji Restoration, Shibusawa spent the years 1869 through 1873 in the Ministry of Finance, rising to the position of assistant to the vice-minister. Shibusawa resigned from the government to go into business. He founded the First Bank of Japan, the Oji Paper Company, the Tokyo Gas Company, the Osaka Spinning Company, and a wide variety of other concerns. Altogether, he was involved in starting over 200 business enterprises. Shibusawa also helped form business organizations, the Tokyo Bankers' Association, and chambers of commerce in Tokyo and Osaka. Shibusawa sought to place the cloak of the public-spirited samurai on the shoulders of Japan's new business leaders. By helping Japan modernize, business leaders were, he argued, worthy of public respect.

But how typical was Shibusawa? There can be no doubt that he and some other business leaders viewed their actions as building up Japan or that some of the Japanese public also adopted this point of view. However, not all changed their attitudes overnight. Moreover, many business leaders were less public-spirited than Shibusawa. A desire for private profits and individual glory motivated them. Nakamigawa, the head of Mitsui in the 1890s, ordered a subordinate to collect debts the government owed Mitsui, even though doing so went against the government's interests.

To starkly characterize Japanese business leaders as community-centered and American executives as profit-centered oversimplifies the situation. Business leaders in both nations, and other nations as well, were motivated by a wide variety of factors. Classic Anglo-American works on self-advancement, such as *Self Help* by Samuel Smiles and *Pushing to the Front* by Orison Swett Marden, were best sellers in Meiji Japan. These books emphasized individualism as the key to success, not group cooperation. Letters written by young men to the *Eisai Shinshi*, a Tokyo magazine of the 1870s, also revealed a widespread desire for individual prosperity.

Labor Relations in Industrializing Japan

Confusion has often existed about Japan's system of labor relations. It has sometimes been incorrectly assumed that the system, with its emphasis on cooperation between managers and workers (with workers having lifetime employment and wages and promotions based mainly on seniority and, in return, giving loyal service to their companies), was simply a holdover from a family notion of business that existed in Tokugawa times, or that there was something unique to the culture of Japan that encouraged such close cooperation.

At the outset three points need to be stressed. First, even in its heyday of the 1950s and 1960s, the system applied to only about one-third of Japan's industrial workers: mainly to men employed full-time by large corporations, even though some smaller firms tried to move in this direction. Second, modern labor relations in Japan developed in response to specific challenges in the late nineteenth and twentieth centuries. The system did not grow out of innate characteristics of Japanese society or culture; there was nothing inherently family-like that predetermined the development of Japan's system of industrial relations. Finally, it is important to realize that there has never been a single model for labor relations in Japan, even among large firms.

Labor relations in Japan have, in fact, long been complex. While merchant houses operated as family enterprises, with clerks and other employees usually treated almost as family members, not all Tokugawa businesses were run this way. Artisans and skilled workers often labored on a contractual basis, frequently moving from firm to firm looking for higher pay and better opportunities. Unskilled laborers were often hired on contracts for seasonal projects or for specific tasks. For most of these workers lifetime employment and seniority-based wages were unheard of.

Cotton textile and silk reeling mills led in the creation of the factory system in Japan. In 1919 textile mills employed 794,000 of Japan's 1,391,000 industrial workers. Women composed 62 percent of Japan's industrial workforce in 1909, and most textile workers were women. Neither lifetime employment nor seniority-based wages were in effect for them. Management regulated nearly all aspects of the textile workers' lives; women lived in company housing and needed passes to leave company property, a situation that led some observers to label their lives slave-like. In many other industries nascent factories subcontracted the recruitment and supervision of workers to outside labor bosses, much as had been done in the United States into the 1880s. As late as 1890, for example, large shipyards and iron foundries relied on this system to provide gangs of sixty to 300 men at a time. Few permanent ties held these workers to their firms.

Dissatisfied workers responded to their situation in several ways. Some women ran away from the textile mills, leading to high turnover rates. Other workers continued to move from company to company in quest of better jobs; still others rioted and went on strike. As early as the 1880s isolated strikes occurred among workers in silk reeling and cotton textile mills. In the 1890s workers in a few industries, influenced by union development in the United States and sometimes aided by the American Federation of Labor, began establishing Western-style craft unions. By 1919 Japanese workers had formed 187 unions, and by 1923 the number had grown to 432. In 1921 Japanese workers organized the Sodomei (Japan General Federation of Labor), and within four years its member unions represented 250,000 workers.

Members of these unions participated in strikes during the twentieth century. Labor unrest spread through many industries in 1906–7, as companies sought to rationalize (that is, make more efficient) their factory operations in the aftermath of the Russo-Japanese War of 1904–5, a time of rising inflation and industrial instability. Amid renewed inflation and a growing demand for skilled workers during World War I, more industrial laborers went on strike.

To dampen labor unrest, and especially to avoid strikes and to lower turnover rates, some industrialists resorted to strategies similar to those used in Great Britain and the United States. A few sought to institute aspects of scientific management, for by the time of World War I Frederick Taylor's ideas about increasing labor efficiency were fairly well known in Japan. Industrialists achieved only limited success in this effort, for Japanese workers, like their British and American counterparts, resisted scientific management as a speed-up ploy and as an infringement on workers' prerogatives. Control of the shop floor, while contested, remained mainly in the hands of skilled workers.

A few firms belonging to the Japan Industrial Club, which was dominated by zaibatsu and companies in heavy industry, began offering seniority bonuses during World War I, and some started forming company unions and engaging in aspects of corporate welfare work. Some employer associations, most notably the Osaka Industrial Association, called on the government to pass a law recognizing the right of craft unions to exist and bargain collectively with management, reasoning that it would be easier to bargain with disciplined unions than with undisciplined, unorganized workers. The Japanese government was, nonetheless, generally hostile to the formation of unions. The Diet passed a Factory Law designed to improve working conditions in 1911, but in doing so was motivated more by a desire to bolster the health of workers needed for the armed forces than to help workers deal with difficult working conditions. In these business efforts around the time of World War I, then, one might see the bare beginnings of a labor relations system that would evolve throughout the twentieth century.

Businesses in Industrializing China

As in Japan, China's government tried to spur economic development to catch up with the West; but it proved less effective than the Japanese government. China's imperial government did not often wholeheartedly embrace economic development, at least not to the degree that the Japanese government did. The government of the Republic, beginning in 1912, sought to link nationalism with democracy and adopted the goal of economic development more completely but lacked the power to fully carry out modernization. Instead, entrepreneurs of various sorts led in the formation of new types of business enterprises in China during the late Imperial and early Republican years. Hindering their advance was the fact that they worked in competition with foreign multinational companies (MNCs) in many fields, especially in the Shanghai region, since the Chinese government was too weak to exclude the MNCs.

Chinese Governments and Economic Development

Japan's defeat of China in the Sino-Japanese War of 1894–95 shocked the Chinese, partly because China had been industrializing with the help of foreign advisers since the 1860s. However, the defeat did not bring fundamental changes to the Qing dynasty, which had ruled since 1644. Instead, the Japanese victory, combined with a growing dislike of foreigners, led to a conservative backlash against foreigners in China, called the Boxer Rebellion of 1899–1900, in which some 200 Western missionaries and thousands of Christian Chinese lost their lives. Backed by the Qing rulers, this rebellion against foreigners was defeated by a combination of Japanese and Western troops who took Beijing. The Boxer Protocol of 1901 imposed $334 million in fines called indemnities, a very large sum for the struggling nation, on the Chinese government and awakened government officials to the need for reforms if China were to catch up with the West and Japan economically and militarily.

By 1900 China had a population of about 450 million people, some 80 percent of whom labored on the land. The standard of living of the average Chinese had been on par with that of people in Western Europe as late as 1750, but it slipped in relative terms in the nineteenth century. The peace that Qing rulers achieved in the 1600s, the development of new agricultural techniques, and China's participation in world trade allowed the nation's population to increase from about 100 million people in 1600 to 300 million people by 1800, with another 150 million joining their ranks in the nineteenth century. This population rise, along with a major conflict called the Taiping Rebellion (1850–64) and foreign encroachments, severely strained the Chinese government. By the late nineteenth and early twentieth centuries, about one hundred Chinese cities contained concessions that foreigners directly administered. There were in addition five leaseholds granted to foreigners covering more extensive territories: a large part of Shandong to Germany, the Liaodong Peninsula to Russia, Guangzhouwan to France, the New Territories adjacent to Hong Kong and the port of Weihaiwei to Great Britain. Altogether, about 400,000 foreigners lived in China in 1920.

To reestablish their nation's sovereignty and to encourage economic growth, the Qing dynasty considered reforms in its last years: changes to the education systems, the establishment of a modern infrastructure, and the drafting of a constitution. Some alterations occurred. The traditional civil service examination system based on knowledge of the classics was abolished in 1905. A new educational system came into existence. China possessed 4,222 public and private academies in 1905, and by 1911 there were

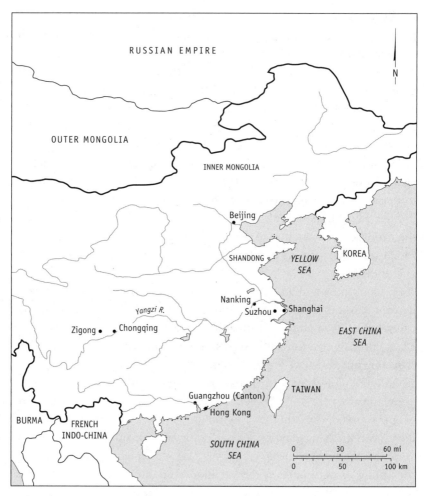

China, around 1910

52,348. Moreover, some laws sought to directly benefit business. In 1903 the Qing dynasty created China's first Ministry of Commerce, and in 1904 a Company Registration Bureau recognized five different types of firms, including limited-liability corporations. However, in general the changes that took place in Qing China were a case of too little, too late.

In 1911 a revolution replaced the Qing dynasty with a republican government, ending 2,100 years of imperial rule in China. The leading republican, Sun Yat-sen, emphasized three principles in his overthrow of the Qing: nationalism, republicanism, and the nationalization of land (a vague form of state planning). In January 1912 Sun Yat-sen, who had been living abroad, returned to China to be named the provisional president of a new Republic of China, and within two months the Qing dynasty abdicated. (Many Chinese intellectuals favored some sort of socialism, reasoning that the state would have to take a leading role in economic modernization, as they imagined had occurred in Meiji Japan, and because they saw in socialism a way to unify different groups in China.) In what historians are increasingly realizing was a complicated development, the gentry and wealthy merchants supported the revolution, along with most army officers and soldiers. Chinese revolutionaries viewed the emperor as having lost his mandate from heaven because of his failure to defend China against foreigners. However, even more was involved, as the revolutionaries sought to create not simply another dynasty, as had happened many times in China's past, but a new form of government.

Yuan Shikai, who controlled the largest army in China, assumed the presidency of the Republic from Sun Yat-sen in 1912. Under Yuan, dreams of republican democracy withered, as he came to rule as a military dictator. Yuan established a top-down type of administration, which stifled local initiative and democracy. Nonetheless, Yuan did try to reform the judiciary and the financial organs of the central government and to modernize China's educational system. Facing a crushing load in the payment of indemnities to foreign nations, Yuan failed to reform China's tax system (and even lost control of the land tax, once the major source of revenue for China's central government, to local governments). Moreover, he failed to raise tariff duties because of the opposition of Japan and Western powers. Yuan relied increasingly on loans from foreign banks and governments to keep his government afloat, which heightened their importance in China. He died in 1916.

Following Yuan's demise, China broke apart politically into a number of territories governed by warlords, a situation that lasted into the late 1920s and 1930s when Chiang Kai-shek superficially unified the nation again. For about a decade and a half, China existed as a nation in name only, and even under Chiang Kai-shek's rule unity proved more elusive than real.

Like its imperial predecessor, China's republican government sought to stimulate business growth. The new national government, together with many provincial governments, held industrial expositions to showcase the products of Chinese industry and promote Chinese businesses. Government officials also backed, sometimes directly, at other times more surreptitiously, boycotts mounted by Chinese consumers against Western and Japanese goods. Japanese demands for territorial concessions in China mounted from World War I on, and boycotts grew in number and, perhaps, effectiveness. Nonetheless, none of the government's efforts amounted to the extent of aid that either Western nations or Japan gave their business enterprises. Weakened by warlords, China's national government was unable to resist imperialistic nations carving out territorial concessions and foreign businesses seeking unrestricted access to the Chinese market. Not until 1934 did the Chinese government regain the right to set tariff duties on goods imported into China.

Business Development and Economic Growth

Nonetheless, business development and economic growth took place, and, in fact, boomed in some years. In the countryside, agriculture was increasingly commercialized, as networks run by merchants linked different areas and regions, as had been the case from at least the time of the Ming dynasty. Small family farms of about three acres lay at the heart of the Chinese economy. While many farmers still grew most of what they ate, they also engaged in market exchanges, in part because they had to pay taxes in specie, as they had for several hundred years. Thus, tea leaves moved from where they were grown in remote mountains to Shanghai and then abroad to London. Nearly one-third of farm output was sold in markets. As in Japan, farms were also places of artisanal craftsmanship, as farmers made all sorts of items, such as cloth, sandals, rope, and bricks. Growing urban markets stimulated further agricultural development and crop specialization, although some economic disintegration and market erosion accompanied the collapse of China into warlordism. The trends were contradictory. Country markets were also sites for the exchange of labor and credit in the fluid economic situation. By the early 1930s about 42 percent of China's farmland was rented, and 32 percent of farm families owned no land at all.

In the cities — especially Shanghai, the site of over half of China's modern businesses (called *gongsi*) — industrial establishments arose. Prior to 1895 foreigners owned perhaps one hundred small factories in China, all of which were illegal under Chinese law. The Chinese government turned a blind eye to some foreign enterprises such as shipbuilding and repairs, but forbade cotton spinning and weaving. Following the Sino-Japanese War, it became legal for foreigners to invest in Chinese businesses, and by 1938 they had invested $2.56 billion, a very large sum. Only about a dozen sizable Chinese-owned industrial enterprises existed before 1900, most of them started and run by government officials. These were mainly arsenals, mines, and shipyards. However, between 1895 and 1913 Chinese investors formed 549 manufacturing and mining enterprises. By 1911 there also existed 5,600 miles of railroad trackage in the nation. Some of the new firms were corporations established by privatizing former government-sponsored enterprises, much as had occurred in Japan in the 1880s. Some other modern businesses developed out of older family businesses, a bit like the way the House of Mitsui became a modern zaibatsu in Japan. Between 1904 and 1911 some 272 companies registered with the Chinese government, half of them as limited-liability enterprises. Still other modern firms were incorporated regional enterprises. Legal changes, especially the incorporation law of 1904, and, even earlier, the formation of the Shanghai Stock Exchange in 1890, paved the way for the formation of the new-style firms; for many of them required capital beyond what could be raised in traditional ways.

In the 1910s there were about 1.5 million workers in the modern sector of China's economy—shipping, railroads, machine tools, cotton textile mills, and the like. Most of them labored in small-scale enterprises, with only about 116 Chinese-owned and 40 foreign-owned businesses employing more than 500 workers. Armament factories were among the first industrial enterprises built by the state, with foreign help. China's state-owned Jiangnan Arsenal was modern and was probably the largest arsenal in the world when it was constructed in 1861. An iron and steel complex grew up in northern China. Light industry, such as cigarette making and cotton textiles, developed in and around Shanghai. In the late Qing era, many of these were associated with the government, for government officials were active in their foundation and early operation. However, in 1910 and afterward, private entrepreneurs became more important, similar to what also occurred in Japan. Still, it is important not to overemphasize the significance of industry and modern business to China. Before World War I, capital investment in industry and railroads amounted to just 6–7 percent of the investment in agriculture.

Networks were important to business development in all of the nations we have examined, but perhaps nowhere more so than in China. What the Chinese called *guanxi*—relationships based on kinship, sworn brotherhoods, student-teacher relationships, and so on—dominated social and economic life. Especially important, and perhaps unique to China, were native-place associations called *huiguan* and *tongxianghui* (the former was more traditional and elitist, the latter a new type that developed in the Republic period and which was less elitist). Where a person was born, or even where his/her parents were born, remained important for life. A person could call on others from the same native-place association for help, including financial aid, regardless of his/her current place of habitation. Even (or perhaps especially) in big cities like Shanghai, native-place associations were of crucial importance. Nor were networks significant only to Chinese. Managers of Western and Japanese companies as varied as Standard Oil, British-American Tobacco, Mitsui, and Nagai Cotton operating in China found it useful to employ Chinese networks to manage their workforces and open markets for their products. The companies often employed a Chinese "Number One" man as a supervisor to recruit workers and handle labor affairs through well-established networks. Moreover, in managing their companies' internal affairs, westerners and Japanese combined hierarchical approaches with managerial networks, with management of their Chinese ventures somewhat less "top-down" than in the West.

Shanghai's Industrial Districts

The production of printing machinery, one of China's leading modern industries, demonstrates well the importance of networks. Focused in industrial districts in Shanghai, making printing machinery was tied to the growth of modern book publishing, which grew up in that same city. The evolution of the two industries was symbiotic, as each spurred the other. For most of the nineteenth century Chinese publishers in Shanghai relied on the importation of printing machinery from the West as they moved into modern publication methods. However, from 1895 Chinese entrepreneurs set up workshops to repair broken machinery, a step that soon led them into making their own printing presses and selling them to Chinese publishers. By the 1920s and 1930s they also reached Japanese and South Asian markets with sales of their printing presses, a circumstance in which the Chinese government took a great deal of pride.

Shanghai became the center for machine making in China, and the production of printing machinery was a large segment of that industry. Between 1895 and 1913 six printing machine workshops were established by Chinese owners. Most of the owners had worked in the trade previously, allowing them to identify the niche market. Thirteen additional printing machine workshops were opened between 1914 and 1924, with still more workshops being established over the next decade. Most of the printing machinery workshops were small. Only a handful employed as many as one hundred workers, many of whom were unpaid or underpaid apprentices living on the premises. Some even slept under their machinery. By 1933 Shanghai was home to 456 Chinese-owned machine-industry workshops employing a total of about 8,000 laborers. Thirty-two of those shops made printing and publishing machinery. The workshops formed part of the network of Chinese firms supplying the large Chinese newspaper plants and publishing houses. Their zenith occurred in the early 1930s. As part of its imperialistic expansion into China, Japan bombed Shanghai in 1932 and then occupied the Chinese parts of the city five years later. Most of the city's machine shops were destroyed or moved inland to escape the Japanese occupiers. In 1949 only 9 of the 308 printing presses made in Shanghai were produced by Chinese companies.

While book publishing in Shanghai illustrates the importance of networks, it also shows how Chinese business leaders often combined old and new ways of making industrial goods. As with the Japanese, the Chinese did not import technologies and business methods uncritically. More commonly, the Chinese imported Western and Japanese methods and then adapted them to their own needs. For example, China's evolution from traditional wood-block printing to Western-style mechanized printing was indirect. In the late nineteenth and early twentieth centuries, many Chinese printers turned to lithography (printing on stone presses) as their medium, before later embracing letter-press printing (movable lead-type printing). Lithography was a halfway house between the old and the new, which allowed publishers to move from wood-block printing to mechanized printing without having to make large capital investments.

The years 1876–1905 were the golden age of lithography in Shanghai. One hundred lithographic printers established businesses in that city, and many of them lasted until the close of the 1930s. However, from 1905 on lithographers were eclipsed by Chinese printers making use of new types of Western-style machinery. Advances in Western-style printing machinery, increasingly made in Shanghai workshops, eroded the appeal of lithography, and lithography faded in relative importance. Large incorporated Chinese publishing companies, which often derived their financing from modern-style Chinese banks, grew up, for those firms could afford the new publishing machinery.

The Dasheng Cotton Textile Mills

However, the direct importation of Western processes did sometimes occur, as in the construction and operation of cotton textile mills in the Dasheng region near Shanghai on the Yangzi River—a good example of the importance of regional enterprises in China's industrialization. The story began in 1895 with Zhang Jian's ideas for a cotton mill in Nantong, home to artisanal cottage spinning and weaving. The actual operations of the mill, the first in what was to become a complex of spinning and weaving establishments, started in 1899.

Zhang's concern was part of a larger trend toward establishment of private industrial businesses in China. Only five cotton-spinning mills had been established in China by this time, but by 1916 thirty were in operation, all owned by merchants. (Zhang Jian held the highest imperial degree, so he was no "mere merchant.") Similarly, the number of weaving establishments rose from one to eighty-one in about the same years. Born in 1853, Zhang started his enterprise with government help made possible by his gentry connections, but his Dasheng mill soon became a private enterprise, registered as a limited liability company in 1907. Zhang became a full-time business leader. Buying cotton grown in the surrounding area, Zhang's mills grew in importance, using convenient water transportation to bring in the raw cotton and ship out finished cloth — as, from the first, the Dasheng mills spun and wove cotton with Western machinery.

Connections were important to Zhang. He used his own funds and ties of friendship to attract funding from local merchants. Then, too, ties he possessed due to his gentry status helped him with government officials, who provided some of the initial financing. Native-place associations were important in organizing the movement and sale of the cotton. And, finally, foremen were in charge of most hiring, doing so through their own personal networks.

The Dasheng mills were modern factories, using machinery from Lowell, Massachusetts, installed with the help of Western engineers. The Dasheng mills introduced large-scale industrial production to the countryside and new types of labor organization to the shop floor. By the 1920s, 8,000 workers labored in the Dasheng No. 1 Cotton Mill, long the core of the Dasheng business complex, on a tight daily schedule. About half of them had earlier been engaged in hand weaving. Over three-quarters of the workers were women, similar to the situations in other nations, especially Japan. The mill had an administrative staff of another 400 people. In the Dasheng mills work was organized in a strict hierarchical fashion, with the mainly unskilled workers thinking only of their particular tasks, not about their development as professionals.

Success in cotton textile production led Zhang to expand his business. In the years before World War I, his company opened several more cotton textile mills and then went on to establish a mill to make oil from crushed cotton seeds, a steamship company, a land reclamation company (to provide land on which cotton could be grown), a publishing house, a soap factory, an iron-making workshop, and a flour mill. By 1910 there were seventeen affiliated companies in the Dasheng group.

In running the Dasheng mills and the growing group of affiliated companies, Zhang adopted an authoritarian management style. He delegated supervisory jobs to mill managers, but kept decision-making powers in his hands. The management structure of Dasheng Cotton No. 1 Mill is suggestive. The mill was divided into four functional departments — material acquisition and goods distribution, shop-floor production, miscellaneous tasks, and finance — each headed by a manager who reported solely to Zhang. Networking by itself did not explain how the Dasheng mill or other enterprises worked. Within the Dasheng complex, the No. 1 Cotton Mill initially served as a holding company owning controlling shares in the other affiliated businesses. The mill's manager also took active roles in running the affiliated firms. A bit later, a controlling share of stocks in the mill and other companies came to be owned by Zhang's Shanghai office company, which acted as the head of the business complex. The Shanghai office also served as the paymaster for the affiliated companies and took charge of the transportation and sale of many of their products. There was a board of directors to oversee all of the companies. However, the board's members usually rubber-stamped Zhang's decisions, giving investors little real say in matters.

The Shanghai office stood at the center of the Dasheng business complex, which was similar in many ways to a Japanese zaibatsu of about the same period. Zhang's family lay at the core of the business empire, just as families controlled zaibatsu. While ministering to a modern business, the Shanghai office used many traditional business practices. It employed traditional accounting practices which were not transparent. Most important, it mixed Zhang's personal financial transactions with those of the Dasheng enterprises, in the manner of preindustrial merchants.

This autocratic management arrangement worked at the Dasheng combine as China's economy boomed through World War I, but it ran into difficulties in later years. Interest payments on debts incurred to pay for expansion, combined with a slump in demand for cotton goods, bit deeply into profits in the 1920s, as did rising prices for raw materials. Then, too, the mills and companies, working though the Shanghai office, made unsecured loans to Zhang and his friends, a situation that further endangered the Dasheng enterprises. Events came to a head in the early and mid-1920s, when bankers, fearful of losing their loans, took control of the Dasheng firms and forced Zhang out. The banks then cut expenses, sold parts of the business empire, and stopped paying dividends to investors. Zhang was never again important in the enterprises, and he died in 1926. Many of the companies he had started continued to function, although more as independent enterprises than as part of a combine, until taken over by invading Japanese in the 1930s and 1940s. What remained of the Dasheng businesses was nationalized by the victorious Communist government in the 1950s.

Conclusions

With the development of zaibatsu such as Mitsui and Mitsubishi, big business arrived in Japan. As in the United States, the rise of big business changed Japanese business firms. Large businesses began adopting bureaucratic management systems. Nonetheless, as the examples of Mitsui and Mitsubishi also demonstrated, family control remained strong longer in Japan than in the United States, and in this respect Japanese big businesses resembled their counterparts in Great Britain, Germany, and China more than those in the United States. The continued importance of smaller firms in industry, as well as in sales and services, illustrates the complexity of Japan's business situation during industrialization. Companies of many sizes and sorts contributed to the development of Japan's economy. Such was the case in China as well. Some large combines, such as the Dasheng enterprises, emerged, but a multitude of smaller firms long remained important.

While recognizing that complexities existed in all the nations we have examined — and especially that small and medium-size companies, as well as their larger brethren, played important roles — generalizations are in order as we conclude our look at the relationships between business development and industrialization. As a very rough generalization, one may say that just as zaibatsu allowed Japan to compete with other industrializing countries, universal banks and cartels helped Germany in that competition. Moreover, as a gross generalization, one can say that large vertically integrated manufacturing companies, while not uniquely American, were most pronounced in the United States. Similarly, smaller firms, often linked in regional groupings, while existing in all of our countries, were most important in Great Britain and China. Family ties, regional groupings, and networks of other sorts remained important everywhere, although a bit less so in the United States. As we have seen, geography and political and legal systems, along with historical circumstances unique to each nation, influenced these business developments. Many complex factors converged to create the similarities and differences among the business firms of the world's industrializing nations.

Suggested Readings

Mishima Yasuo, *The Mitsubishi: Its Challenge and Strategy* (Greenwich, 1989), Morikawa Hidemasa, "The Organizational Structure of Mitsubishi and Mitsui Zaibatsu, 1868–1922: A Comparative Study," *Business History Review* 44 (Spring 1970), 62–83, William Wray, *Mitsubishi and the N.Y.K., 1870–1914* (Cambridge, Mass., 1984), and Yui Tsunehiko, "The Personality and Career of Hikojiro Nakamigawa, 1887–1901," *Business History Review* 44 (Spring 1970), 39–61, analyze the development of Mitsubishi and Mitsui. William Wray, ed., *Managing Industrial Enterprise: Cases from Japan's Prewar Experience* (Cambridge, Mass., 1989), is an important collection of case studies. Penelope Francks, *Japanese Economic Development: Theory and Practice* (London, 1992), chapter 13, offers a valuable look at small business in industrializing Japan. On smaller firms, see also Takeuchi Johzen, *The Role of Labour-Intensive Sectors in Japanese Industrialization* (Tokyo, 1991). Yoshihara Kunio, *Sogo Shosha: The Vanguard of the Japanese Economy* (New York, 1982), and M. Y. Yoshino and Thomas Lifson, *The Invisible Link: Japan's Sogo Shosha and the Organization of Trade* (Cambridge, Mass., 1986), are useful studies. For a valuable collection of essays on business and technological change in Japan, see Janet Hunter and Cornelia Storz, eds., *Institutional and Technological Change in Japan's Economy: Past and Present* (London, 2006).

Earl Kinmouth, *The Self-Made Man in Meiji Japanese Thought: From Samurai to Salary Man* (Berkeley, 1981), looks at business ideology in the Meiji period. Sheldon Garon, *The State and Labor in Modern Japan* (Berkeley, 1988), and Andrew Gordon, *The Evolution of Labor Relations in Japan: Heavy Industry, 1853–1955* (Cambridge, Mass., 1985), provide insights into the development of labor relations. E. Patricia Tsurumi, *Factory Girls: Women in the Thread Mills of Meiji Japan* (Princeton, 1990), is revealing on the role of women in Japan's industrial development.

Scholars have recently been exploring Chinese business history. Peter Zarrow, *China in War and Revolution, 1895–1949* (London, 2005), is an overview of political, economic, social, and cultural change. For an introduction to trends in Chinese business history, see the five essays composing *Enterprise & Society* 6 (Sept. 2006). The classic work on Chinese industrialization remains Albert Feuerwerker, *China's Early Industrialization: Sheng Hsuan-Huai (1844–1916) and Mandarin Enterprise* (Cambridge, Mass., 1958), but many of its findings are being revised in the present day. Elizabeth Koll, *From Cotton Mill to Business Empire: The Emergence of Regional Enterprises in Modern China* (Cambridge, Mass., 2003), is a valuable case study about industrialization and business development, looking at the Dasheng business group. Christopher A. Reed, *Gutenberg in Shanghai: Chinese Print Capitalism, 1876–1937* (Honolulu, 2004), and Sherman Cochran, *Encountering Chinese Networks: Western, Japanese, and Chinese Corporations in China, 1880–1937* (Berkeley, 2000), emphasize the importance of networks. For a study of a foreign multinational enterprise in China, see Sherman Cochran, *Big Business in China: Sino-Foreign Rivalry in the Cigarette Industry, 1890–1930* (Cambridge, Mass., 1980).

CHAPTER 6

American, British, and German Businesses in the Interwar Period

In a front-page article on 7 October 1929, the editors of the American investment newsletter *Moody's* advised their readers that "fundamentals are sound . . . there can be no real or long depression." For neither the first nor last time in American history, the experts were wrong, as the stock market crash of that fall developed into the Great Depression of the 1930s. In fact, the entire interwar period was a tumultuous economic time, with lots of ups and downs. Nor were the swings limited to the United States. As would be expected in an interconnected world, what occurred in American business affected European developments and vice versa, making the interwar years roller-coaster ones economically. As Western business executives faced new challenges during the interwar years, they continued to alter the nature of their companies and their nations' business systems. Still, as in earlier periods, continuity as well as change characterized the development of business practices. The same was true in Great Britain and Germany, as companies in those countries tried to deal with difficult times. Also as in the past, the differing cultures, social systems, and political situations decreed that, while there would be many similarities in the responses of business leaders to their difficulties and opportunities, there would be marked differences as well.

American Business

A recession right after World War I hit American companies hard, revealing basic deficiencies in the management of large manufacturing businesses. None had anticipated the onset of the recession, and most responded sluggishly to it. The recession exposed serious management problems previously hidden during a period of prosperity. However, over time some large manufacturers developed a new management system called decentralized management, designed to allow their companies to react quickly to market changes. Adopted sparingly in the interwar years, decentralized management came to characterize large American industrial firms after World

War II. And, it spread well beyond the United States. Smaller firms experienced fewer changes in how they operated during the interwar years, although some alterations did occur, particularly in sales.

Diversification and Decentralization

During the opening decades of the twentieth century, many large manufacturing companies produced a widening range of consumer durable goods. These were products meant to last for a number of years, and many were big-ticket items: automobiles, electric stoves, refrigerators, radios, and the like. They were made for more and more markets. In the 1920s the United States was rapidly becoming a consumer society, with consumer durables bought on time through installment payments becoming central to the nation's economy. The American economy, more than ever before, was tied to consumerism and consumer buying. Not surprisingly, advertising and marketing became big businesses in their own rights. Both General Motors and Ford helped buyers purchase automobiles by setting up financial agencies to loan them money, such as the General Motors Acceptance Corporation.

A product of the Second Industrial Revolution, the automobile was the most important example of the significance of consumer durable goods to the American economy. In 1914 Henry Ford began using conveyer-belt mass-production techniques to turn out his famous Model T's, producing 15 million of the cars by 1928. This revolutionary concept, in which assembly lines brought work to laborers at fixed stations in factories, built on earlier advances in using interchangeable parts in American factories throughout the nineteenth century. General Motors and other firms adopted mass-production methods in the 1920s, and in 1929 American companies sold a record 4.6 million automobiles to domestic consumers. Americans' rapid adoption of the automobile affected their nation's culture, as increased mobility brought town and countryside together as never before. Among other things, people shared the same jokes. One oldster requested that he be buried in his Model T. When asked why, he replied, "Oh, because the darned thing pulled me out of every hole I ever got into, and it ought to pull me out of this one." Songs were sung praising the democratizing influence of the Model T:

> Now Henry Jones and a pretty little queen
> Took a ride one day in his big limousine,
> The car kicked up and the engine wouldn't crank
> There wasn't any gas in the gasoline tank.

About that time along came Nord in his little old Ford
And he stole that queen as his engine sang a song
And his little Ford rambled right along.

As manufacturing businesses became more diversified in terms of their products and markets, and more directly affected by the ups and downs of consumer buying, centralized management could no longer adequately run the companies, a point driven home by a postwar slump. The executives of big businesses were so tied up in the daily affairs of their companies that they were not planning for the future. Companies as varied in their operations as Goodyear Rubber, Ford, General Motors, Armour Meats, DuPont, and Sears, Roebuck encountered severe problems when Americans temporarily stopped buying their products. When new car sales collapsed, General Motors was forced to borrow $83 million in short-term notes to survive and Ford Motors sold all nonessential equipment, including 600 telephones, to raise ready cash.

In coping with their difficulties, some businesses developed decentralized management systems. In decentralized management the head office came to concentrate upon planning for the entire company and on coordinating the operations of its different parts. The daily operations of the company were delegated to managers of divisions, with the divisions usually organized around product lines or regions. As part of their reorganization, these diversified big businesses improved greatly their accounting systems, financial controls, and market forecasting. In short, no longer did a few people or a few committees in the head office run all aspects of a firm's business.

General Motors: Pioneer in Decentralized Management

General Motors pioneered decentralized management. William Durant was the father of General Motors. He first became interested in automobiles in 1904, when he took over the Buick Company in Flint, Michigan. Durant used Buick as his base to found General Motors, and between 1908 and 1910 he brought together over twenty-five previously independent companies — including Olds, Oakland, and Cadillac — as the General Motors Corporation. A second period of growth occurred in 1918–20, as Durant added Chevrolet, Fisher Body, a tractor company, an electric refrigerator company, and a number of smaller concerns to General Motors. While an energetic empire builder, Durant failed to provide his company with adequate management. He tried to run the company as a one-man show, making both grand policy and daily operating decisions by himself, but, as the firm grew in size and complexity, major decisions on investment, expansion, marketing, and the like often simply were not made.

The postwar recession disclosed the managerial weaknesses that had developed at General Motors. Lacking any form of market forecasting, each division invested large sums in new plants to build more cars, even as sales dropped 20 percent in one year. Moreover, each division continued to buy large inventories of raw materials with which to produce its cars. Cash-flow difficulties made problems even worse. Each division maintained its own bank account, making it hard for the head office to move funds internally within the company. Buick, in particular, was reluctant to give up its cash to the head office, even when that cash was desperately needed to keep the company afloat. Underlying these various difficulties was the basic problem of control, for the head office was unable either to plan for the future of the company or coordinate the work of its different parts.

Management changes ensued. In late 1920 Durant resigned as president of General Motors, and Pierre S. DuPont, recently retired from the DuPont Company, became the new president of General Motors. Looking for investment opportunities for substantial wartime profits, the DuPont Company had by 1919 purchased 29 percent of General Motors' stock. In rebuilding General Motors, DuPont was greatly assisted by Alfred P. Sloan Jr., a graduate of the Massachusetts Institute of Technology and a vice-president and major stockholder in General Motors.

Frustrated by Durant's chaotic way of doing business, Sloan prepared an "Organization Study" that contained a plan to revamp the management of General Motors even before the crisis of 1920. DuPont and others in top management adopted it in late 1920. This plan introduced decentralized management to General Motors by clearly delineating the duties and responsibilities of the head office and the divisions and by providing for effective communications among the different parts of the company. The plan's goal was to combine divisional autonomy with supervision by a strong central office.

Sloan and DuPont made significant changes at the operational level. Each division was now clearly defined by a distinct product line. Market segmentation in modern industrial firms began at General Motors. As the automobile market matured, Sloan and DuPont recognized the need to differentiate their cars, ranging from Chevrolet to Cadillac, from each other and from those of their competitors. They eliminated overlap in the prices, products, and markets of the divisions. Advertising and annual model changes identified each make of car. Run by a general manager, each division controlled its own engineering, production, and sales organizations, and each enjoyed a considerable degree of freedom in its daily operations.

To ensure coordination in the work of the divisions, DuPont and Sloan created the office of group vice-president. Freed from specific daily operating responsibilities, the group vice-presidents supervised the work of related divisions and helped set policies for the entire company. Four groups were established: accessories, affiliated companies, export, and car and truck. The officers in these divisions and groups were line officers.

Sloan and DuPont also created a strong central or head office (called the corporate office) for General Motors. General officers, working through executive and finance committees, coordinated the work of the four groups, made policy decisions for the company, and planned for its future. In doing so, they were assisted by a vastly enlarged staff made up of financial and legal experts. Neither the general officers nor the staff officers concerned themselves with daily operating matters.

To arrive at cooperation and understanding between management in the divisional and the central offices, Sloan and DuPont established a number of interdivisional relations committees. Officers from all levels belonged to these committees which met at regular intervals to discuss common problems. Both staff and divisional engineers, for instance, composed the general technical committee that sought solutions for common engineering problems the different divisions encountered in designing and producing cars.

Finally, Sloan and DuPont improved financial reporting and statistical controls, creating a model long followed by other diversified corporations. Three innovations were of special importance. First, the central office received weekly and monthly production reports from each group and division. Under Durant, no such data had been available. Second, the central office received reports every ten days from dealers on how many cars were actually being sold, and this information made market forecasting possible (the ten-day period of reporting sales is still the standard period in the automobile industry). Finally, the work of each division was assessed by the central office, using new accounting techniques that measured its rate of return on investment, making it easier for those on top to decide where to expand or contract the company's operations. (Figure 3 outlines decentralized management at General Motors.)

The decentralized management system instituted at General Motors in the 1920s worked well for decades. The company's share of the American

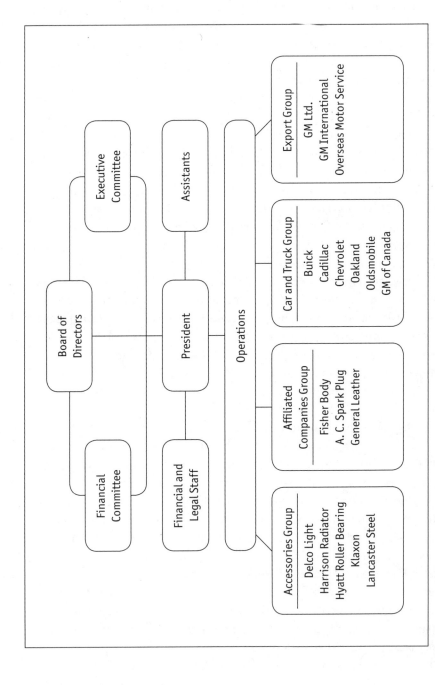

FIGURE 3 *Decentralized management at General Motors in 1924 (adapted from Management and Administration 7 [May 1924]: 525, courtesy of Houghton Mifflin)*

automobile market increased from 19 percent in 1924 to 43 percent three years later, by which time its annual net profit amounted to an impressive $276 million. The Great Depression provided the acid test for the new organization. Although its sales fell by two-thirds between 1929 and 1932, General Motors continued to show a profit and to pay dividends every year throughout the 1930s. With only minor changes, the decentralized management structure pioneered in the 1920s remained the basic administrative framework of General Motors into the 1970s.

The Spread of Decentralized Management: Strategy and Structure

Over time, many big businesses in the United States and abroad followed the route pioneered by General Motors. Structure followed strategy in American business. The more diversified a company was in terms of its products and markets, the more likely it was to establish some form of decentralized management. International Harvester adopted decentralized management in 1943, and both Chrysler and Ford did so right after World War II. In the chemicals industry DuPont led the way in the 1920s as it began making a broad range of consumer goods such as rayon, with Hercules and Monsanto following in the 1930s. As they moved into the production of many new household electrical appliances, Westinghouse adopted decentralized management in 1934 and General Electric did so in the 1950s.

While needed and appropriate for many firms in the mid-twentieth century, decentralized management eventually created problems for American companies. Over several decades, too many layers of management were created in many of the companies using decentralized management systems. Companies ossified and reacted only sluggishly to market changes; and this slowness hurt, as those changes came with increasing rapidity in the global market, especially in the 1970s and 1980s. Then, too, the use of decentralized management, with its tremendous dependence on reports, placed a premium on having top managers in the corporate office well versed in financial management methods, a situation that could lead companies to place too much emphasis on short-term financial objectives at the expense of longer-term goals. Too often managers in the corporate office lost touch with what was going on in their companies' factories, as too few of them understood operational management. These problems became noticeable in the 1970s and later years. The same problems affected companies that followed the American model in Great Britain and other lands.

Small Business in Manufacturing

Small businesses experienced a long-term decline in their relative importance in American manufacturing between 1880 and 1970. With the rise of large manufacturing companies, the shares of small firms in both industrial employment and output dropped. However, not all small manufacturers suffered. Small businesses continued to thrive in areas in which they could carve out market niches, fields in which flexibility, especially the capability to turn out rapidly small batches of goods in short production runs, was of most significance.

The metal-fabricating and machinery-making industry of New England between 1890 and 1957 was one such field. Of the eighty firms composing the industry, all but eighteen employed fewer than 100 workers, only fifteen possessed tangible assets exceeding $500,000, and only ten had a net worth of more than $500,000. Success came through the development of specialty products for niche markets. Some entrepreneurs specialized in products with only a limited demand, thus avoiding competition with big businesses disdaining to enter such unappealing fields. Others engaged in just one process, such as metal stamping, heat treating, or electroplating. By performing custom work, they secured nonstandardized orders overlooked by larger mass-production firms. Still others differentiated their products by providing extraordinary service and by building up reputations for dependability.

Personal ties held these small businesses together. Most of the founders, like those in small businesses in other industries and in other times, began their enterprises as partnerships or single-owner proprietorships, although all except six eventually reorganized their businesses as corporations. Whatever legal forms they assumed, nearly all the businesses were directly run by their owner-founders. Family enterprises in which fathers and sons or brothers jointly handled affairs frequently existed. Sometimes wives participated, usually looking after the finances of the operations.

This personal approach to business carried over into financing and labor relations. Personal savings, supplemented by family funds, funds from local business acquaintances, and, to a much lesser extent, bank borrowing, provided the initial capital. Very few companies borrowed from federal government agencies. Capital used to finance expansion came mainly from retained earnings and debt financing. Few of the entrepreneurs had access to equity markets. Even if they had had such access, few would have made use of it, for they were not willing to dilute their ownership and managerial control over their companies. Over one-half of the companies began with five or fewer employees. As the firms developed, they were able to acquire and keep their growing number of employees through a combination of monetary and nonmonetary incentives. Some offered more than the prevailing wage rate. Others provided chances for rapid advancement and opportunities to learn new skills, and in all firms the owner-managers continued to know their workers individually.

Big and Small Business in Industry

The continued development of big business in industry dramatically changed the world of the small manufacturer. Before the Civil War, nearly all American businesses had been small firms, single-unit enterprises without managerial hierarchies. With the acceleration in industrialization that occurred after the Civil War, this situation changed. Large companies benefiting from economies of scale and scope supplanted small firms in mass-production fields. While continuing to grow in absolute numbers and while remaining important in niche markets, small manufacturers became proportionally less important to America's overall economy.

The spread of large companies with decentralized management systems accelerated the trend toward concentration and the growth of oligopoly in the United States. The nation experienced its second major merger movement in the 1920s, as 5,846 mergers occurred in 1925–31. In some manufacturing fields there was a decrease in price competition, as prices in oligopolistic industries became less responsive to market forces. In those fields the decisions of the managers of big businesses rather than market forces determined the prices and quantities of goods produced. The visible hand of management became increasingly important in determining how part of America's business system functioned. It was in the interwar years that the American automobile industry, once composed of dozens of companies, came to be dominated by the Big Three—General Motors, Ford, and Chrysler.

Businesses in Sales and Services

Small businesses remained dominant longer in sales and services than in manufacturing. However, the interwar years brought changes in business organization to these fields, especially to sales, as the continued development of chain stores and the rise of supermarkets eroded the importance of independent retailers. The most notable change lay in the rapid increase in the importance of chain stores in retailing, such as the Great Atlantic and Pacific Tea Company (A&P), Woolworth, and J. C. Penney. The spread of chain stores was part of a more general trend in retailing, the growth in importance of large-scale stores. By 1949, in addition to the 20 percent of the nation's retail sales made by chain stores, department stores accounted for 8 percent, supermarkets 7 percent, and mail order houses 1 percent. Independent retailers, who had handled nearly all the sales as late as 1890, accounted for less than two-thirds of the sales.

What accounted for this dramatic rise in the chains? Probably most important, chain stores gave lower prices to consumers while still earning substantial profits. They did so by providing fewer personal services to customers than independents, by making no deliveries, by dealing strictly in cash, and by dispensing fewer premiums and trading stamps. Chains engaged in the most up-to-date business practices: the use of new accounting methods to keep track of inventories, new store layouts, and new forms of advertising. The scale of operations allowed the chains to pass on savings in costs to their customers, much like Wal-Mart at a later date. Many chains cut out middlemen in distribution, dealing instead directly with the growers and producers of goods. Chains also engaged in extensive backward vertical integration. A&P possessed subsidiaries that controlled many of its sources of milk, cheese, coffee, canned salmon, and bread.

Small service businesses also came under increasing pressure from large firms in some fields, although not to as great an extent as did small retailers. Possessing fewer economies of scale than stores selling goods, service industries were less conducive to the spread of large firms. Banking, for example, remained dominated by small businesses, although the trend was toward consolidation. The number of commercial banks in the United States fell by half during the 1930s, and then stabilized at around 15,000 through the 1980s. The coming of federal deposit insurance in 1933 enhanced the safety of small banks and gave them a new lease on life. In the interwar years branch banking also came to the United States in a major way. In 1920 less than 5 percent of banking offices were branches. Only twenty-one states permitted branch banking at that date, and until the passage of the McFadden Act by Congress in 1927 branch banking was forbidden across state lines. With the liberalization of the laws by the McFadden Act and later legislation, banks with branches came to compose one-fifth of the total by 1935, and in 1957 over one-half of the 13,617 commercial banks had branches.

From Associationalism to the Welfare State

One reason for the merger movement of the 1920s and a more general business rationalization movement — an attempt to make businesses more efficient and productive — in the 1920s and 1930s was that the federal government favored them. To be sure, the federal government continued to regulate business as it had begun to in the Progressive Era. However, there was more cooperation between government and business, to the extent that historians often label the nature of government-business relations in the United States during the interwar years "associationalism."

During World War I government officials and business executives worked together as equals through government agencies, the most important of which was the War Industries Board, to mobilize industry for the war effort. After the war, Herbert Hoover, first as secretary of commerce, and then as president between 1929 and 1933, sought to extend government-business cooperation. Hoover tried to set up an associative state as an alternative to either government control of the economy (what he called statism) or cutthroat competition and individualism. Hoover wanted government and business leaders to work together voluntarily to make the nation's economy strong. In Hoover's conception the federal government, aided by private research foundations, would be the source of modern, scientifically derived economic information. The government would pass that information along to business leaders who, in turn, would make rational business decisions in their own and the national interest. Hoover's actions took several major forms. He worked with business leaders to try to reduce waste in their industries. For example, under Hoover's guidance, the lumber industry adopted standard sizes, terms, and grades. Hoover also labored with executives to try to smooth out the ups and downs of the business cycle.

However, the onset of the Great Depression of the 1930s revealed the inadequacy of Hoover's ideas and added important new dimensions to economic rationalization. By 1932 industrial production had fallen to half of what it had been just four years earlier, and unemployment stood at about 25 percent. In this situation of widespread economic distress business rationalization came to mean much more than simply making individual firms more efficient or smoothing out small variations in the business cycle. Rationalization came to include economic recovery, with the recovery efforts led by the federal government.

In trying to solve the problems of the Great Depression, Franklin D. Roosevelt, who took office as president in 1933, built in part upon foundations laid by Hoover. Roosevelt's key solution for the problems of the industrial sector of the economy was a piece of legislation passed by Congress during the summer of the first year in which he held office, the National Industrial Recovery Act (NIRA). This act set up a new federal government agency, the

National Recovery Administration (NRA) modeled upon the War Industries Board of fifteen years before. In the NRA business leaders and government officials voluntarily cooperated to try to bring about economic recovery. Antitrust laws were suspended, and prices and production quotas were set in an attempt to help businesses get back on their feet. However, because its economic principles were faulty (the higher prices resulting from price fixing among manufacturers made it difficult for consumers to buy industrial goods), the NIRA did not work, and Roosevelt allowed it to die after the Supreme Court declared the law unconstitutional in 1935.

Roosevelt moved beyond Hoover's ideas to create with Congress the beginning of a welfare state in America, wherein the federal government assumed responsibility for the general welfare of Americans. A wide variety of federal government programs gave jobs or assistance to those out of work, something not done during the Hoover years. None of these actions, however, ended the Great Depression. While now aided by the federal government, some 10 million Americans remained jobless in 1939.

As long as Roosevelt's efforts at recovery aided them, business leaders supported New Deal measures. The NIRA initially had considerable business support. Nonetheless, much of the business backing had faded by the mid-1930s. Economic leadership by government officials was something many business leaders were unwilling to accept, especially since the New Dealers supported legislation promoting unionization. Then, too, the business community split over many of the New Deal's welfare measures, with few executives supporting the full range of Roosevelt's legislation. When rationalization moved beyond efforts to make companies more efficient and productive and threatened to impinge on management prerogatives, business leaders backed off from the movement.

Many government-business splits were healed during World War II, which brought renewed profits to businesses. Cooperation reached new heights during the conflict, as business executives and government officials worked together in a myriad of federal government agencies, most important the Office of War Mobilization and the Office of Price Administration, to ensure the successful mobilization of industry for the war effort. Federal government spending on the war ended the Great Depression, and unemployment finally dried up in 1942.

Labor Relations
Adversarial relations characterized industrial labor relations in America, as employers sought to wrest control of the workplace away from their em-

ployees, especially skilled workers. With the entrance of the United States into World War I in 1917, many labor leaders hoped that their unions would become more powerful. This proved to be the case, for the federal government struck a new arrangement with trade unions: in return for a pledge to refrain from strikes and to cooperate in achieving full industrial production, the unions were given the right to organize factory workers. During the war the National War Labor Board, a new federal government agency, mediated disputes in 1,100 plants affecting 711,500 employees and established work councils made up of representatives of management and labor in an attempt to prevent disputes from disrupting production.

Many labor officials, joined by a few business leaders, hoped that this type of cooperation, in which the federal government would continue to be involved, would expand after the war. They hoped that a contract of sorts could be reached between labor and management to protect workers' wages and working conditions and thus avoid conflicts in the future. Such was not to be, at least not in the 1920s. When labor leaders sought to unionize the steel industry, then central to America's industrial economy, they were sharply rebuffed and defeated, an outcome that ensured that labor-management relations in mass-production industries would remain much as before the war, with management dictating the terms of employment to workers and with conflict continuing between them.

With the crisis of World War I behind them, most business leaders rejected the idea of bargaining with labor unions. Instead, they tried to destroy them. Union membership peaked in 1920 at over 5 million workers, but then declined to 3.4 million in 1930, only 6.8 percent of America's nonagricultural workforce. Rather than accept independent labor unions, business leaders promoted welfare capitalism, which was based on the premise that the businesses, not independent trade unions, should look after the interests of workers. By the 1920s welfare capitalism encompassed housing, educational, medical, religious, and recreational facilities for employees, profit-sharing plans, and retirement pensions. Welfare capitalism often also involved the establishment of company unions. Although company unions were of some help in improving working conditions, they did not bargain collectively on behalf of workers with management on such fundamental issues as wages and hours of work. Company unions were almost always controlled by management, were limited to individual companies, and mainly provided avenues of communication between management and workers. In short, welfare capitalism and company unions were largely designed to protect the power and prerogatives of management.

Labor relations underwent a fundamental shift in the 1930s, a particularly stressful time in the history of American business and labor. Changes resulted, in part, from the willingness of New Deal political leaders to mitigate the harm of the Great Depression by fostering unionization. Because the Great Depression cut so deep, politicians sought to restore vigor to the business system by granting workers the means, through unions and collective bargaining, of increasing their share of the nation's wealth. In doing so, workers would, it was hoped, purchase products of their own industrial handiwork and thereby stimulate recovery. However, more was involved. Changes also resulted from growing militancy in the workforce. Such militancy produced larger and stronger unions. Politicians were almost forced to respond to the growth in union strength.

The result was the National Labor Relations Act of 1935, which granted workers the right to form unions of their own choice and required businesses to agree to collective bargaining. Partly as a result of the new law, labor struggles broke out in mass-production industries employing great numbers of unskilled and semi-skilled men and women. Led by auto workers, laborers developed a new and very effective strategy designed to improve their standards of living: they sat down on the job and refused to leave their factories, thus shutting down production. On the eve of World War II nearly 9 million American workers, 16 percent of the nonagricultural workforce, belonged to unions.

As workers bargained with management through independent unions, welfare capitalism faded away. Mass-production unions — the United Auto Workers, the United Steelworkers, the United Rubber Workers, and the like — along with the federal government assumed responsibility for the welfare of labor. Labor power rose still more during World War II, until by 1945 the number of workers who were unionized had climbed to over 14 million, nearly 22 percent of the nonagricultural workforce.

British Business

In the interwar years the formation of large companies accelerated in Great Britain. Mergers and efforts to make manufacturing firms more efficient were commonplace, and through the mergers large companies developed in some fields of British manufacturing. With the rise of these big businesses, the nature of the business firm and its management began changing. A handful of companies adopted the decentralized type of management pioneered in America by General Motors. Even so, Great Britain remained primarily a land of smaller companies. In many fields of manufacturing and in much of retailing small firms dominated the business landscape. The British business system, like that of the United States, was complex. While some parts performed well during the interwar years, others lost ground relative to competitors abroad.

Rationalization, Consumerism, and Big Business

From the outset of the 1920s economic distress lay behind much of the rationalization movement in Britain, and economic recovery was one of the movement's goals. The same postwar recession that hit America hurt Great Britain even more. In 1921 unemployment rose to 10 percent and never fell below that mark in the interwar years. In this new situation some of Britain's business leaders looked to rationalization—and to mergers, which they often equated with rationalization and efficiencies—for their salvation. Business leaders sponsored rationalization in part as an alternative to socialism favored by some labor groups. British executives were also influenced by the example of American companies. They observed American subsidiaries, such as that of Ford Motors, using mass-production methods to make their English plants more efficient. Moreover, they saw American firms leading mergers in Great Britain. General Electric brought together four electrical manufacturers to form Associated Electrical Industries, and General Motors took over Vauxhall Motors to become a large-scale automaker in Britain.

Some government leaders also favored business rationalization. The British government had been less directly involved than either the American or Japanese governments in industrialization and economic development in the nineteenth century. During World War I, however, British government officials and business leaders cooperated closely in the crisis situation. The government encouraged businesses to adopt mass-production methods, a situation that stimulated merger activity, as firms sought to expand their production capacities. Private profits and national economic growth would, it was hoped, advance together. In the 1920s mergers blossomed in Great Britain. Prodded by an organization of manufacturers, the Federation of British Industries, the government allowed mergers to take place. About 4,000 British companies merged during the 1920s and 1930s, especially in the foodstuffs, chemicals, metal manufacturing, shipbuilding, electrical engineering, and building materials industries.

A growth in consumerism also spurred business development, as in the

United States. An expansion in shopping opportunities, along with a spread of tourism and spectator sports, suggested the development of consumerism in Great Britain from the 1880s onward. Indeed, at times in the twentieth century organized consumers, working through such bodies as nationwide buying cooperatives, came to be recognized as a "third force" in British society, separate from either business or labor interests. Most concretely, rising real incomes enjoyed by many in interwar Great Britain, despite the persistent unemployment of some, led to increased consumer demand for goods.

Something approaching the mass consumption of the United States arose in Great Britain. For example, between 1927 and 1939 the number of people owning radios soared from 2.2 million to 9 million. However, as in the United States, it was the automobile that was the foremost symbol of increased consumerism. Both the Morris Company and Austin Motors, Great Britain's two largest automakers, moved in the direction of mass production in the interwar years, with Morris going the farthest by setting up a complete moving assembly line at its Cowley works in 1934. Ford of Great Britain was the third largest producer, even though Henry Ford, who could be very stubborn, refused for years to produce an automobile suitable for British roads, one with right-hand drive (an automobile having its steering wheel on the right-hand side). Automobile production in Great Britain rose from 147,000 vehicles in 1924, to 238,000 cars and trucks in 1929, to 593,000 vehicles in 1937. These figures compared to the 4.6 million automobiles produced in the United States in 1929. Although not going as far as in America, increased consumer demand created the possibility of economies of scale in some British industries, encouraging the growth of larger factories and firms.

With these mergers big businesses became more common. In 1919 only one British company was capitalized at as much as £32 million, Coats Sewing. By 1930 an additional six firms were: Unilever, Imperial Tobacco, Imperial Chemical Industries, Distillers, Courtaulds, and Guinness. By 1930, as well, at least ten British firms employed more than 30,000 workers. Industry became more concentrated. In 1909 the largest 100 companies accounted for 16 percent of Britain's industrial output, but they accounted for 24 percent by 1935, about the same proportion as in the United States. Even so, however, most British manufacturers remained considerably smaller than their American counterparts. In 1930 only the fifty largest British industrial companies would have made the list of the top 200 such firms in the United States.

Changing Business Management

As time progressed, more and more of the large British companies established centralized bureaucratic management systems. Within their head offices a division in management occurred. Entrepreneurial peak coordinators, business leaders roughly equivalent to senior vice-presidents in the United States, took charge of making grand policy and coordinating the different activities of their companies. They were assisted by specialists in personnel, finance, accounting, and technical matters who took responsibility for the routine functions of the firms. However, as in the United States, centralized management could not adequately handle the growing complexity of the affairs of the largest of the big businesses in Great Britain. Two British companies, Imperial Chemical Industries and Unilever, influenced by what General Motors and other American firms were doing, turned to decentralized management. Activities were organized on a divisional basis, with the divisions set up by region or product. The division chiefs reported to peak coordinators in the head office who controlled financial matters and grand strategy for their companies. Increasingly sophisticated accounting and record keeping bound together the different parts of these companies.

Where did the managers come from to staff Great Britain's growing number of big businesses? At the highest level, that of peak executives, many came from business families, much more so than was the case in the United States. Some companies also recruited their top managers from government ministries — Imperial Chemical Industries recruited from Inland Revenue — or from the military, as did Vickers, Britain's leading armaments maker. Technicians, the functional specialists, usually received on-the-job training within their firms. Accountancy was one common avenue of advancement for such middle-level managers. As in times past, British business leadership tended to be self-replicating. In the years 1930 through 1949 about 45 percent of the nation's business leaders were the sons of businessmen, 10 percent were the sons of farmers, 28 percent the sons of public officials, and only 17 percent the sons of clerical workers or laborers.

Imperial Chemical Industries

Imperial Chemical Industries (ICI) presents a glimpse at how a few large British businesses diversified their operations and adopted decentralized management during the interwar years. Formed as part of the business rationalization movement, the firm expanded its operations in the 1920s and 1930s to become one of Great Britain's largest and most complex companies. As their firm grew, ICI's executives found it necessary to alter its management system, and centralized management gave way to decentralized management.

The formation of ICI in 1926 can be traced to a lunchtime discussion between Harry McGowan, the chairman and managing director of Nobel Industries Ltd., and Reginald McKenna, a high-ranking government official. Both wanted to strengthen the British chemical industry in its growing competition with American companies like DuPont and German companies like I.G. Farben. From this conversation and lengthy negotiations came ICI as a merger of the four largest British chemical companies: Nobel Industries, the United Alkali Company, British Dyestuffs, and Brunner, Mond. In the 1920s and 1930s ICI was the largest manufacturing company in Great Britain and one of the largest chemical companies in the world. ICI employed 47,000 people in Great Britain alone and possessed plants in Canada, South Africa, Australia, and South America producing heavy chemicals, explosives, dyes, and fertilizers.

ICI expanded its activities as time progressed, with two related projects receiving special attention. It moved into the synthetic production of ammonia. Ammonia could be used as a source of nitrogen, and nitrogen was used in making fertilizers and explosives. Employing a related chemical process, ICI also started producing synthetic gasoline out of coal. In 1931 ICI entered into an agreement with I.G. Farben to obtain the technical process of hydrogenation, and with government support began making synthetic gasoline in 1936. World War II brought further expansion to these and other projects, and between 1937 and 1943 ICI invested the large sum of £58 million on twenty-five new factories.

Of the four companies merging to form ICI, Nobel Industries had the greatest influence on its management practices. Nobel had itself been created as a result of a merger of more than thirty companies in 1920. To rationalize this originally loose collection of firms, those at Nobel established a centralized management system. They set up a central research laboratory, centralized production in the most efficient factories, and established a strong central office to run the entire company as one entity. Within Nobel's head office functional departments handled publicity, personnel, purchasing, legal issues, and taxation matters for the entire company. However, by the mid-1920s Nobel was beginning to move in the direction of decentralized management by having the head office shift some responsibilities for the company's daily operations to product divisions. What had occurred at Nobel was repeated at ICI, which is not surprising since Nobel men occupied many of the key managerial positions at ICI.

ICI began with a strong central management system in 1926. A Finance Committee and an Executive Committee controlled capital expenditures and made all policy decisions. Banking, purchasing, commercial, and statistical control policies were all standardized and centralized in the head office. In the field, operations were centralized in the most efficient factories. While this system of management succeeded in lowering production costs, it had flaws. ICI was simply too complex in terms of its products and markets to be run well by a centralized management system.

In the late 1920s and early 1930s ICI's executives replaced centralized management with decentralized management. They established eight groups based upon products, very similar to the product divisions set up at General Motors. These groups were given responsibility for daily operations. A General Administration Committee composed of those officers in charge of the groups plus officers from the head office coordinated the work of the eight groups. Two committees in the central office, the General Purposes Committee and the Finance Committee, composed of the president and directors, made the large strategic decisions for ICI.

The Limits of Rationalization

However, even with the merger movement, the growth in size of some industrial firms, and the adoption by some firms of new management methods and structures, neither business nor political proponents of rationalization achieved as much as they desired. Old habits died hard. The continued atomization of most industries into dozens, even hundreds, of small firms proved difficult to change. Moreover, it soon turned out to be the case that those big firms that did result from mergers were not necessarily as efficient as they might be. As in the United States, many business executives, while eager to support rationalization aimed at increasing the profitability of their individual firms, were often unwilling to support rationalization measures that might impinge on their prerogatives.

The Failure of Rationalization in the Steel Industry

What occurred in Great Britain's steel industry illustrates the limitations of industrial rationalization. Most business and political leaders agreed that this industry needed to be reshaped if it were to remain competitive internationally, but disagreements among steelmakers, bankers, and government officials meant that, while some new approaches were tried, little was ultimately accomplished during the interwar years.

There were aspects of both stagnation and growth in Britain's steel industry. The output of Britain's steel industry rose by 62 percent between 1913 and 1936–37, a growth spurt greater than the 37 percent increase of steel production in Europe as a whole or the 36 percent rise in German steel output. Nonetheless, the British steel industry experienced tremendous fluctuations in output from year to year, suffered from stagnation in exports, and came to possess a great deal of excess capacity, which translated into high unemployment for its workers.

Like much of British manufacturing, the British steel industry had developed in the nineteenth century mainly as a disparate collection of small, nonintegrated firms; and so the industry remained in the early 1920s. Despite the continuing growth of their industry, British steelmakers felt intensifying pressure from large vertically integrated American and German competitors in many markets (an increasing share of Britain's production went to Commonwealth markets, made up of countries associated with the British Empire).

Even under the gun of rising foreign competition, attempts by steelmakers to rationalize their firms were disappointing. There were places where the merger of companies with overlapping capabilities might have led to the implementation of more efficient production methods and the elimination of excess capacity, among steelmakers of Britain's northeast coast, for example. Such did not occur. Well-entrenched family interests in the many small companies made mergers difficult, as did conflicts about how to proceed among various groups of creditors, shareholders, and customers. Even when mergers were possible, they did not necessarily result in efficiently run firms, as was true for Britain's largest steel company, United Steel. Formed through the merger of four iron and steel firms between 1917 and 1920, this company was unified in name only. Throughout the 1920s the four steelmakers composing it operated almost as independent entities, with little managerial coordination of their work and few economies of scale. Only in 1928, faced with mounting financial losses, did United Steel begin centralizing its management and making its plants more efficient.

During the interwar years British banks became more involved in the management of manufacturing concerns than they had previously been and might have provided leadership in rationalizing steelmaking. City of London, regional, and local banks had long invested in industry. British banks had not, however, taken much of a role in managerial decision making in those companies, especially when compared to the more active roles taken by German universal banks and the banks of Japanese zaibatsu. This began to change during the interwar years. In the early 1930s the Bank of

England mapped out plans by which British steelmakers might form large vertically integrated regional amalgamations in the interests of production efficiencies, but the bank ultimately drew back from involvement in any such schemes. The bank did not want to invest in an unprofitable industry, lacked the management know-how to bring about rationalization, and did not want to engage in activities that might make it more accountable to the British government.

Finally, the British government might have promoted rationalization schemes for the steel industry, abandoning its traditional stance of avoiding direct involvement in industrial matters. Like the Bank of England, the British government did, in fact, become more engaged than before; but, again like the bank, the government did not go far enough. The government wanted the elimination of excessive competition in the steel industry, yet also feared the development of regional steel monopolies. As a result, for years the government tried to foster mergers that would result in a more efficient industry, but long refused to pass a protective tariff for steel. Only in 1932, at the nadir of the Great Depression and in response to similar actions by many other industrial nations, did the British government enact a protective tariff. In the 1930s the government sought also to form cartels in the steel industry; these efforts, however, accomplished little in the way of rationalization and increased efficiencies.

Labor Relations

As we have seen, trade unions developed rapidly in some fields in Great Britain, becoming considerably more powerful than they were in the United States. Craft unions in such trades as iron and steelmaking, cotton textiles, coal mining, shipbuilding, and construction, established in the 1880s or earlier, were joined by so-called "new unions" first set up in the 1890s. Made up of less-skilled workers, the new unions were less craft-based and more industry-based. This situation led to the formation of broad industrial unions such as the Miners' Federation in 1908, the Transport Workers' Federation in 1910, and the National Union of Railwaymen in 1913. Trade union membership rose from 750,000 in 1888, 6 percent of the industrial workforce, to 2.6 million in 1910, perhaps 30 percent of the industrial workforce.

Unlike the situation in the United States, where until the 1930s the government often opposed the formation of unions, the British government accepted and, indirectly at least, promoted the establishment of trade unions. Especially important was the passage by Parliament of the Conciliation Act of 1896. Through this act the government could appoint an official to work as an arbitrator between labor unions and management. While neither management nor labor had to use the services of an arbitrator and while the findings of an arbitrator (when used) were not binding, the act encouraged the development of collective bargaining. In the years before World War I, most bargaining was regional in nature. During the conflict the British government became increasingly involved in labor disputes, and arbitration became compulsory. Bargaining shifted to the national level during the war and remained there in the interwar years, with national trade unions bargaining collectively with national employers associations.

The growth of trade unions may have hurt productivity in some fields of British industry. In the automobile industry many British manufacturers rejected the American example of high throughput, capital-intensive technology, accompanied by the payment of relatively high wages. (As we have seen, some, such as Morris and Austin, did take this route.) Fearing the resistance of workers to the introduction of labor-saving machinery, many British automakers used more labor-intensive production methods that enabled workers to retain considerable control of work processes. Automobile manufacturers in Britain balanced the relatively low productivity of their workers by paying lower wages than automakers in the United States.

There was more to industrial relations than simply adjusting pay scales. Associated with labor relations was a failure on the part of both business and government to invest in advancing labor skills. Practical skills rather than academic training were seen as the proper basis for business success for both workers and managers. A much smaller proportion of British workers and managers received an education in engineering or the sciences, or any education beyond elementary education, than did their counterparts in Germany or the United States. The gap was greatest for workers. Only 230 junior technical schools had been established in Great Britain by 1937–38, in which children leaving grammar (elementary) school might learn basic sciences before entering factory occupations. As industrialization became more technologically complex with the development of such fields as chemicals, synthetic fibers, automobiles, and electrical equipment, this shortcoming hurt Great Britain.

Retailing in Great Britain

New forms of retailing developed in Great Britain from the mid-nineteenth century, as the nation's consumer culture expanded: department stores, chain stores (multiples), and cooperatives. Yet, even as these types of retail outlets grew during the interwar years, small retailers continued to predominate in sales. As late as the 1930s independent retailers accounted for 80 percent of the sales of such new consumer durables as automobiles and electrical goods, along with a similar percentage of the sales of fruit and vegetables, fish, chocolates, and tobacco products. Altogether, over two-thirds of Britain's retail sales were made by single-outlet retailers, about the same proportion as in the United States.

Several factors limited the rise of big business in retailing. Families often did not want to expand their enterprises to a size larger than they could easily oversee, which often limited department stores and multiples to growth in single regions. Rather than extending their stores into new areas, families invested in other types of local enterprises such as housing and factories. In addition, the ability of organizations of independent retailers to enforce resale price maintenance agreements, agreements by which manufacturers refused to allow their products to be sold below certain prices, undercut advantages larger retailers might try to obtain by purchasing and selling in bulk. Unlike the situation in the United States, where such agreements could not usually be enforced, in Britain resale price maintenance agreements meant that large retailers could not lower prices to compete with mom-and-pop stores. Competition had to take place in terms of service, where small retailers close to their customers often had the advantage. Finally, the regionally fragmented nature of the British market slowed the growth of large national retailers, so that only after World War II did many develop.

Business and City Planning in Great Britain and the United States
Even as people in Great Britain and the United States tried to deal with their changing business environments by reworking their firms, they also sought to control their economic, social, and cultural environments through urban planning. Not surprisingly, business people and professionals were deeply involved in both endeavors, with reformers crossing and recrossing the Atlantic to share ideas. City reform and urban planning efforts took numerous forms. From the 1880s into the twentieth century, a growing number of cities on both sides of the Atlantic began providing a broader range of services to their residents through municipal ownership of water supplies, sewer systems, and public utilities such as electrical systems. Some built streetcar systems. In addition, several broader planning concepts emerged.

Influenced especially by Baron Georges Haussmann's work in redesigning Paris during the mid-nineteenth century, American reformers sought to remake cities in comprehensive ways through a "City Beautiful" movement in the early twentieth century. Few British city councils adopted comprehensive city beautiful planning in this time period, preferring to work in more piecemeal ways. (There were, nonetheless, some comprehensive experiments in Great Britain, as in the establishment of so-called "garden cities," such as Ebenezer Howard's Letchworth in 1903.) Typically, American city beautiful plans, drafted by the country's first group of expert, professional urban planners, included new street and harbor systems designed to move traffic more efficiently, civic centers for city government buildings and auditoriums, and new park and boulevard systems. Washington, D.C., Chicago, and San Francisco were three of the over one hundred American cities to have urban plans drawn up. The plans were intended to make the cities more efficient economically, move them ahead of their urban rivals (business boosterism was a big part of planning), and extend the social influence of business people and professionals over working-class residents. However, none of the plans were implemented in their entirety. While urbanites could agree on the value of planning in the abstract, they usually disagreed on its particulars, such as where to place a new road or civic center. Then, too, workers disliked implications of social control by business people and opposed the plans for that reason.

More long-lived and much broader in scope was the development of urban zoning—the separation of industrial, commercial, and living activities into different parts or "zones" of a city by the stipulation of different building codes for various areas in cities. Zoning remains the most common form of city planning worldwide today. Frankfurt, Germany, is usually recognized as the first city to engage in comprehensive zoning, doing so in 1891. In Great Britain, paternalistic employers set up strictly zoned company towns, such as William Lever's Port Sunlight near Liverpool, just a short time later. (Lever was a soap maker, and his firm was a precursor of Unilever.) However, not until 1932 did Parliament pass legislation permitting towns and cities to really begin zoning, and only with the passage of the Town and Country Planning Act of 1947 was zoning fully embraced nationwide. In the United States, zoning spread through the passage of city ordinances, not through national or state legislation. (Hawai'i became the only state to have statewide zoning, adopting a land-use system modeled on Great Britain's after World War II.) Los Angeles and New York City were the first large American cities to adopt comprehensive zoning, doing so around the time of World War I. Eagerly embraced by local realtors, more than four hundred American cities adopted zoning by 1925, and nine hundred cities had done so by 1930. As we shall see in the next chapter, the Japanese also turned to zoning as a way to control their urban development during the interwar years.

German Business

What occurred in Germany offers a valuable comparison to the course of events in Great Britain and the United States during the interwar period. Despite the devastation of World War I, many German businesses recovered in the 1920s to regain leading places in the world economy. Already in 1929 German firms produced 134,000 automobiles and trucks, for example. During the interwar years, too, the German state, especially under the Nazis, increased its involvement in economic affairs, until businesses, especially those in heavy industry, became almost simply part of the state apparatus.

German Business during the 1920s

World War I left many German industrial firms in ruins. Runaway inflation and high interest rates (20 percent per day in 1923!) added to problems in the early 1920s, making it impossible for German business leaders to plan for the future. In this chaotic situation German manufacturers found the loose cartels and the universal banks that had earlier been of great help less useful, and turned to tighter business associations and their own internal resources to rebuild and expand. With general economic stability returning to Germany from 1924, industrial firms were able to regroup and then move ahead. Generally speaking, those German companies that had built strong foundations before the war—large, efficient manufacturing plants, extensive marketing systems, and competent management teams—recovered most rapidly and fully. In the industries of the Second Industrial Revolution—in such varied fields as alloyed metals, chemicals, and machinery—German firms were soon driving their British counterparts from world markets. The same was true of some German companies in light industries, such as those making rayon.

World War I brought changes to government-business relations in Germany. As in the United States and Great Britain, the government became increasingly involved in business affairs. After the war a new government, the Weimar Republic, was formed; and under its aegis a compromise was reached between employer and employee associations, giving Germany the most complete system of social welfare programs and industrial relations in the world. Basically, German manufacturers agreed to some of labor's demands to avoid even more radical changes. Backed by labor more than by business, efforts were made to rationalize German industry; large nation-wide business organizations appeared and many smaller regional cartels developed. Even so, the continued importance of smaller firms in industry limited the effectiveness of German rationalization attempts; and, as in other nations, rationalization was only partially fulfilled. Business and government actions brought prosperity to Germany in the mid- and late 1920s.

German Business and the Nazis

That prosperity vanished with the coming of the Great Depression; unemployment rose to 10 percent in 1929 and to 33 percent in the winter of 1932–33. It was in these hard times that Adolf Hitler's National Socialists (Nazis) came to power, with Hitler appointed chancellor in early 1933. The roles played by big business leaders in facilitating Hitler's rise to power are controversial. Some business leaders may have thought they could use Hitler to achieve ends of their own; other executives may have backed Hitler as they turned away from Weimar democracy. Business support for Hitler was, however, far from unanimous; and more was involved than business backing in Hitler's ascent. In the chaotic economic times of the early 1930s Hitler garnered substantial popular support. The Nazis won less than 3 percent of the national vote in 1928, but increased their share to 18 percent in 1930 and then to 37 percent in April 1932.

Under Hitler the Weimar constitution was abandoned, and the government became a dictatorship. The Nazi government forced all major industries to form cartels, with the cartels becoming not independent business associations, but arms of the state (as did labor unions). Government control of business, especially heavy industry, tightened as Hitler prepared for war. During World War II, especially from 1942, when Albert Speer became Minister of Armaments, efforts were made to rationalize industry more fully. Product "rings" composed of business and government leaders were formed to design and produce simplified weapons with long production runs.

Even so, smaller firms remained important in Germany's economic mobilization. As in Japan, medium-size and small manufacturers were joined into networks of subcontractors for big businesses. In fact, about one-half of Germany's armament companies had no more than one hundred employees. Moreover, the Nazi government sought to aid small retailers, one of its sources of support. In 1933 it placed a temporary ban on the opening of additional retail outlets and controlled their establishment thereafter.

Enforceable retail price maintenance laws, as in Britain, also favored small retailers. In 1933 German retail shops had an average of 2.6 employees.

Conclusions

Developments during the interwar years, especially in Great Britain, raise the important issue of international competitiveness. Only a handful of Britain's industrial firms rationalized their operations and management systems as dramatically as ICI. Most big British manufacturers were loosely run confederations of formerly independent companies with lax central direction over their operations. United Steel epitomized this approach to management for about a decade. Family connections and influence remained pronounced in Britain's large manufacturing firms, considerably stronger than in their American counterparts. Beyond the world of large companies lay the realm of small business. Despite the merger movement, small firms remained the norm in Great Britain, even in manufacturing.

Did the continuing family nature of British business and the smallness of many of its industrial companies hurt Great Britain in international competition with nations like the United States and Germany? Did larger, better managed, better organized, more efficient companies in other nations destroy Great Britain's industrial dominance? These questions, first voiced in the late nineteenth century, were more commonly asked during the interwar years, and swelled to become a loud refrain after World War II. In some industries during the interwar years the answers were probably "yes." However, Great Britain's overall industrial picture was ambiguous, as the steel story suggests. Steel's inability to rationalize fully was due, in part, to the continued dominance of relatively small, family-owned companies — but only in part. Banks and the government must also bear some of the blame for the failure to form a truly efficient industry. Moreover, it is worth remembering that, for all of its problems, Britain's steel industry expanded faster than that of any of its major European competitors in the 1920s and 1930s.

The issue of national economic decline, in Great Britain or in any nation, is complex. There is, first of all, the question of what is meant by decline. Britain lost ground *relative* to some other nations in some heavy industries in the interwar years, especially in the more technologically advanced fields of the Second Industrial Revolution, such as chemicals. However, even in these fields British output generally increased, although at a slower rate than in some other countries. Overall, the British economy continued to grow in the interwar years, and did so after World War II. Up to World War II

Britain's gross domestic product, a measure of a nation's economic output, remained substantially larger than that of Germany or France.

In some fields of business, especially those beyond heavy industry, the British excelled. City of London institutions continued to lead the world in financial services during the interwar years. Then, too, Great Britain remained, as it had been in the nineteenth century, the world leader in foreign direct investment (FDI)—that is, investments in overseas mining, service, and manufacturing establishments—with FDI totaling $10.5 billion in 1938. British investment groups, such as Matheson and Butterfield & Swire, diversified into international trade and manufacturing with sophisticated management practices. The number of British multinational manufacturers (British companies having at least some of their factories overseas) rose from just over 200 in 1914 to 448 in 1939.

In those areas in which Great Britain lost ground relative to some other nations there was generally more than one cause. Certainly more was involved than shortcomings in the personal nature of family management during the interwar years; there is no convincing proof that managerial failures were widespread in family-run firms. Both financial institutions and multinationals did well with family-style management. Just which factors contributed to Great Britain's relative decline in some areas of heavy industry is a hotly debated topic. Sometimes management failed to adopt the most up-to-date production methods. In cotton textiles, for reasons that seemed to make sense at the time, British manufacturers stayed with older spinning and weaving methods longer than their counterparts in some other nations. The failure of the British government to provide adequate education in the sciences and technologies, often reinforced by a failure of businesses to invest in human skills, was probably even more important in causing problems in heavy industries—in steelmaking and automaking, for example. And, as we have seen in steelmaking, the inability of British industrial, banking, and government leaders to agree on courses of actions thwarted efforts to make industries more competitive.

Suggested Readings

Alfred D. Chandler Jr., has written extensively about the development of decentralized management in the United States in his *Strategy and Structure* (Cambridge, Mass., 1962). Alfred P. Sloan Jr., *My Years with General Motors* (New York, 1965), provides an inside look at managerial change. Much has been written about Henry Ford and the history of Ford Motors. For a close look at the impact of the Model T on America, see Reynold Wik, *Henry*

Ford and Grass-Roots America (Ann Arbor, 1972). James Soltow, "Origins of Small Business: Metal Fabricators and Machinery Makers in New England, 1890–1957," *Transactions of the American Philosophical Society* 55 (December 1965): 1–58, is a seminal study on the history of small business in industry in the United States. Martha Olney, *Buy Now, Pay Later: Advertising, Credit, and Consumer Durables in the 1920s* (Chapel Hill, 1991), and Charles McGovern, *Sold American: Consumption and Citizenship, 1890–1945* (Chapel Hill, 2006), examine the relationship between the development of a consumer society and business change. Ellis Hawley, *The New Deal and the Problem of Monopoly* (Princeton, 1966), and Collin Gordon, *New Deals: Business, Labor, and Politics in America, 1920–1935* (Cambridge, 1994), examine government-business relations. For a masterly overview, see David M. Kennedy, *Freedom from Fear: The American People in Depression and War, 1929–1945* (New York, 1999).

Leslie Hannah, *The Rise of the Corporate Economy* (Baltimore, 1976), is an essential account about British business. Derek H. Aldcroft, *The Inter-War Economy: Britain, 1919–1939* (New York, 1970), surveys economic changes. W. J. Reader, *Imperial Chemical Industries: A History*, 2 vols. (Oxford, 1970 and 1975), is a solid examination of a leading British firm. Michael Dintenfass, *Managing Industrial Decline: Entrepreneurship in the British Coal Industry between the Wars* (Columbus, 1992), and Steven Tolliday, *Business, Banking and Politics: The Case of British Steel, 1918–1939* (Cambridge, Mass., 1987), are valuable case studies. On the development of a consumer society in Great Britain, see John Benson, *The Rise of Consumer Society in Britain, 1880–1980* (London, 1994), and Matthew Hilton, *Consumerism in 20th-Century Britain* (Cambridge, 2003). For two valuable comparative studies, see Ellen Furlough and Carl Strikwerda, eds., *Consumers against Capitalism? Consumer Cooperation in Europe, North America, and Japan, 1840–1990* (New York, 1999), and Susan Strasser, Charles McGovern, and Matthias Judt, eds., *Getting and Spending: European and American Consumer Societies in the Twentieth Century* (Cambridge, 1998). For an overview of the history of European automaking, see James Laux, *The European Automobile Industry* (New York, 1992).

On transatlantic city reform and urban planning, see especially Daniel Rogers, *Atlantic Crossings: Social Politics in a Progressive Age* (Cambridge, Mass., 1998). On developments in Great Britain, see John Sheail, *An Environmental History of Twentieth Century Britain* (Houndmills, 2002), chapter 2, and T. C. Smout, *Nature Contested: Environmental History in Scotland and Northern England since 1600* (Edinburgh, 2002), chapter 6. On American planning efforts, see Mansel G. Blackford, *The Lost Dream: Businessmen and City Planning on the Pacific Coast, 1890–1920* (Columbus, 1993), Marc A. Weiss, *The Rise of the Community Builders: The American Real Estate Industry and Urban Land Planning* (New York, 1987), and William H. Wilson, *The City Beautiful Movement* (Baltimore, 1989). Mel Scott, *American City Planning since 1890* (Berkeley, 1969), remains a standard work.

The development of business and its relationship to government in Germany may be examined in R. J. Overy, *War and Economy in the Third Reich* (New York, 1994). Valuable case studies include John Gillingham, *Industry and Politics in the Third Reich: Ruhr Coal, Hitler, and Europe* (New York, 1985), Peter Hayes, *Industry and Ideology: IG Farben in the Nazi Era* (New York, 1987), Wilfried Feldenkirchen, *Siemens, 1918–1945* (Columbus, 1999), and Ray Stokes, "The Oil Industry in Nazi Germany, 1936–1945," *Business History Review* 59 (Summer 1985), 254–78. Henry Ashby Turner Jr., *German Big Business and the Rise of Hitler* (New York, 1985), is controversial.

Japanese and Chinese Businesses in the Interwar Period

In 1921 Japan's largest trading company, Suzuki Shoten, found itself in deep financial difficulties. Like many Japanese firms, Suzuki had expanded rapidly during World War I, only to face hard times in the worldwide economic contraction following the conflict. Suzuki failed in 1927, and only later did forty former employees of Suzuki establish a new and successful firm, Nissho, from its ashes. As the example of Suzuki Shoten suggests, the interwar years, the 1920s and 1930s, were unstable economic times for Asian businesses. A recession of varying intensity and duration hit the different nations following World War I, and business recovery in the mid-1920s was cut short by the global depression of the 1930s. The deepest and most widespread depression in world history, these hard times ended only as nations prepared for World War II. Adding to uncertainties, especially for Chinese businesses, was Japan's aggressive military expansion. Hostilities with Japan began in 1931-32, when Japan took over Manchuria, and in 1937 Japan began a widespread invasion and occupation of China proper, which ended only with Japan's defeat in World War II.

Japanese Business

Like other industrial nations, Japan experienced tremendous economic ups and downs during the interwar years. World War I brought an economic boom to Japan, as Asian markets were thrown open by the inability of Western nations like Great Britain to supply them with goods. However, this boom collapsed in 1920, and Japan was caught up in the worldwide recession. The 1920s were perilous times for Japanese businesses, for a series of financial panics interrupted economic recovery. The 1930s initially brought little relief; for, as world trade stagnated, Japan found demand for its chief exports — silk, cotton, and tea — drying up. Economic recovery in the mid- and late 1930s revolved around two developments. There was a revival of Japanese exports when the country left the gold standard and devalued the yen in 1931, and government spending for military goods rose dramatically.

In 1931–32 the Japanese army occupied southern Manchuria, a full-scale war broke out between Japan and China in 1937, and Japan's attack on the United States in 1941 signaled the spread of World War II to the Pacific. Government spending on military goods rose dramatically, and by 1934 Japan's GNP had recovered from a nadir in 1931. Consumerism played some role in Japan's economic recovery, but it was much less important in Japan than in the United States or Great Britain.

Japanese business and political leaders responded to the economic swings, especially the downturns, in ways roughly similar to their Western counterparts. They worked together to rationalize their firms and industries, but, as in the West, with only partial success. Business people and politicians also sought to stimulate consumerism, so long as it furthered their nationalistic goals. Business leaders, often aided by politicians, established new zaibatsu based on heavy industries and experimented with new types of labor relations. Small manufacturers became increasingly important as subcontractors to their larger brethren. Yet, as in Great Britain and the United States, there was also continuity in Japanese business. Many small manufacturers continued operations as independents, and small firms remained dominant in sales.

Business Rationalization

As in Great Britain and the United States, a business rationalization movement took place in Japan during the interwar years, as political and business leaders tried to deal with economic shocks. At the level of the individual firm, many companies redesigned their factory layouts, imported new technologies, and standardized production methods. At the industry level, companies joined cartels to fix prices and limit production. The Japanese government backed the formation of cartels as a way to make Japanese business strong in world trade. A Major Industries Control Law of 1931 sought to create a cartel for every large-scale industry, and by 1932 Japan possessed thirty-three cartels in heavy industry, thirty-one in chemicals, eleven in textiles, eight in food processing, and eighteen in finance.

The cartels varied tremendously in their effectiveness. Generally, the efforts of the Japanese government to bring about recovery through cartelization were only partly successful. As in Great Britain and the United States, companies tended to support their government's rationalization efforts only when they perceived direct benefits from doing so. When cartelization did not fit in with their plans, companies found ways to avoid it. It was more government spending on war industries, as in the United States, than the success of cartelization and rationalization that brought revival to Japan's economy, as may be seen in looking at what happened in the steel industry.

For all intents and purposes, Japan's modern steel industry began with the operations of Yawata Iron and Steel, a government works, in 1901. World War I, with its great demand for steel, led to a major expansion of Japanese steel production. When Yawata failed to keep up with the soaring demand, private companies entered the steel business. By the end of the war 200 private companies were turning out 60 percent of Japan's raw steel. However, the wartime boom in steelmaking became a bust in the 1920s, as the Japanese companies faced renewed imports of pig iron from India and steel from Western nations.

Japanese steelmakers tried to counter international competition with a rationalization movement. They introduced new, more efficient ways of producing iron and steel; and companies merged, until there were only about ten major steelmakers in Japan by 1926. Between 1926 and 1930 these companies formed various cartels, but the cartels proved unable to deal with the slump in demand for steel that accompanied the depression of the 1930s. Finally, in 1933 the Japanese Diet passed the Nihon Iron and Steel Company Act, which aimed at consolidating all Japanese steelmakers into one company. However, despite this legislation, enough companies remained outside of the consolidated enterprise to limit its effectiveness. It was only military orders for steel products from the mid-1930s on that lifted Japan's steel industry out of its depression.

The New Zaibatsu: Nissan and the Riken Group

The growth of heavy industry was a particularly noticeable aspect of economic recovery and military spending in Japan during the 1930s. The collapse of foreign markets for silk, cotton, and other products of light industry combined with military purchases of steel, chemicals, machinery, and the like to build up heavy industry. As late as 1928 light industry accounted for more than twice as much of Japan's total industrial output as did heavy industry, but by 1935 heavy industry was more important than light industry.

As Japan's economy changed, alterations occurred in the nature of its business firms, especially big businesses. A major development during the interwar years was the establishment of so-called "new zaibatsu," business complexes firmly based upon heavy industries — steel, chemicals, engineering, electrical machinery, and automobiles. Japan Nitrogen, Nissan, Nakajima Aircraft, and Toyota were among the most important. The new zaibatsu were less diversified than the older zaibatsu such as Mitsui and Mitsubishi, often lacking their own banks or trading companies, and they were more closely allied with the government's military expansion.

Nissan, the largest of the new zaibatsu, originated in mining. Nissan can be traced to the Hitachi Copper Mine, which was modernized and incorporated as the Kuhara Mining Company a few years before World War I. During the war boom Kuhara Mining became one of Japan's leading industrial firms. When the war ended, the company diversified into new fields, including shipping and trading. However, a fall in the price of copper and problems encountered in diversification brought Kuhara close to bankruptcy in the mid-1920s. In 1926 Ayukawa Yoshisuke, who was in the cast steel business, bought Kuhara, reorganized it, and renamed it Nihon Sangyo, soon shortened to Nissan. By selling some stock in Nissan to the public he raised funds for expansion, and by concentrating the company's efforts on heavy industry he was able to secure still more from retained earnings. By the mid-1930s the Nissan zaibatsu had grown to consist of over eighty companies, mainly in heavy industry.

Like Nissan, the Riken Group was a new zaibatsu that came into being in the 1920s, and its development illustrates well the close ties that often existed between the Japanese government and heavy industry. The Riken Group originated in discussions between Takamine Jokichi, a well-known Japanese chemist, and Shibusawa Eiichi, both of whom lamented the fact that Japan lagged behind in the development of a chemical industry necessary for the expansion of heavy industry and the growth of national power. World War I cut off the importation of many drugs and industrial products from Western nations, leading the Japanese government to look favorably on the establishment of a chemical research program. Out of these concerns came the formation of the Institute (Riken) of Physical and Chemical Research in 1917. The government provided three-fifths of the funding for the Institute, with the rest coming from private businesses. The Institute's goal was to make Japan self-sufficient in the development of military supplies and industrial materials.

The Institute developed a number of drugs, vitamins, and chemicals in the 1920s and was soon searching for a way to produce them commercially and expand their use in the Japanese economy. The result was the formation in 1927 of the Rikagaku Industrial Company, funded mainly by leading zaibatsu—Mitsui, Mitsubishi, Sumitomo, Yasuda, and Okura. The Institute and its director also bought shares in Rikagaku. By 1936 the Institute had developed 167 major products, including drugs, synthetic sake, photographic printing paper, and corundum. Particularly important for the military was the development of new ways of making magnesium and piston rings for internal combustion engines.

The Riken Industrial Group, as it came to be called, took form in the late 1930s with Rikagaku as its nucleus. Rikagaku acted as a holding company owning stock in subsidiary companies and providing some coordination of their activities. By 1940 the Riken Group consisted of fifty-eight major companies, including Riken Magnesium, Riken Piston Ring, Riken Special Steel, Riken Electric Wire, and Riken Corundum, some of which also controlled subsidiary companies. Very important to Japan's war efforts in the late 1930s and early 1940s, the Riken Group filled its role in helping to build up heavy industry so necessary for military expansion. Broken up by American authorities after World War II, the Riken Group later partially reformed with new goals.

Consumerism and Nationalism

Not all of the large firms that formed or expanded in interwar Japan were new zaibatsu associated with the government's push to develop heavy industry and the military. Some, although far fewer than in the West, produced consumer products. Kikkoman's history illustrates well this different path. Kikkoman did not make consumer durable goods such as automobiles, stoves, or washing machines. As was typical of Japanese firms making consumer goods, it produced a consumer nondurable good, a product not meant to last for long: soy sauce.

Kikkoman traced its origins to the Tokugawa period. As cities like Edo became major consumption centers, the demand for shoyu (soy sauce) increased greatly, and new shoyu producers set up rural plants in response to this demand. One such place was the area around Noda in central Honshu. Noda possessed a good river link to Edo, which practically assured its rise as Edo continued to grow. In the Tokugawa and Meiji periods, the technology for brewing shoyu remained traditional. It involved the mixing of roasted wheat and steamed soybeans, setting aside this mixture to mold, adding salt water to the mixture as it was molding, allowing this mixture to ferment for one or two years, and then extracting the liquid shoyu from the fermented result. There were about 14,000 makers of shoyu in Japan in 1910, mostly small-scale.

Among those going into shoyu production in Noda were the Takanashi and Mogi families, who began operations in the early 1660s and who became interrelated by marriages. The families soon dominated shoyu production in Noda by setting up branch households to run more and more new shoyu-making plants, not by setting up larger plants, since, given the technologies of the day, there were few economies of scale. There was a division of responsibilities, including a separation of ownership from management, among the households. Some families provided the capital for the shoyu factories but did not play an active role in running the operations. Other households bought the raw materials and sold the shoyu. Still other households were in charge of the actual production processes. In these circumstances there was a lack of coordination—a situation that could be endured when traditional, small-scale production was the norm, but that could not be permitted as the Mogis and Takanashis began moving into large-batch production.

Technological improvements began in the late Meiji period and continued in the Taisho and early Showa periods—that is, during the 1920s and 1930s. Machinery and heat were applied wherever possible to speed up the production process. Large-batch production in new factories dwarfed earlier traditional production efforts. In 1926 the company opened the biggest factory of any type in Japan and three years later opened a still larger one. As production facilities became larger and more complicated, better coordination between them and their sales outlets were needed. In 1917 the heads of the Mogi and Takanashi families met to discuss amalgamation. After a year of negotiations the result was a merger of many of the separate family production facilities into one new company, the Noda Shoyu Company (the immediate predecessor of Kikkoman).

Noda Shoyu was set up as a joint-stock company in 1918, embracing 1,000 workers, fifty managers, scores of plants, research facilities, sales offices, and transportation and storage sites. Still owned exclusively by the Mogi and Takanashi families, Noda Shoyu centralized its management. Functional committees within the company's head office sought to handle all planning, coordinate all business operations, and standardize production methods. The three most important committees were those of managerial coordination, sales, and research. Business methods were standardized; in 1922 the first codification of company rules and regulations was issued. As part of its efforts to become more efficient, Noda Shoyu reduced the number of its brands of shoyu from thirty-four to just sixteen.

In 1925 a very important legal change was made, and from this alteration Noda Shoyu emerged as a zaibatsu, although, unlike Nissan or the Riken Group, a zaibatsu not closely associated with the Japanese government. An unlimited partnership called Senshusha, owned by the Mogi and Takanashi families, was set up. Senshusha owned 60 percent of the shares in Noda

Shoyu and six other concerns. Some of these other enterprises were food production companies, but they also included a bank and trading company. By the early 1930s Senshusha was only slightly smaller than Furukawa, the smallest of Japan's so-called "Big Eight" zaibatsu. Noda Shoyu remained the most important manufacturing company in the Senshusha group. By 1930 Noda Shoyu was one of the fifty largest manufacturing companies in Japan. More and more salaried professional managers were introduced into the management of Senshusha and Noda Shoyu, and the involvement of Mogi and Takanashi family members in daily management operations lessened.

Kikkoman (the name Noda Shoyu assumed in 1964) survived World War II and, after solving critical problems, prospered in the postwar years. In 1946 the old holding company Senshusha was dissolved, much as Mitsui and Mitsubishi were, in the interests of economic democracy. Kikkoman officially became an independent company, no longer having any official connection to the bank or trading company that had been owned by Senshusha. However, democratization was more apparent than real. The Mogis and Takanashis still owned 20 percent of the stock in Kikkoman, and companies in which they had interests held an additional 20 percent. After World War II, Kikkoman first focused on making soy sauce. It further mechanized operations in the 1950s and 1960s, and in doing so moved from large-batch to continuous-process production. By 1973 it made nearly one-third of the shoyu produced in Japan. Kikkoman diversified its efforts, as per capita Japanese consumption of soy sauce declined due to dietary changes. By 1980 Kikkoman sold three dozen different food and food-related products in Japan and abroad, and a year later shoyu accounted for only 62 percent of Kikkoman's total sales.

Despite the growth of many new industrial businesses in the postwar period, Kikkoman was still one of Japan's 200 largest industrial firms in 1980, with sales of $600 million and an employment of 4,000. Kikkoman's history shows the continuing importance of successful family businesses to Japan's business system, especially when compared to the United States. However, Kikkoman's history also illustrates that changes did take place. The demands of technology and market, as Kikkoman moved from small-scale to large-batch and then to continuous-process production, led to the development of new legal and managerial forms and forced the employment of more professional managers, sorely needed to coordinate the work of the company's different parts.

While Kikkoman's growth illustrates changes occurring in the making of consumer nondurables, the emergence of companies in radios and automobiles shows the nascent development of consumer durable enterprises in Japan. This was consumerism with a nationalistic twist. The Japanese government was vitally interested in both radios and automobiles. Government officials favored automobiles and trucks as necessary for the nation's military buildup and saw in the dispersal of radios throughout cities and countryside a means of spreading their views of world affairs. Japanese consumerism thus differed substantially from Western consumerism, which was market-driven and not closely related to governmental needs.

Automobiles were available in Japan during most of the interwar years from Western, mainly American, manufacturers. In the early 1930s Ford and General Motors accounted for about 93 percent of the automobiles sold in Japan. Car parts were produced in Detroit, shipped to the Tokyo area as "knock-down" sets, and assembled there for sale throughout the nation. As part of Japan's wartime movement toward autarchy (self-sufficiency), members of the Diet passed legislation in 1936 making it virtually impossible for foreign firms to bring knock-down sets into Japan, an action opening the way for nascent Japanese automakers. Nissan, the new zaibatsu, moved into making cars and trucks. Toyota, a well-known producer of cotton-textile looms, had also been experimenting with automobile production for several years by this time and increased its output in the late 1930s. The Japanese military insisted on boosting truck production for the army, a preference quickly reflected in production statistics. In 1940 Toyota made 14,519 trucks, but only 268 automobiles. When they clashed, military desires trumped consumerism.

The story was somewhat similar for radios in Japan. Broadcasting began in 1925 over a government-owned network, the Nihon Hoso Kyokai (NHK). The government made a major effort to push radio ownership, spending 10 million yen, a large sum, between 1926 and 1934 in just the first stage of developing the NHK. Eventually, the NHK established fifty relay stations of 500 to 10,000 watts apiece to disperse radio waves throughout the nation as a way to reach citizens with the government's take on the news. By 1935, 35 percent of urban homes possessed radios, as did 6 percent of rural homes. In 1938 the government began a campaign of "one household, one radio." It worked. By 1945, 62 percent of urban households and 39 percent of rural ones had radios. Not until well after World War II did the first commercial, nongovernmental radio and television stations and networks develop in Japan.

Small Businesses in Manufacturing

Even with the development of zaibatsu such as Nissan, the Riken group, and Senshusha, small and medium-size firms were important to Japan's industrial growth. Despite the rationalization and concentration that occurred, small businesses remained significant industrial employers. In 1930, 58 percent of Japan's industrial workforce labored in factories with four or fewer employees, and in 1934 companies with no more than 500 workers accounted for 62 percent of Japan's industrial output.

More than in earlier times, small manufacturers acted as subcontractors for larger industrial companies. The heavy-industry companies of older zaibatsu such as Mitsui and Mitsubishi controlled scores of small subcontractors, as did many of the new zaibatsu. Toyota employed Honda Motors as a subcontractor making piston rings for its engines. Large firms used smaller enterprises as subcontractors to take advantage of their lower wages, technical strengths, and underemployed workers. They increasingly relied on networks of suppliers for raw materials, semi-finished goods, and components — a strategy very different from the one of vertical integration followed by large American manufacturers. In the mid-1930s at least 20 percent of the manufacturing value of products in Japan's automobile, textile-weaving, and electrical equipment industries came from subcontractors.

The use of subcontractors helped Japanese industrialists compete with their Western counterparts, for through the establishment of networks of suppliers large firms could avoid the tremendous capital outlays involved in doing all the manufacturing and marketing by themselves. By working through networks, large firms could also avoid, to some extent, the need to establish complex managerial systems. As they did in zaibatsu, these business networks extended beyond relationships between mother companies and subcontractors. Many types of financial and marketing networks developed, leading one commentator to note that by the close of the interwar years, it was the existence of constellations of firms that most characterized Japanese manufacturing.

Still, many small industrialists operated as independent firms not tied to any one large manufacturer. While growing in importance during the interwar years, subcontracting would become still more significant for the Japanese economy after World War II. Throughout the 1920s and 1930s independent small industrialists were important in heavy industries as well as light industries, and small firms got ahead with little government aid. Indeed, some small firms prospered despite government efforts to try to force them to join cartels and merge with their larger brethren in the interests of business rationalization and productivity. What occurred in the machine tool industry provides a look at independent small business manufacturing in interwar Japan. Zaibatsu and their affiliated subsidiaries were not important.

Many small entrepreneurial firms dominated the machine tool industry. Of the machine tool industry's 1,978 companies in 1938, only 93 had more than a hundred workers, and 1,531 had no more than thirty. These firms resisted government efforts to merge them or organize them into cartels. As occurred in the iron and steel industry, firms in the machine tool industry found ways to avoid joining cartels decreed by the Major Industries Control Law of 1931. And, a licensing scheme embedded in a Machine Tool Industry Law of 1938 did not make the industry more efficient or productive.

Resistance to government rationalization work continued even during World War II. In 1941 the Japanese government sought to consolidate strategic military industries into control councils. It was hoped that small firms could be forced to merge with larger ones and that resulting economies of scale would make the production of war goods more efficient. Such did not occur, at least not in the machine tool industry. Instead, many of the smaller producers formed regional groupings which then successfully brought pressure on the control councils to keep supplying them with raw materials needed to make military goods.

Businesses in Marketing

Marketing continued to develop along lines established before World War I. Older zaibatsu used their *sogo shosha* (trading companies) to sell their goods abroad, and also sometimes inside Japan; and independent *sogo shosha* handled foreign sales for non-zaibatsu manufacturers. With regard to marketing in Japan, differences in how the makers of traditional and nontraditional products sold their goods, already apparent before World War I, widened during the interwar years.

Most makers of traditional products, such as sake and soy sauce (including even Noda Shoyu), sold their goods through Japan's elaborate system of wholesalers and retailers. While department stores expanded and some chain stores began operations, the most typical retail outlet remained the mom-and-pop store. In 1937 the Diet, responding to pressures small retailers were feeling from encroachments of department stores and other large-scale retailers, passed a Department Store Law limiting the size of stores. Legislation of this sort persisted into the 1980s.

Most producers of traditional goods made items for local or regional markets. Only a few traditional goods producers went further before World War II. Fukusuke Tabi, a maker of footwear, was one of those few. Established in 1885, the company had within a decade started making footwear with sewing machines imported from Germany; and three years later it established the factory system of production, to which the moving assembly line was added in 1923. After encountering problems in trying to sell its footwear through established marketers, including competition between sales agents and profit-destroying discounts, Fukusuke Tabi set up its own national distribution system in the late 1920s and the 1930s. All its wholesalers and many of its retailers were integrated into the Fukusuke organization.

For companies manufacturing Western-style goods, Japan's established distribution system often proved unworkable, and an increasing number of them set up their own distribution channels. Established in 1898, Morinaga and Company manufactured marshmallows, caramels, and chocolates by Western methods, at first selling the candies through 250 wholesalers in Tokyo and Osaka. However, when those wholesalers competed by invading each others' territories, the resulting chaotic sales situation bit into Morinaga's profits. The situation worsened when Morinaga set up a factory using continuous production methods in 1925, leading to an outpouring of candies. Morinaga's solution was twofold. The firm worked with wholesalers across Japan to set up candy retail outlets as joint ventures, with the wholesalers putting up 90 percent of the capital for the stores. And, in 1928 Morinaga organized a group of existing independent retailers, who were beginning to feel the pinch of competition from department stores and chain stores, into its marketing network.

As manufacturers of many new products in the United States had already discovered, producers of nontraditional goods in Japan found that wholesalers and retailers dealing with many different items could not provide the specialized services — demonstrations, sales, and, in the case of big-ticket items such as sewing machines, financing and after-sales repairs — needed to introduce new products to the emerging national market. Increasingly, therefore, they organized their own sales networks. Still, Japanese manufacturers rarely exercised as high a degree of control over sales as Morinaga. Most simply reorganized existing wholesalers into sales companies, with the wholesalers putting up most of the capital, for manufacturers were hard-pressed simply to build their factories. Usually, the sales companies remained legally and financially independent of the manufacturers. Few manufacturers set up their own retail outlets; Morinaga was exceptional in this respect.

Business, Government, Society, and Labor in Japan

Despite their growing association with the Japanese government's military efforts, business leaders dropped in public esteem in the interwar years. The heads of the zaibatsu, in particular, came under intense criticism for supposedly following their own interests to the detriment of those of the Japanese nation. The zaibatsu and big businesses in general were accused of corrupting politics. It was a common saying, if an exaggeration, that whenever Mitsui or Mitsubishi caught a cold the Diet came down with pneumonia. Antagonism came to a climax with the assassination of the head of Mitsui by a group of young army officers in 1932. This anti-zaibatsu sentiment had some influence on business. The zaibatsu made voluntary donations, actually forced gifts, of funds to the Japanese government; and, at the request of the government, some accelerated their movement into heavy industry.

Under pressure, large firms also extended labor practices incorporating long-term employment and seniority-based promotions and wages to a growing number of managers and employees. Managers and workers were increasingly recruited right out of school and then given additional training in their companies, as firms sought to heighten bonds of company loyalty. Companies provided more benefits for their workers — dining rooms, assembly halls, club houses, and housing — much as those British and American companies embracing welfare capitalism were doing.

The pressures on the companies came from several sources. There was a continuing scarcity of skilled workers in some fields, especially in heavy industry, and a corresponding desire by employers to keep workers loyal to their firms. In addition, the power of organized labor increased into the mid-1920s. By 1925 the Sodomei, the Japan General Federation of Labor, had 250,000 members. For awhile there were prospects for the passage by the Diet of a law recognizing the rights of workers to form independent unions to bargain collectively with management. Even some employer associations supported the establishment of such unions around the time of World War I as a way of stabilizing their nation's chaotic labor situation. However, this possibility faded in the late 1920s and disappeared in the early 1930s. A revival of traditional values in Japan, combined with the increasing power of the army and accompanying crackdowns on leftist leaders, eroded the strength of Japan's labor movement.

Large companies resisted bargaining collectively with their workers. During the interwar years more Japanese executives instead turned to scientific management to rationalize labor practices, with somewhat more success than before World War I. Most common were the adoption of time/

motion studies and the rearrangement of production facilities, both of which took shop-floor power away from skilled workers and placed it in the hands of managers. These efforts were part of the business rationalization movement.

In addition, influenced by the formation of work councils in Great Britain and company unions in the United States, Japanese business leaders set up work councils to mediate differences between management and labor. By 1929, 112 work councils composed of managers and workers existed. The work councils were forerunners of enterprise unions, which became common in Japan after World War II. These were unions organized around companies, not industries. The enterprise unions tended to reinforce company loyalty and did not really bargain collectively with management on the part of workers. They resembled in many ways the company unions common in the United States in the 1920s.

The extension of the new system of labor relations was achieved only painfully, as can be seen in the case of Noda Shoyu. At Noda Shoyu a short strike in 1923 was followed by a much longer and more serious one in 1927–28. The major issue was who would control the pace and nature of work, as production processes were modernized and standardized: workers or managers? The 1927–28 strike lasted seven months and resulted in the firing of 1,100 workers. It was the most celebrated (or notorious) of all of the many strikes in Japan in the interwar years. Management won; but to improve its public image, to keep skilled workers loyal to the company, and to avoid labor unrest in the future, Noda Shoyu began putting in place seniority-based wages and promotion, a wide range of benefits, and works councils.

Toward a Dual Economy

Neither long-term employment nor seniority-based promotions and wages were usually extended to workers in small firms. The lives of workers in small firms were often tenuous and unstable. In the interwar years relationships between large and small manufacturers were one-sided. During recessions it was the small subcontractors, not the larger manufacturers, that laid off workers. Most small companies paid wages lower than those offered by their larger counterparts, and that gap widened through the interwar years. By 1932–33 workers in firms with 5–9 employees earned wages equal to only 61 percent of the wages of employees in companies with at least 100 workers, workers in companies with 10–29 employees earned 74 percent, those in firms with 30–49 employees 81 percent, and workers in companies with 50–99 employees 89 percent.

The spread of wage differentials signaled a larger trend, the development of what has often been called a "dual economy" in Japan. While small firms remained important in some fields as independent manufacturers, as in the machine tool industry, the overall significance of small independent industrialists lessened in the interwar years. Japan's industrial economy tended to divide. Large efficient firms geared to the export market and to Japan's military needs came to dominate smaller subcontractors serving them and Japan's home market. This trend began in the early 1900s and accelerated during the interwar years. It remained a characteristic of the Japanese economy into the years after World War II, but without the military aspect.

Japanese Business during World War II

The Japanese government used public dissatisfaction with big business and the needs of war to increase its powers over the economy. A government planning office was set up in 1937 to begin coordinating the work of the different parts of Japan's wartime economy. The Diet passed a General Mobilization Law in 1938, giving the government broad powers to control wages, prices, and the allocation of raw materials in the economy. In addition, many detailed laws determined what businesses could and could not do in specific industries. These laws did not always work as well as was intended. Just as firms in some industries evaded the Major Industries Control Law of 1931, they also thwarted government efforts to control them during World War II.

Nonetheless, the laws were important, not only for what they did accomplish during the war years, but for the precedents they set. To some extent, the laws served as models for legislation passed by the Diet after World War II. That legislation sought to provide government guidance of the Japanese economy in the 1950s and 1960s (although, as we shall see, much of the postwar legislation met with the same sort of mixed response from businesses as did the legislation of the interwar years).

Urban Planning in Interwar Japan

Urban planning was a key way by which Japanese sought to control their socioeconomic environment during the interwar years, just as it was for people in Western nations. Much more than in the United States and Great Britain, changes occurred in a top-down manner. In the interwar years, prefectural governors, mayors of cities, and other city officials were generally appointed, not elected by local residents. The Home Ministry of the national government tightly controlled regional and local governmental developments, with prefectural governors usually appointed from that ministry's roster of bureaucrats. Decisions made in Tokyo and prefectural offices were most important in shaping Japan's expanding urban areas. Those decisions emphasized the need to reduce the risk of fire, build broad, straight, paved streets, and improve water supplies, as Japan sought in urban affairs, as in other matters, to catch up with the West.

The importance of Japan's central government in urban planning was most apparent in the Diet's passage of City Planning and Urban Building Laws for the entire nation in 1919. Administered by the Home Ministry, the laws admitted little room for local variance. Growing out of earlier efforts to remake Tokyo, and influenced by Western ideas, these laws were a first attempt at a comprehensive planning system that applied to whole urban areas and all major cities. With only minor changes, the measures remained in effect into the late 1960s.

The 1919 laws had five major provisions. First, they divided urban lands into four zones: residential, commercial, industrial, and unrestricted. This effort came about a decade after major American cities led by New York and Los Angeles had embraced zoning. The system in Japan differed from zoning in the United States in two major ways. In Japan, zoning was imposed from above — in the United States each city worked out its own zoning scheme — and was much less exclusive than American zoning schemes. That is, there was more intermixture of land uses in Japan than in the United States, with, for example, workers' housing continuing to be built right next to factories. Second, the legislation set building codes for construction in the different zones — such as allowable building materials, building heights, and building lot coverage. Third, the laws established building lines by designating the edges of roads as building lines and stipulating that construction could occur only on lots fronting those lines. Fourth, the measures provided for the designation and construction of public facilities ranging from parks to sewer systems. Finally, the laws, expanding on earlier practices and stiffened by additional legislation passed in 1923, included land readjustment schemes, especially for the development of land on the outskirts of cities. The government could require landowners to donate up to 10 percent of their holdings for public purposes, such as the construction of roads, without compensation, the assumption being that they would benefit from the improvements.

The measures accomplished less than had been hoped in remaking cities. Destruction of much of Tokyo by an earthquake and fire in 1923 required that Japan's national government focus planning efforts and funding on the capital for the rest of the decade, leaving little in the way of national planning expertise and money for other cities. Moreover, the opposition of local landowners to land readjustment schemes stymied some planning efforts. Finally, despite the growth in population and size of their cities, many Japanese simply did not think that their areas yet needed much in the way of planning and found ways to delay its onset. Zoning was adopted slowly, with just twenty-seven of the largest ninety-seven urban areas having established zoning plans by 1930. The Great Depression of the 1930s and World War II (and recovery from that conflict during the 1940s and 1950s) precluded much in the way of experimentation with urban planning for decades.

Only in the late 1960s, with their nation benefiting from high-speed economic growth, did most Japanese return to urban planning. The Diet passed laws in 1968 and 1970 that sought to alter urban planning in Japan fundamentally, the first major changes since 1919. Responding to grassroots citizens' protests and legal suits about air and water pollution, resulting diseases and deaths, and continuing rampant urban sprawl, the laws aimed to give much more power to local municipalities to control growth, including powers to force developers to pay for infrastructural improvements. The laws also expanded the nation's zoning system to eight land-use zones. As in the West, the planning laws aimed to take a regional approach to urban problems. This basic change in Japan's urban planning legislation set the tone for planning into the twenty-first century.

Chinese Businesses

Two elements dominated China's politics and political economy during the interwar years: efforts to unite the country internally and attempts by Japan to establish hegemony over the nation. Both elements affected business growth. Some modern firms continued to develop along lines laid down over previous decades, but many others were deeply affected by political developments, even uprooting factories to move inland to escape Japanese domination.

Government and Business

Two political parties sought to unify China in the wake of World War I. One was Sun Yat-sen's Nationalist Party (the Guomindang or GMD), which had been started in a limited way before the conflict. Chiang Kai-shek emerged as the foremost leader of the GMD after Sun's death in 1925. Trained in Japan by the Japanese military, Chiang organized the GMD along strict centralized lines. With the aid of Soviet advisers, Sun had set up the Whampoa

Military Academy in southern China, and Chiang became its first commandant. Chiang would henceforth always be a military commander at heart, with economic matters taking a backseat to military affairs. The second was the new Chinese Communist Party (CCP). Helped by Soviet advisers, several Chinese established study groups and then in 1921 founded the CCP. From the first, Mao Zedong was involved in the party, but he did not emerge as its predominant leader until the late 1930s and 1940s.

Japanese aggression against China developed piecemeal. In the North, the Japanese took over German concessions in Shandong during and after World War I. Japanese had also been active in Manchuria from at least the early twentieth century, as a result of their nation's victory over Russia in 1905. They overran the region in 1931–32, setting up a puppet state called Manchukuo, with many of its rich natural resources flowing to Japan. Japanese aggression farther south began with the bombing of Shanghai in 1932. From 1937 Japan was at war with all of China, with Shanghai falling to Japanese troops that year.

In the mid-1920s the GMD and the CCP cooperated in an effort to unify China and to oppose Japanese aggression. In 1926 a combined GMD-CCP force moved north from Canton in what was known as the "Northern Expedition" to defeat warlords and unify China, successfully reaching the Yangzi River and Shanghai in 1927. Northern China, including Beijing, was brought under control by late 1928, allowing Chiang to claim that he had unified China under one government. However, destroying the CCP was always more important to Chiang than defeating Japan; and in 1927, aided by the criminal Green Gang in Shanghai, he turned on the Communists in that city and elsewhere, killing thousands. Survivors fled the city and other areas under attack by Nationalist forces, generally moving south and west. For about seven years, different groups of Communists sought to control various sanctuaries, sponsoring land reform and redistribution, only to come under attack from Nationalist armies. Finally, in 1934–35 most Communists joined in the "Long March" to Shaanxi in northwestern China. Here they were relatively safe from both Nationalist Chinese and Japanese attacks, but in retreating the CCP gave up most of China to the GMD. Meanwhile, Chiang established his headquarters at Nanking for the decade of 1927–37. Losing large numbers of soldiers in the fall of Shanghai to the Japanese in 1937, Nationalist forces withdrew farther inland to Wuhan and then to Chongqing, which remained headquarters for the GMD for the duration of World War II.

Chiang's government, which claimed to control most of those parts of

China not occupied by the Japanese, helped business development in some ways. The Nationalists regained formal control over tariff duties from foreign governments (although some nations, especially Japan, persuaded the Chinese government to keep tariffs low on many of their products), at least until the Japanese takeover of China's seacoast in the late 1930s. Moreover, the Nationalists eliminated most internal tariff barriers. The Nationalists also reformed their nation's tax system and sought to stabilize their nation's currency. Some infrastructure improvements took place, as the government built highways to connect major cities, although much less was done to improve railroads. The weakening of the CCP and labor unions, especially in Shanghai, pleased capitalists. In addition, the Nationalist government backed consumer boycotts of Japanese goods and efforts to promote consumer purchases of Chinese-made products more enthusiastically than in earlier years, with the efforts amounting to a "National Products Movement." While the economic effectiveness of that movement is difficult to assess definitively, it did contribute to the formation of a sense of Chinese national identity. As in Japan, consumerism had marked nationalistic overtones in China.

Yet there was a negative side to the ledger. The Nationalist government did little to help farmers. As Chiang moved increasingly to the political right in the late 1920s and the 1930s, he lost sight of land reform, one of Sun's original goals. In fact, the military always came first, with up to 80 percent of Chiang's budget used to support an army of 5 million people. Over time, many business leaders, especially those heading modern banks and industrial companies, came to resent forced loans and new taxes levied on their firms, especially since the levies came at unpredictable intervals that made it hard for business leaders to plan for the future. Some historians have argued that, in fact, Chiang and the GMD were basically anticapitalist and used their powers to extort funds from business leaders, especially those in Shanghai, to support the GMD's military campaigns. Then, too, the national unity that had proven to be so elusive in the 1910s remained difficult to achieve. Especially in the North, Chiang had made arrangements to coopt warlords into his government rather than fight them in the field; and some warlords consequently remained in effective control of their regions. It was also in the North (and West and Center) that the Communists began building or rebuilding bases of popular support. What these circumstances meant for business people was that China's unity — including laws and taxes — was more apparent than real, making it difficult for them to operate on a truly national level.

Into the early 1930s much of China's modern business was located in Shanghai. Some 53 percent of the nation's foreign trade and 26 percent of all of its domestic and foreign shipping passed through the city. About 1,200 of China's 2,400 modern, Western-style factories were there, including 61 of the country's 127 modern cotton textile mills. Cotton textile mills employed 57 percent of the nation's industrial workers. Many labored in foreign-owned, especially Japanese, mills. Foreign-owned mills accounted for 44 percent of the yarn spindles, 67 percent of the thread spindles, and 51 percent of the looms in China. In addition, Shanghai's modern banks accounted for 64 percent of the capital invested in such banks in China. The twenty-six modern banks belonging to the Shanghai Bankers Association controlled over three-quarters of the resources held by modern banks in China. Most of these businesses prospered into the early years of the Great Depression but suffered from the mid-1930s onward, and were hurt additionally by Japan's takeover of Shanghai in 1937.

The war with Japan brought drastic changes to Chinese business, as Nationalist controls over businesses increased even more. Many of the businesses in Shanghai moved inland to try to escape from the invading Japanese. As in all the nations we are examining, the national government became increasingly involved in business during wartime. Already in 1935 the Nationalist government owned outright about 11 percent of the industry that registered with its Ministry of Industry, especially in such fields as munitions and heavy industry (and especially in iron and steel). Government involvement broadened during the late 1930s and 1940s. However, Nationalist efforts never amounted to a fully articulated or implemented program of economic development. Governmental industrial policies probably accomplished less in China than in Japan, and even in Japan the effectiveness of governmental policies, as in rationalization efforts, has generally been overrated by most historians.

Nor did Nationalist politicians ever fully control businesses. For example, throughout the 1930s and 1940s Chinese entrepreneurs selling both modern Western medicines and traditional Chinese remedies found numerous ways to circumvent governmental restrictions on their efforts and managed, despite all the disruptions of those decades, to expand throughout China and into Southeast Asia. They typically did so through their very astute use of print media to advertise their goods, helping create in China the beginnings of a consumer culture, at least for nondurable goods. As they expanded, the medicine companies showed that business penetration into China by Western firms such as British American Tobacco and Standard Oil was not a one-way street. Chinese businesses also expanded abroad well before World War II. Nor were the medicine companies alone. The China Egg Produce Company, for instance, developed extensive markets for its refrigerated products throughout Europe and the United States between 1923 and 1950.

Business Forms

As in earlier decades, businesses, especially modern ones, took many forms in interwar China. Networks, especially *guanxi* ties based on a person's native place, remained very important for both traditional and modern Chinese businesses. However, as the nation's economy modernized, other types of networks grew in prominence.

In the mid-1930s, for example, China possessed a modern banking sector composed of a relatively small number of very large banks — such as the Central Bank, the Bank of China, the Bank of Communications, and the Farmers Bank of China — that were associated with the government and that had nationwide banking networks, and a much larger number of smaller banks. Altogether there existed 164 modern banks in China in 1936, about half of which were headquartered in Shanghai. Networks of interlocking directorates linked these banks. Some 80 percent had interlocking directorates, meaning that they shared at least one director with another bank. These interconnected banks fell into four groups. Three small groups of banks corresponded to geographic areas in China, but the majority of the banks belonged to one primary, nationwide network stretching across all of China. This network was based more on the shared professional interests of the modern-style bankers than on *guanxi* ties. Many of the directors had studied in Japan and considered themselves to be professional bankers.

Such modern networks were hardly unique to Chinese businesses. They were, for example, common in the United States. Major commercial and investment banks often shared numerous directors, and they also shared directors with many large industrial businesses. Indeed, the linkages were so common in the early and mid-twentieth century that reformers urged the passage of legislation breaking up the ties in the interests of industrial democracy.

Few other Chinese businesses went as far as the modern banks in belonging to national networks. Some firms developed almost independently of the types of networks to which banks belonged. Such was especially the case for those companies belonging to China's nascent state enterprise system, which developed especially between 1937 and 1945, when Japan's invasion forced Nationalist leaders to rethink the nature of their nation's economic system. Although China's government may not have been as successful as some other nations in mobilizing industry for war, it did control state-owned enterprises, especially in weapons making in arsenals and, more generally, in heavy industry. These enterprises were important, not just in the 1930s and 1940s, but also to some extent as models for state-owned enterprises after Communists won control of China in 1949. There were indigenous sources for Mao Zedong's Communist economic enterprises; ideas about industrial enterprises did not have to be imported solely from the Soviet Union.

Japan's attacks led Nationalist leaders to move arsenals from their seaside locations to inland ones such as the city of Chongqing. Twelve of China's arsenals were relocated to Chongqing by 1941. Nationalist leaders assumed the management of the arsenals, many of which had earlier been in private or provincial government hands. Supported by the Nationalist government, the arsenals succeeded in boosting their output of munitions. The same story took place in some of China's heavy industries. Between 1936 and 1945 the Nationalist government took over or established 130 enterprises in heavy industries, including metallurgy, electrical equipment, chemicals, mining, and energy. The government wholly owned and managed seventy-five of them, partially owned or managed another thirty-seven, and invested in eighteen. As in the case of the arsenals, these enterprises moved inland to avoid Japanese attack and occupation. The largest was the Dadukou Iron and Steel Works (DISW), which in 1943 had seven manufacturing plants employing 22,000 workers. The DISW engaged in vertical integration, having its own iron and coal mines near Chongqing. As a result, the public sector, which had lagged behind the private sector in the ownership of heavy-industry enterprises in 1933, came to overshadow the private sector in heavy-industry ownership just nine years later.

Even so, a note of caution is needed. In all those parts of China still controlled by the Nationalists in 1942, only 69,000 workers labored in heavy industry. Even the DISW turned out only 12,000 tons of iron and just 2,200 tons of steel in that year. These products were essential to the Nationalists and amounted to more than the CCP could make in its enclaves, but they were far from representing a full modernization of the Chinese economy. The accomplishments of the Nationalists, while very real, must not be overemphasized.

State enterprises shared several characteristics. They had formal administrative bureaucracies, possessing a governance system characterized by administrative units composed of divisions and departments ranked according to their size and importance within the administrative hierarchy. These were functional units, such as divisions of work affairs, technology, accounting, and welfare. Technocrats replaced traditional bureaucrats in managing the enterprises. During World War II, they introduced new accounting methods based on real cost calculations. The DISW, for example, did so in 1942, basically replicating what Carnegie Steel had accomplished in the United States about sixty years earlier. State enterprises provided a broad range of services for their workers, continuing a trend from the 1890s, much as some large Western and Japanese firms did. They typically provided housing, education, child care, savings plans, recreational facilities, and consumer organizations (especially consumer buying cooperatives through which members could purchase daily necessities at reduced prices). The enterprises were, thus, both production and consumption units for many Chinese. Nor was this situation limited to state-owned enterprises. By 1946, 1,354 Chinese enterprises, including many privately owned and operated ones, provided 10,890 social service and welfare institutions for their employees. Whether state-owned or private, these work units were called *danwei*.

Conclusions

During the interwar years, wide swings in national economies combined with market changes to alter business firms and their management globally. As big businesses became more diversified in terms of their products and markets — particularly in the United States, but to some degree in other nations as well — some adopted new management systems. In Japan, special circumstances spurred the growth of zaibatsu, and here too, changes occurred, as new zaibatsu based upon heavy industry grew in importance. Large and small firms came increasingly to occupy different spheres in manufacturing, with smaller companies either acting as subcontractors for larger ones or producing as independents for niche, not mass, markets. Still, the business systems of nations remained complex, with smaller firms continuing to play significant roles in sales.

More than individual companies changed during the interwar years; so did the business systems of each nation. As they sought to mitigate the impacts of recessions and depressions and as they prepared for World War II, governments became more involved in the workings of their economies and in the operations of specific industries. Government-sponsored rationalization movements sought, although with only limited success, to make individual firms, industries, and entire economies more efficient and productive. Spending during depressions and even more spending during World War II led governments to become deeply involved in economic matters. That involvement continued after the conflict.

In the interwar actions of the national governments there was a marked movement toward autarchy, especially during the depression decade of the 1930s. As nations left the gold standard and as they threw up trade barriers against each other's goods, they practiced "beggar thy neighbor" policies. Especially from 1931 onward, international cooperation waned, replaced by economic and military competition. It is sometimes argued that globalization — the free flow of goods, capital, and people across national boundaries — is inevitable in modern economies. However, as events in the 1920s and 1930s clearly showed, it is not. After moving toward economic integration in the long nineteenth century up to 1914, the global economy moved away from it during the interwar years and World War II. Globalization is as much a political construction as an economic one. It was revived after World War II.

Suggested Readings

Nakamura Takafusa, *Economic Growth in Prewar Japan* (New Haven, 1983), provides an overview of economic changes before World War II. Mark Fruin, *Kikkoman: Company, Clan and Community* (Cambridge, Mass., 1983), Michael Cusumano, *The Japanese Automobile Industry: Technology & Management at Nissan & Toyota* (Cambridge, Mass., 1985), and Barbara Molony, *Technology and Investment: The Prewar Japanese Chemical Industry* (Cambridge, Mass, 1990), examine big businesses. David Friedman, *The Misunderstood Miracle: Industrial Development and Political Change in Japan* (Ithaca, 1988), looks at small firms in Japan's machine tool industry. Simon Partner, *Assembled in Japan: Electric Goods and the Making of the Japanese Consumer* (Berkeley, 1999), surveys the beginnings of consumerism. Kawabe Nobuo, "The Development of Distribution Systems in Japan before World War II," in *Business and Economic History* (Williamsburg, 1989), ed. William Hausman, is an excellent survey. Andre Sorensen, *The Making of Urban Japan: Cities and Planning from Edo to the Twenty-First Century* (London, 2002), and Carola Hein, Jeffrey Diefendorf, and Ishida Yorifusa, eds., *Rebuilding Urban Japan after 1945* (London, 2003), examine the history of urban planning in Japan. Parkes M. Coble Jr., *The Shanghai Capitalists and the Nationalist Govern-*

ment, 1927–1937 (Cambridge, Mass., 1986), Karl Gerth, *China Made: Consumer Culture and the Creation of the Nation* (Cambridge, Mass., 2003), Sherman Cochran, *Chinese Medicine Men: Consumer Culture in China and South East Asia* (Cambridge, Mass., 2006), and Morris L. Bian, *The Making of the State Enterprise System in Modern China* (Cambridge, Mass., 2005), examine Chinese business development from various angles.

National Businesses in an Expanding International Economy

Even as the final phase of World War II began, allied leaders met at Bretton Woods, a resort in the White Mountains of New Hampshire, to plan what they hoped would be a financial system that would facilitate the development of a prosperous international economy after the war. In the summer of 1944 the Bretton Woods Agreement was completed by representatives of the forty-four nations present. Shortly thereafter, United Nations governments, without the participation of the Communist bloc, sought to reduce trade barriers among themselves, an effort culminating in 1947 with the General Agreement on Tariffs and Trade (GATT), which Japan joined in 1955. The goals of the Bretton Woods Agreement and the GATT were similar: to stimulate the growth of the national economies around the globe and through this stimulation to remove what was believed to be one of the major causes of war, economic recession.

The goal was a more prosperous international economy of nations trading freely with each other, for Western policy makers believed that only in a situation of world prosperity could democracies endure and world peace prevail. Turning away from the movement toward autarchy that had characterized the 1930s and early 1940s, they embraced internationalism, returning to the global political and economic situation that had prevailed before World War I. Their goals, then, were certainly not brand new in the 1940s, but policy makers did more to make them a reality in the 1950s and 1960s than in previous decades. With the Bretton Woods Agreement came the creation of two institutions, the International Monetary Fund and the International Bank for Reconstruction and Development (the World Bank). These organizations labored to stabilize currency exchange rates among nations and sought to promote economic development in war-ravaged and underdeveloped nations. The nations adhering to the GATT took part in a series of negotiations called "rounds" that lowered tariff barriers on a wide variety of products around the world in an effort to expand trade. An agreement in

1967 resulting from the Kennedy Round lowered tariff duties an average of 35 percent on 60,000 items, for example.

The Bretton Woods Agreement and the GATT helped to link national economies as never before. World trade rose at an average annual rate of about 4 percent in the century before 1945, but at a much higher 7 percent over the next twenty-five years. The value of world trade increased fivefold between 1950 and 1970! Foreign trade became more and more important for the economies of nations around the world. In 1950 the United States sold 9 percent of its production abroad, but by 1970 about 13 percent. For Great Britain the comparable figures were 43 percent and 48 percent, for Japan 18 percent and 30 percent. There was a major exception to this turn of events, however: Communist nations, including China, did not participate in these international agreements that had their origins in the early years of the Cold War. As such, Communist nations traded among themselves but were not involved in extensive trade with the United States and its allies. Nonetheless, international economic growth reshaped many Western business firms and policies in the 1950s and 1960s, and it is to these changes that most of this chapter is devoted.

American Business

New market opportunities led large American industrialists to diversify in terms of their products and markets, and, as the companies diversified, they adopted decentralized management systems, extending a trend from the 1920s. The federal government was important in continuing business growth at home and abroad, as it both promoted and regulated businesses. As in earlier times, the development of large firms did not mean the extinction of smaller ones. Small industrialists persisted when they could develop specialty products for niche markets. However, when compared to what had occurred in earlier times, small businesses in manufacturing and sales declined rapidly relative to larger companies.

Sources of Business Growth

Government actions continued greatly to influence American business developments in the postwar years. The federal government actively promoted business development. For example, most of the financing for airports and interstate highways came from the federal government. At the same time, the federal government continued to regulate businesses through a host of independent regulatory commissions, such as the Securities and Exchange Commission, set up in 1934. Government-business cooperation, with business executives joined together in groups such as the Business Round Table, also continued, in a manner similar to associationalism under Herbert Hoover in the 1920s. Business leaders played a major role in the writing of the Employment and Production Act of 1946, by which the federal government assumed responsibility for trying to manage the overall level of economic prosperity in the United States for the first time.

American governmental actions at the international level also greatly affected business in the postwar period. The Bretton Woods Agreement and the GATT, both strongly promoted by the U.S. government, sought to create a prosperous international economy open to American trade. America's Marshall Plan of 1948 had similar goals. The Marshall Plan used a blend of public aid from the federal government and private technical assistance from American businesses to promote the economic recovery of Europe. The objective, largely successful, was to ensure the creation of prosperous democracies in Western Europe. Through various programs, including massive purchases of supplies for the Korean War of the early 1950s, the federal government also helped revive the Japanese economy, which lay prostrate after World War II. These governmental actions all contributed to the economic revival of much of the world in the postwar years and this revival in turn opened new markets to American business.

Economic growth also came from the continuing development of a consumer society in America, with its insatiable demand for consumer goods — television sets, automobiles, and household appliances — and, increasingly, for services. The United States developed what may rightly be called a "consumer-amenity" society after World War II. People wanted more and better consumer goods than they had in the 1920s — color television sets, not radios or black-and-white televisions, for example. Americans continued to develop identities as consumers rather than simply as producers of goods. They came, among other matters, to view nature as a commodity to be consumed in their leisure time and pushed for environmental legislation for clean air and water as part of their plans for a consumer-amenity society.

As a result of both favorable governmental policies and consumer buying, the economy of the United States experienced rapid growth during the first twenty-five years after World War II. Between 1945 and 1960 America's GNP increased by 52 percent, and the nation's per capita GNP rose by 19 percent. Then, in the 1960s the GNP of the United States climbed 46 percent, and the per capita GNP grew by 29 percent. For a decade or two, the United States bestrode the globe. In 1951 Americans owned 80 percent of the world's electrical goods and consumed more than 40 percent of its electricity. They made 66 percent of the world's steel. They built 99 percent of all of the automobiles sold in the United States. The average American ate 50 percent more than his or her counterpart in Europe. Americans composed 5 percent of the world's population, but possessed more wealth than the other 95 percent.

Labor in the Immediate Postwar Decades

The immediate postwar decades saw changes in America's labor situation, as large businesses sought to roll back gains made by workers in the New Deal. The National Association of Manufacturers, joined by the Business Council, the Chamber of Commerce, and other business associations, led an effort to revise the National Labor Relations Act of 1935. The business groups sought to reshape the law to restrict union activities and to retard future union growth.

When Congress passed the Taft-Hartley Act in 1947, it responded to the desires of business leaders. This law required union leaders to swear that they were not members of the Communist Party, to account for their organization's finances, and to refrain from making political contributions. The law prohibited the closed shop but allowed the open shop, thereby preserving management's right to hire whomever it chose. Unions had to provide a sixty-day notice before launching a strike; and the federal government, when it deemed that disputes hurt the public interest, could order striking workers to return to their jobs for eighty days while bargaining continued. To slow the growth of unions, the new law allowed states to require the open shop by enacting so-called "right-to-work" laws. That is, workers could not be forced to join unions.

The passage of the Taft-Hartley Act had important consequences. Union membership began a period of long-term decline, falling from a peak of almost 36 percent of the nonagricultural workforce in 1945 to slightly more than 25 percent in 1980. In manufacturing fields that had arisen with the Industrial Revolution there was still occasional labor-management conflict, but the common pattern of management behavior in dealing with labor was one of aggressive realism. In effect, a new social contract was struck. As long as the economy was experiencing long-term growth, management was generally willing to grant higher wages (which could be accommodated by automation, productivity growth, and higher prices for consumers). In return, unions gave up any aspirations to affect how executives ran their companies and worked to discipline local leaders and rank-and-file members who supported disruptions of production processes. The relinquishment of authority by unions was not usually voluntary. Most often management dictated the terms of the bargains, continuing an effort to dominate labor-management relations dating back to at least the 1920s and 1930s.

Business Diversification: Multinationals and Conglomerates

The expansion of the international economy combined with the continued development of America's domestic market to open new opportunities for business. Accordingly, a growing proportion of businesses chose diversification as its growth strategy. An increasing number entered foreign markets, and many set up overseas manufacturing operations to become multinational corporations. Those emphasizing the domestic scene also diversified, often by both product and market. As they diversified, American companies adopted decentralized, multidivisional management systems similar to the one pioneered by General Motors in the 1920s. By 1970, 86 percent of the 500 largest industrial companies in the United States were diversified to the extent that they possessed at least three major divisions, and most of these firms had adopted some form of decentralized management.

Multinational corporations (MNCs), usually defined as companies with production facilities in more than one country, were a major response of American business leaders to expanding business opportunities around the world. MNCs had long existed, but they increased in numbers and in the scope of their activities in the immediate postwar period. By 1970 over 3,500 American companies possessed direct foreign investments in some 15,000 overseas enterprises, and in that year the direct foreign investments of American companies amounted to about $78 billion, a sum equal to roughly 8 percent of their nation's GNP.

International Telephone & Telegraph (ITT) was one of the most far-flung of American MNCs. The company's president, Harold Geneen, and forty members of his New York headquarters staff jetted to Europe to go over reports with the company officers there each month. Some joked that the initials ITT stood for International Travel and Talk. Geneen believed that only through detailed face-to-face meetings could he achieve one of his prime goals in running his company: "no surprises." With 200,000 employees in Europe by 1970, ITT Europe had become the seventeenth-largest company on the continent. Not surprisingly, Europeans complained of the American "invasion" of Europe. ITT had by the late 1960s also become a conglomerate, for by the close of that decade it was an extremely diversified company with interests in car rentals, house building, hotels, and glassmaking, in addition to its businesses in communications.

Conglomerates were an extreme form of business diversification that appeared in the United States in the postwar years. Conglomerates were companies with many different divisions, at least eight, producing and selling unrelated goods and services. Thus, conglomerate businesses resembled the geologic formations from which they took their name. (A conglomerate rock is composed of fragments varying in size from small pebbles to large boulders in a cement mixture such as hardened clay.) Conglomerates became a major part of the American business scene in the 1960s. In 1966, 60 percent of all mergers in America were conglomerate-type mergers, and by the close of that year forty-six of the nation's largest 500 industrial companies were conglomerates.

The officers of conglomerates claimed that a new type of business executive was developing in the United States. This new breed consisted of young, ambitious managers with generalized management talents and skills, people versatile and adaptable enough to solve any problem in business. Trained especially in financial management, these new business leaders could, it was said, run a company well without knowing much about its products or production methods. However, in reality conglomerates often experienced problems due to faulty management. In 1960 through 1962, for example, General Dynamics lost $425 million, because the corporate office located in New York failed adequately to supervise sloppy work being done by its Convair Division across the continent in Los Angeles. Problems of this type multiplied in the 1970s and 1980s.

The relative decline of small businesses in manufacturing continued in the 1950s and 1960s. Some small firms still succeeded as producers of specialty goods for niche markets, much like the Philadelphia textile makers of the nineteenth century and the New England metal fabricators and machinery makers of the early twentieth century. However, the relatively stable economic situation of the day, combined with the filling of American needs and desires for mass-produced consumer goods, was conducive to the development of large firms using big factories to make a range of fairly standardized goods in long production runs. As a result, small manufacturers declined in importance relative to large ones into the early 1970s.

Sales and Services

Hit hard by the entrance of large chain stores and grocery stores into their fields, small retailers mounted spirited but only partially successful responses. Mom-and-pop grocery stores continued to attract patronage by offering services, such as home delivery, which were no longer provided by the chains and supermarkets. Some specialized in the types of goods they carried. In field after field, many small retailers also banded together in associations to secure some of the benefits, especially the discounts won through high-volume purchases, obtained by large-scale enterprises. In the grocery industry, for example, independent retailers formed voluntary groups, such as the Independent Grocers' Association (IGA), and retailer-owned cooperative warehouses. By the 1940s over one-third of all grocery wholesale sales passed through these institutions.

Changes taking place in hardware sales demonstrate well the alterations occurring in retailing. In the postwar years some hardware retailers joined retailer-owned cooperatives. John Cotter put together one such cooperative as True Value hardware stores. Brought up in the hardware business, Cotter founded True Value in 1948, by which time independent hardware retailers were facing severe competition from chain stores and discount outlets. In this system hundreds of independent retailers came to own Cotter & Company, which in turn acted as their wholesaler. Profits earned at the middleman's sales level were rebated every year to the retailers, which remained independently owned. By the mid-1980s True Value had 7,000 member stores and fourteen major distribution centers, making it the largest hardware distributor in the United States.

The effectiveness of the economic responses of small retailers varied considerably. Most small independent retailers failed to adjust to the new way of selling groceries. In this field, in which low prices were of utmost significance, the chains and supermarkets ruled supreme. By 1971 five large supermarket chains dominated food retailing in the United States by emphasizing rapid turnover of stock, high sales per employee, and large store size. In hardware, a field in which individual customer service remained more important, independents working through groups like True Value did better, at least for a time. The number of retail hardware outlets in the United States declined from 35,000 in 1954 to 26,000 in 1972 but stabilized and even rose a bit in the mid- and late 1970s.

A new phenomenon in the postwar years was the development of discount stores as a challenge to established retailers, large and small. The number of discount outlets in the United States soared from 1,329 in 1960 to 3,503 just six years later. By the mid-1960s discounting was well established in the East and Midwest and was beginning in other parts of the nation. Discount stores were particularly important in sales of toys and infants' clothing, sporting goods, automobile accessories, and housewares. E. J. Korvette was the largest discounter with sales of $594 million and 40 stores, followed by

S. S. Kresge (K-Mart, Jupiter) with 233 stores selling $490 million worth of goods. The top ten retailers each had sales of at least $173 million in 1965. Wal-Mart, just getting under way in the 1960s, took discounting to new heights in later decades, becoming the world's largest retailer, and one of the world's largest businesses, in the 1990s.

The service sector remained home of small businesses more than retailing. Possessing fewer economies of scale than stores selling goods, services were less conducive to the spread of large firms. Most real estate companies were small and closely tied to their local communities. Only with the development of new communications and computer technologies in the 1970s and 1980s did local and regional companies like Century 21 and Coldwell Banker grow to become national giants. Small local businesses also dominated the field of law. As in real estate, it required the development of new media and communications techniques for some law firms to grow large, as did Hyatt Legal Services in the 1980s. However, the power of small companies was eroded in some service industries. National insurance and banking companies expanded their reach. Although small firms continued to thrive in both these fields, their status was less secure than in earlier times.

America's Corporate Business System

The spread of conglomerates and MNCs, together with development of more traditional big businesses, continued a trend begun in the mid-nineteenth century: a relatively few big businesses dominated key segments of the American business system, especially in manufacturing. The distinction between center and peripheral firms widened; by 1962 the fifty largest companies possessed over one-third of America's manufacturing assets, and the top 500 over two-thirds.

As in the past, the business leaders who managed America's big businesses remained something of an elite. A detailed study of the backgrounds of the leaders of the nation's largest 500 companies in 1976 revealed that all except one were men, that all were white, that 85 percent were from middle-class families, and that 71 percent were Protestant. Most were also well educated: 86 percent had graduated from college, 24 percent had earned masters degrees, and 16 percent had received doctorates. Moving from rags to riches remained as unusual as it had been a century earlier.

British Business

In the immediate postwar decades British businesses continued to develop along many of the lines laid down during the interwar years. A renewed rationalization and merger movement led to the development of larger firms, most of which came to be run by decentralized management systems similar to that developed earlier at Imperial Chemical Industries. The national government continued, and indeed increased, its involvement in economic and business affairs, especially when the Labour Party was in power.

Backed by trade unions, the Labour Party engaged the government deeply in general economic planning and business ownership through the nationalization of some basic industries, such as coal mining and steelmaking. The government also developed a welfare state. Three pieces of legislation were of most importance: the National Insurance Act (1946) provided unemployment benefits and retirement pensions; the National Health Service Act (1946) provided free medical and dental care; and the National Housing Act (1947) endorsed the principle of public housing.

Despite the growth of big business and big government — some would say because of their continued development — Great Britain's economy did not advance as rapidly as did that of the United States or Japan. In some fields of heavy industry, especially, Britain continued the relative downward slide that had started during the interwar years, a slide that became a drop during the 1970s.

Government, Business, and the International Economy

During the late 1930s and the 1940s the main thrust of British business was to avoid competition through collective action, a stance that left companies poorly prepared for the intense international competition of the postwar years. The merger movement of the 1920s and early 1930s, which had led to some rationalization in British business, slowed in later years. Instead of combining via mergers, businesses stifled competition by setting up a growing number of cartels and trade associations. Government actions encouraged this shift. In 1935 the government granted tax concessions to businesses working with each other to limit output, and during World War II the government worked with trade associations to plan the economy.

The major change in the business environment faced by British firms in the postwar years was a tremendous increase in competition, both at home and in the world marketplace. British firms faced increasing challenges from multinationals making and selling goods inside their nation's boundaries. The number of American firms having manufacturing subsidiaries in Great Britain rose from 43 in 1907 to 222 in 1935 and to 493 in 1962. By 1962 American MNCs in Britain accounted for over 50 percent of the British market for automobiles, vacuum cleaners, electric shavers, razor blades, sewing machines, typewriters, breakfast cereals, and potato chips, and for 30–50 percent of the market for computers, rubber tires, refrigerators, and washing machines. Actions taken by the British government also increased competition. Reversing its earlier position, the government sought to encourage business competition through new laws: the Monopolies and Restrictive Practices Act of 1948, the Restrictive Trade Practices Act of 1956, and the Restrictive Trade Practices Act of 1968.

British businesses faced growing competition in world trade as well. With the maturation of national independence movements in former colonies such as India, British business lost most of its heavily protected Empire market, which had been a major outlet for British goods before World War II. At the same time, Great Britain's adherence to the Bretton Woods Agreement and the GATT opened the nation to growing imports. In 1952 Great Britain held 22 percent by value of world trade in manufactures, but by 1969 only 11 percent.

The Spread of Diversified, Decentralized Big Businesses

British business leaders responded to the increase in competition by renewed rationalization. A major merger movement began in the 1950s and, like America's conglomerate movement, peaked in 1968. Between 1957 and 1967, 38 percent of the companies traded on the London Stock Exchange were acquired by other quoted companies. The British government encouraged some of these mergers in hopes of making British companies more competitive in world trade. The government sought to create "national champions." The government backed the formation of the British Aircraft Corporation in 1960 as a merger of Vickers-Armstrong, English Electric, and Bristol Aeroplane and supported the creation of the British Steel Corporation seven years later as a merger of fourteen previously independent firms.

While often not bringing about the increases in economic efficiency hoped for (just as the rationalization movement of the 1920s had failed to), the mergers did increase the power of big business in Great Britain. British companies became large by international standards. In 1972, thirty British manufacturing enterprises employed at least 40,000 people apiece. This figure was nearly as great as the number of such companies in all of the six original nations of the European Common Market, but less than the eighty-nine such companies in the United States. Of the largest two hundred companies in the world outside of America in 1969, over one-fifth were British. Of the largest three hundred manufacturers in Western Europe in 1969, about one-third were British. British big businesses clustered in many of the same fields as in the United States—food processing, chemicals, metals, electrical machinery, and transportation equipment—fields in which economies of scale and scope mattered.

Pushed by competition and pulled by new market opportunities, British companies diversified their product ranges and decentralized their management structures. By 1970, ninety-four of Great Britain's largest one hundred companies had diversified to some degree. Diversification came later to Great Britain than to the United States and, at first, was slower to spread in Great Britain. However, when diversification occurred, it took place rapidly, in the single decade of the 1960s. The rapidity was due, in part, to the work of McKinsey & Company, an American management consultant firm. Hired by many British companies to give advice on what growth strategies to follow, the American consultants usually suggested diversification by products or markets. As in the United States, diversified companies in Great Britain adopted decentralized management structures to handle the growing complexity of their operations. By 1970 seventy-two of the one hundred largest British companies were being run by some form of multidivisional, decentralized management. Few British firms, only six of the top one hundred, went so far as to become conglomerates, however.

Great Britain's diversified, decentralized companies possessed structures like those of similar companies in America. General managers in the corporate office, advised by staff officers, made the grand policy decisions. Divisional officers ran daily operations. However, there were some differences. Divisional managers often took part in policy making in British companies, not just operations. This situation raised doubts about their objectivity in measuring the performance of the various divisions of companies. Second, financial controls were not as well developed in Great Britain. Annual budgets were not the control devices they had earlier become at American companies like General Motors. Then, too, managerial hierarchies were less fully developed in Great Britain. As late as 1968 two-thirds of Great Britain's largest 120 companies possessed no hierarchy beyond that of chairman and managing director.

Ironically, as leading British companies adopted American management practices and structures, they fell prey to some of the same problems afflicting U.S. firms. During the 1970s and 1980s some large multidivisional, decentralized British companies became hidebound. With their many layers of management and with executives trained increasingly in finance, the British firms, like their American cousins, had difficulty dealing with the rapid economic changes taking place in the global marketplace. In the 1960s, however, most managerial weaknesses were papered over by the worldwide economic expansion of the immediate postwar decades.

British Multinationals

Like their American counterparts, British executives expanded MNCs. The world's leader in foreign direct investment (FDI) before World War II, Britain fell to second place after the conflict, trailing the United States. Perhaps 40 percent of British FDI was lost between 1938 and 1956 as a result of wartime destruction, sequestrations, and forced sales. Even so, in 1971 Britain controlled 14 percent of the world's accumulated FDI — behind the 48 percent share of the United States, but ahead of Germany's 4 percent and Japan's 3 percent. During the first fifteen years after World War II the lion's share of British FDI went to Commonwealth countries, but from the 1960s more went into Western Europe and the United States.

As in the case of MNCs in other nations, the existence of MNCs headquartered in Great Britain raised questions about their control. Could a national government adequately regulate the affairs of international companies? To whom, if anyone, were MNCs responsible? These issues were placed in the spotlight in 1965, when Prime Minister Harold Wilson sought to impose economic sanctions, including an oil embargo, on white rebels in the newly formed African nation of Rhodesia. Working against the wishes of the British government, Royal Dutch Shell and British Petroleum, Great Britain's two leading MNCs, found ways to ship oil into Rhodesia. A bit later, the oil companies worked against the intentions of the British government by supplying oil to the Union of South Africa, which insisted on maintaining the policy of apartheid.

Smaller Industrial Firms

As large firms grew in importance in British manufacturing, smaller companies declined in significance, even more rapidly than was occurring in either the United States or Japan. Manufacturing establishments with 200 or fewer employees dropped in number from 103,000 in 1948 to just 83,000 in 1971. During the same years the proportion of industrial workers employed in Britain by smaller manufacturing firms fell from 37 percent to just 28 percent. By the mid-1970s small industrialists accounted for only one-quarter of Great Britain's output of manufactured goods.

Several reasons accounted for the decline. Few government policies aided small firms in the immediate postwar decades; only in 1971 did the British government mount a concerted effort to foster small-business growth. In fact, most government policies in the 1950s and 1960s worked to the disadvantage of smaller companies, as the government favored mergers and rationalization in pursuit of imagined production efficiencies. Moreover, as in America, consumer demand for standardized goods favored mass production in big factories operated by big businesses. Small firms were at a disadvantage in this situation.

Sales and Services

Small retailers also lost ground to their larger brethren, due in part to changes in British laws. Legislation passed by Parliament in 1956 and 1964 outlawed retail price maintenance schemes, greatly enhancing competition in retailing. While important, these legal changes probably hastened trends already under way. Owning small retail businesses became less attractive than in the interwar years. As Great Britain became more of a welfare state with considerable aid given to citizens out of work, going into retailing as an alternative to unemployment was less appealing. Then, too, technological and social changes — the growing use of refrigeration in the distribution of foodstuffs, an increased acceptance of self-service and prepackaging, and the development of a better national road system — bit into sales made by small retailers.

By the mid-1980s small shops accounted for only about one-third of Britain's retail sales, and only 13 percent of grocery sales. Multiples (chain stores) were big gainers, especially in such fields as consumer durables, clothing, and alcohol. By the close of the 1980s the four largest grocery chains accounted for 80 percent of all sales in that field. Much the same trend was apparent in services. The Big Five banks that dominated Britain as early as 1914 became the Big Four in 1968, and these four banks accounted for 92 percent of Britain's bank deposits by the mid-1970s.

British Business Leaders and Labor

What of Britain's business leaders, those who headed the new diversified companies and MNCs? Family businesses became less important than before. As late as 1950 one-half of Great Britain's largest one hundred businesses were controlled by families, but twenty years later only one-third were. By the late 1960s and early 1970s the average company director in big business was fifty-six years old and not very mobile. He (very few were women) had an average salary of £11,000 (about $26,000) in 1970, much less than the average $210,000 earned by the heads of the largest 500 American companies just a few years later in 1976.

In terms of background, business leaders had most likely attended a public school (that is, in reality, a private school; in Britain private schools were and are called public schools). Only about one-half possessed a university education, most commonly from Oxford or Cambridge. This proportion of top executives going to a university was much less than the 89 percent in France, the 83 percent in the United States, or the 78 percent in West Germany and Italy. Perhaps most startling, as late as 1970 only 9 percent had received any professional education in business management. Although more open than in the past, Great Britain's business leadership remained elite in the postwar years. In the 1950s, 36 percent of the nation's business leaders were the sons of businessmen, another 36 percent the sons of clerical workers or laborers, 21 percent the sons of public officials, and 7 percent the sons of farmers.

Poorly educated, Britain's business leaders failed, as they had during the interwar years, to invest in the education of the workforce. In stark contrast to what occurred in Japan, executives did little to upgrade the training of their workers. The idea that the practical man, a person untrained in theory, could adequately design and make products continued to hold sway in Britain's manufacturing enterprises. Nor did improvements in public education compensate for the lack of on-the-job training. The British government increased funding for education (at least before 1979), but the educational improvements that occurred benefited industry little. For instance, technical schools, which might have imparted skills valuable for industrial work, dropped in number from 321 in 1947 to just 225 in 1962. Workers in many industries, lacking skills and knowledge that might have allowed them to adjust to new ways of doing things, resisted automation and other innovations in factory operations. This deficiency, apparent much earlier, became pronounced in the 1970s and 1980s. Already by the mid-1970s the productivity of British industrial workers lagged that of their West German counterparts by about 50 percent, with an even wider gap separating British from Japanese workers.

Japanese Business

Even more than in the United States and in sharp contrast to Great Britain, high-speed growth characterized the Japanese economy in the 1950s and 1960s. That this would be so was not apparent in the immediate postwar years. Japan was a defeated nation with widespread unemployment, rampant inflation, and shortages of food and fuel. It was feared that thousands might starve. Japan's recovery from this low point was remarkable, aptly

labeled by many as an "economic miracle." In the 1950s and 1960s investment in plants and equipment rose 22 percent per year, and Japan's GNP
soared by an average of 10 percent annually! The full development of consumerism in Japan — similar to what had been occurring in the United
States since the 1920s — fueled much of this economic growth. A surge in
demand for what the Japanese called the Three Cs — cars, color televisions,
and air-conditioners — was especially important. By 1970 Japan's real national income was six times greater than it had been in the mid-1930s, and
industrial output was ten times larger. Unemployment had dried up, and
inflation disappeared. Despite a 42 percent increase in Japan's population,
the nation's standard of living was far above that of the prewar years.

Japan's economic expansion opened new opportunities for business.
Older zaibatsu — Mitsui, Mitsubishi, Kikkoman, and Nissan, among others
— were broken up in the interests of economic democracy by American authorities in the 1940s, but they reorganized in new ways in the 1950s and
1960s. In addition, there was more room in the Japanese economy than
in earlier times for entrepreneurial firms. Then, too, smaller companies,
whether operating as independents or as subcontractors, remained an important part of Japan's mix of businesses. In general, companies in heavy
industry expanded more rapidly than those in light industries, continuing
a trend begun in the late 1920s. The availability of relatively cheap raw materials and oil encouraged this trend. With business expansion Japan possessed the world's third-largest economy by 1968, trailing only the United
States and the Soviet Union. No single factor explains Japan's dramatic rise
from the ashes of defeat to the status of economic superpower. Rather, a
coincidence of many elements led to the nation's economic recovery and
expansion.

The External Environment
Factors external to Japan's economy were important. The same worldwide
movement toward free trade that helped American companies and which
increased business competition in Great Britain aided Japanese firms. Only
with large parts of the world available as sources of raw materials and as
markets for its finished products could Japan, now stripped of its colonial
possessions, survive and prosper. The GATT was of particular importance.
While reaping the benefits of markets open to its goods, Japan was able by
special arrangements to restrict foreign investments in its companies and
limit the entrance of unwanted goods into the Japanese market until the
1970s and 1980s. Legislation enacted in 1949 and 1950, and liberalized only

in the late 1960s and 1970s, limited imports into Japan and restricted foreign investments in the nation.

American policies also helped rebuild Japan. The United States government, which dictated economic policy to Japan between 1945 and 1952, sought to democratize Japan's business system. Some business leaders lost their jobs, some zaibatsu were dissolved, and an antimonopoly law was passed. However, as the Cold War began, American leaders revised their attitudes toward Japan. Americans sought to revitalize Japan as a bastion of pro-Western capitalism in the Far East, especially after Communists won control of China in 1949. Americans also desired an economically strong Japan so that Japan would be able to import goods made in America (until 1968 the United States enjoyed a trade surplus with Japan). The zaibatsu were allowed to reorganize in the 1950s, the antimonopoly law was ignored, and most American leaders favored an extension of Japanese exports throughout the world. Even more specifically, American military expenditures in Japan, especially for the Korean War, allowed the Japanese to finance a major increase in their imports.

Government-Business Relations

Changes occurring within Japan spurred economic growth as well. Often remarked upon was the positive nature of government-business relations. Observers thought they discerned a particularly cooperative relationship between government and business, in which the government provided valuable guidance for the expansion of Japan's economy. In fact, there was often considerable cooperation between government and business in the postwar period, and this cooperation did in some cases spur business growth.

The Japanese government, working especially through the Ministry of Finance and the Ministry of International Trade and Industry (MITI), sought to guide the development of the nation's economy. The MITI, in particular, tried to provide planning for economic development, most often in the realm of heavy industry. This planning was attempted, not by government order or fiat, but by government guidance through the provision of incentives for business development. Thus, the Japanese government sought a middle way between the heavy-handed government ownership of industry and centralized government economic planning that characterized the Soviet Union, on the one hand, and the open, free-market economy of the United States, on the other hand.

The attempted guidance of economic growth was not brand new, nor were the institutions devised to do so. The MITI's origins date to 1881, when the

Ministry of Agriculture and Commerce was formed to stimulate and guide Japan's economic growth by indirect methods as part of the shift away from direct controls begun by the new minister of finance, Matsukata Masayoshi, in 1880. The Ministry of Agriculture and Commerce split into two parts in 1925, with one of the new parts becoming the Ministry of Commerce and Industry. The Ministry of Commerce and Industry led much of the rationalization program of the interwar years and was significant in encouraging the switch from light to heavy industry. Reorganized in 1939, the Ministry of Commerce and Industry helped mobilize the Japanese economy for war and was converted into the Ministry of Munitions in 1943. With the defeat of Japan, the Ministry of Munitions went through several changes that resulted finally in the establishment of the MITI in 1949.

After World War II the Japanese government took numerous actions to encourage and guide business development. The national and prefectural governments improved Japan's economic infrastructure: harbors, highways, railroads, electric power grids, and so forth. Government banks, backed ultimately by the Bank of Japan, loaned funds to large private city banks that in turn loaned to business. Laws passed by the Diet also helped business. A 1952 law gave subsidies and quick tax write-offs to companies investing in new equipment and research, and a 1956 income tax reduction stimulated consumer spending.

The MITI's work was of considerable importance. The MITI labored to rationalize inefficient companies and industries and could be forceful in doing so. In 1952 the MITI advised ten large cotton spinners to reduce their output by 40 percent and informed them that a failure to lower production would lead to a cutoff in the foreign exchange allocation needed for their importation of raw cotton. MITI's guidance also meant targeting companies for growth, helping them secure technology, capital, and markets. Many of the specific laws by which the MITI sought to guide Japan's economic growth in the 1950s and 1960s had predecessors in the interwar years. A 1937 trade law served as the precedent for legislation in 1949 giving the MITI power over Japan's foreign exchange. The Petroleum Industry Law of 1934 served as a direct model for legislation with exactly the same title in 1962. Laws encouraging industrywide rationalization and stabilization efforts in the 1920s and 1930s paved the way for similar legislation in the 1950s and 1960s.

Governmental actions encouraged economic growth and business development. However, it is difficult to judge precisely how important government aid was in Japan's postwar economic recovery and expansion. The

MITI's actions, while significant, should not be overstressed. Many other factors were involved, for the business situation in Japan was complex. The coal industry, targeted for nurturing by the MITI, never fully developed. Then, too, some companies, such as Honda Motors, prospered despite their opposition to MITI's desires and actions. Japan recovered economically from its wartime devastation and then surged ahead at least as much through the actions of its business leaders and industrial workers as through steps taken by its government officials.

The Variety of Businesses in Manufacturing

As in the United States, economic growth in the 1950s and 1960s opened new opportunities for business leaders in Japan, opportunities of which they were quick to take advantage. Their actions in turn caused additional growth. Japan's business situation was fluid after World War II, a situation that encouraged business experimentation and entrepreneurship. As they sought out new opportunities, Japanese executives shaped new types of companies, making the business picture in their nation diverse.

Typical of the rebirth of entrepreneurship was Honda Soichiro and Honda Motors. Notorious as a playboy in his youth — Honda was a lover of fast driving, geisha houses, sake, and traditional epic poetry — Honda rebuilt his destroyed factory in a new mode after World War II. He was one of the first to recognize the need for cheap, reliable transportation in Japan, at a time when gasoline was scarce and streets congested. He began by attaching war-surplus engines to bicycles. In 1949 Honda produced his first motorcycle, and by the late 1950s his company was mass-producing small motorcycles for Japan's urban market. Honda invaded the American market in 1959 and a decade later boasted 1,600 dealers in the United States. Automobiles, the Honda Civic and Accord, came in the 1970s.

Honda built his company as an independent entrepreneur. He avoided tie-ups with other firms, breaking a prewar arrangement with Toyota and avoiding bank loans wherever possible. He prospered despite conflicts with the Japanese government. In 1951 Honda refused to take part in an attempt at government-business cooperation designed to boost Japanese exports, and in the early 1960s Honda successfully opposed a MITI initiative to merge Japanese automakers into just a few large companies.

Japan's more traditional big businesses also reorganized, after some efforts to break them up, in the postwar years. Between 1946 and 1948 twenty-eight holding companies with family control were dissolved. However, with the advent of the Cold War this American-led effort ended, and by 1971 six major business groups had reorganized: Mitsubishi with eighty-six major firms, Sumitomo with eighty, Mitsui with seventy-one, Fuji with seventy-one, Sanwa with fifty-two, and Dai Ichi with twenty-seven. As in the prewar zaibatsu, these groupings usually consisted of a bank, a trading company, and many manufacturing companies. However, there were important differences. These new groupings lacked any central headquarters or holding company owning stock in subsidiary companies. Instead, the groupings — often called *keiretsu* — were much looser, held together by informal meetings of the heads of the various companies and by some stock interchanges among the companies.

The formation and expansion of MNCs, as in Great Britain and America, was yet another response of business leaders in Japan to the economically open postwar world. Even before World War II, Japanese businesses had set up some overseas production facilities. However, most were located in Japanese colonies and were limited to mining, communications, and some types of heavy industry. Many more overseas production facilities were established during the 1950s and 1960s. The direct foreign investment of Japanese firms climbed from $447 million in 1961 to $1.45 billion just six years later and soared to $3.5 billion by 1973. The average annual growth rate of Japan's direct investment in overseas ventures came to 31 percent between 1967 and 1973, much more than West Germany's 26 percent, America's 10 percent, or Great Britain's 9 percent. The sudden increase in Japan's overseas investments in the late 1960s and early 1970s came mainly from investments in the United States, especially in the commercial and service sectors of the American economy.

One reason Japan's large manufacturers were able to expand rapidly at home and abroad was their increased use of subcontractors. Subcontracting became increasingly common after World War II. By 1971, 59 percent of all the small industrial companies in Japan were acting as subcontractors for larger concerns, and ten years later the proportion had risen to 66 percent. By the late 1970s and the 1980s, 82 percent of Japan's manufacturing firms with more than 300 employees used subcontractors, employing an average of sixty-eight subcontractors apiece. The importance of subcontracting differentiated the Japanese system of manufacturing from the American one. In the United States, as in the past, large manufacturing companies were more likely to be vertically integrated and less likely to depend heavily on subcontracting.

Subcontracting was particularly well developed in Japan's automobile industry. Toyota and Nissan, for example, turned to subcontracting as a way to meet the growing demand for their cars from the mid-1950s on. In the 1950s Toyota and Nissan accounted for about 50 percent of the manufacturing costs for each car sold under their names, the other 50 percent coming from their subcontractors. By the late 1970s and early 1980s the contribution of Toyota and Nissan had dropped to about 30 percent, with subcontractors accounting for 70 percent. In 1977 Toyota had 168 first-level subcontractors; these companies in turn controlled 5,437 second-level subcontractors; and the second-level subcontractors had 41,703 third-level subcontractors.

By using subcontractors, Toyota and other companies were able to expand production greatly at little cost. The use of subcontractors allowed them to keep their capital investments and labor costs lower than they would otherwise have been. In 1989 Toyota produced 4.5 million cars with 65,000 employees; by way of contrast, in the same year General Motors used 750,000 employees to make 7.9 million cars. Toyota made its system work by cooperating very closely with its subcontractors, especially the first-level ones — providing them with technical help, financing, and other skills. In turn, the subcontractors provided high-quality parts and subassemblies to Toyota on time, as needed. However, the growing importance of subcontracting was a mixed blessing for smaller firms. Increasingly, the larger companies dictated the terms of doing business to the smaller firms. In recessions it was the subcontractors that suffered most, accepting price cuts for their products and laying off employees. As a consequence, wages and productivity were usually lower at subcontractors than at the mother companies.

Businesses in Sales

In retailing, mom-and-pop enterprises continued to grow in absolute numbers in Japan but, as in the United States and Great Britain, lost ground relative to larger retail outlets. Pressures on small retailers, apparent before World War II, increased after the conflict. More manufacturers, including Nissan and Toyota, set up their own nationwide distribution and sales channels to bypass Japan's cumbersome, many-layered system of wholesalers and retailers. In 1983 Toyota possessed 318 dealerships that had 3,665 sales outlets employing 116,000 people, and Nissan had 258 dealerships with 3,265 outlets employing 82,000. In general, companies making technologically advanced products found, as had many American firms at earlier dates, that general wholesalers and retailers could not adequately demonstrate, sell, finance, and service their goods — leading them to enter sales.

Then, too, large department store and superstore chains grew in importance. As part of Japan's postwar consumer revolution, department stores increased their share of Japan's retail sales from less than 1 percent in 1945 to nearly 10 percent fifteen years later. Superstores combined general-merchandise and supermarket sales under one roof. Borrowing directly from American supermarkets, superstores stressed chain operations, self-service in product selection, checkout lanes using cash registers, heavy advertising, and high-volume sales with low profit margins. In 1972 there were over 2,000 superstores in Japan, and five years later there were 3,100. Superstores surpassed department stores in total sales in 1973.

Responding to the cries of small retailers, the Diet passed the Department Store Law in 1956, modeled on a 1937 law with an identical title. The 1956 law required permission from the MITI for the opening or expansion of any retail store with more than 1,500 square meters of floor space (or 3,000 square meters in some large cities), and such permission was rarely given. However, there were ways to get around this law. Some entrepreneurs — Isao Nakauchi of Daiei, for example — created their department stores and superstores by limiting each floor to 1,500 square meters and setting up each floor as a legally separate company. By 1972 Daiei was the leading retailer in Japan. Even so, as late as 1976, 1.6 million retail outlets employing 5.6 million workers served Japan's population of 112 million. Despite the inroads of large department stores, superstores, and the like, Japan had many more retailers per capita than most other industrial nations. As a result, the Japanese paid higher prices for their consumer goods. Service by small-scale retail outlets was expensive.

The Tsutsumi Family and the Seibu-Saison Enterprises

Members of the Tsutsumi family were among the first business people to see clearly new opportunities in retailing and leisure activities in Japan. They rode and, to some degree, directed their nation's postwar consumer revolution. Tsutsumi Yasujiro founded the family businesses during the interwar and immediate postwar years, basing them mainly on the development of resorts for Japan's emerging middle class, Tokyo's Seibu Railroad, which possessed valuable landholdings, and a fledgling department store. Like Honda, he built his business empire with little government help and by operating outside of zaibatsu groups. When Yasujiro died in 1964, two of his sons greatly expanded the businesses he had started.

Tsutsumi Yoshiaki took charge of what became the Seibu Railway Group. By the early 1990s the railroad carried about 2 million passengers daily, along with thousands of tons of freight. By then the railroad group had also parlayed its landholdings into Japan's largest group of luxury hotels (the forty-one Prince Hotels in Japan, along with six Princes overseas) and was developing the nation's most extensive chain of ski, golf, and vacation resorts. In the mid-1990s the Seibu Group employed about 45,000 people and had annual revenues of about $7.2 billion. Yoshiaki was by some estimates for a while the world's richest private person, worth $280 billion in 1990, mainly because of the value of the landholdings of his companies.

His brother, Tsutsumi Seiji, controlled a second complex of enterprises that became known as the Saison Group. This group evolved from a Tokyo dry-goods store purchased in 1940, from which came one of Japan's leading department store chains, Seibu Department Stores. In the 1960s Seibu became the first department store group to move into superstores, the Seiyu stores, which trailed only Daiei in superstore sales by 1972. In the 1970s and 1980s Seibu, by then called Saison, diversified into a broad range of consumer services — insurance, credit, information networking, consulting, and so on. By the mid-1990s the Saison Group employed nearly 150,000 workers and had annual net sales of $35 billion, which compared to Nissan's $43 billion and Toshiba's $33 billion.

Seiji and Yoshiaki took important leaves from their father's book. Both expanded their businesses outside of the work of *keiretsu* and with little government aid. And neither played much of a role in business associations in Japan. Their strategies worked for several decades, but their companies — like so many others — became fatally entwined in a decade-long economic downturn in Japan during the 1990s. Parts of the family business empire went bankrupt.

The Management and Organization of Businesses

Like the companies themselves, Japanese business management methods were diverse. In the entrepreneurial firms the word of the owner-founder was law. Tsutsumi Yasujiro ruled his railroad and resort empire as an autocrat. Under him there was no president's office in any Seibu company, no director's offices, nor even any rooms set aside for department or section chiefs. Known within the company simply as "the boss," Yasujiro held board meetings at his private residence in Tokyo. His sons delegated some responsibilities to others as their enterprises grew in the 1970s and 1980s, but not many. Yoshiaki, in particular, continued to rule by himself, visiting his enterprises by helicopter.

In many of Japan's large business groups, however, consensus decision making was more the norm. An important aspect of this type of management was the *ringi* system, meaning "circular discussion" system. A *ringi* was a proposal put forward by a manager of one department that was passed on to managers of related departments and finally to the president. As the proposal was passed around, all those who saw it could make comments on an attached form. When it finally reached the president, he made his decision on how to proceed on the basis of what his subordinates had written. Closely related to the *ringi* system was *nemawashi*. Roughly translated as "root binding," *nemawashi* was a term taken from horticulture. It referred to the informal discussion and consultation that occurred in a Japanese company before a formal proposal was presented, much as the roots of a bush must be carefully bound up before a bush is transplanted.

In the immediate postwar decades changes occurred in the management structures of many large Japanese companies. Staff offices — personnel, long-range planning, public relations, and so forth — were added to Japanese firms, largely as a result of American influences. Many Japanese companies also added an operating committee called the *jomukai* to their administrative hierarchies. This body consisted of the president, vice-president, and several senior managing directors; and, as the importance of *jomukai* rose, the significance of boards of directors was correspondingly reduced, as was also taking place in Great Britain and the United States.

Regardless of precise structure, big businesses in Japan, the United States, and Great Britain became more similar in that they were multi-unit enterprises run by bureaucratic management. Nonetheless, significant differences remained. Japanese managerial hierarchies remained much flatter than those in the United States; that is, large Japanese companies had far fewer layers of management than their American counterparts. Then, too, few of Japan's big businesses adopted fully developed decentralized management systems, in contrast to what occurred in the United States or Great Britain. Japanese firms were less diverse in their product offerings and in the markets they served. (Seibu and Saison were exceptions.) At a time when most large American manufacturers produced a wide range of goods, most large Japanese manufacturers made only one or two major products. As a consequence, decentralized management was less necessary, and most Japanese firms did well with centralized management systems. Or, some moved partway into decentralized management. Matsushita Electric Industrial, for example, organized product groups with divisions for product design, engineering, production, and sales, but kept the actual selling of goods at the corporate level. Corporate management also took care of the finances, labor relations, and legal matters for the entire company.

In short, less responsibility was delegated to the divisional level in Japan than in Great Britain or the United States. Instead of becoming large multidivisional, decentralized firms, Japanese big businesses operated more as parts of constellations of firms joined together in various types of business networks, just as they had in times past. Networks linking banks, trading companies, and manufacturers in *keiretsu* were one type of such an arrangement. The linkage between industrial firms and their subcontractors was another. These types of linkages combined with their flatter managerial hierarchies to give Japanese firms advantages over some of their foreign competitors. Japanese companies could often respond quickly to economic changes and market alterations. Only in the 1980s and 1990s did Japanese business become rigid in their management set-ups, forfeiting that advantage and contributing to a long decade of economic stagnation.

Whether heading entrepreneurial firms or companies within the *keiretsu* groups, Japanese business leaders shared several characteristics in the 1950s and 1960s. They were younger and more vigorous than those of the interwar years, for as a result of American actions about 3,600 business leaders were forced to retire in the years 1946 through 1948. Even more than in the interwar period, the top managers of big business were college-educated, some 90 percent by the early 1960s. With big businesses hiring from only a handful of prestigious universities, a new business elite based upon education expanded. These business leaders often came to view themselves as the true saviors of Japan, in a manner reminiscent of early Meiji times. Indeed, their wholehearted pursuit of profits and economic growth helped spur Japan's economic recovery.

Labor Relations

Changes occurring in labor relations both reflected the concern for economic growth and were one reason for that growth. The origins of what became known as the Japanese system of labor relations date back to at least the interwar period. Faced with shortages of skilled workers and worried by labor disruptions, some big businesses offered wages and promotions based on seniority, along with extensive benefits, before World War II. Following the conflict, Japan's labor situation was chaotic, as workers in many industries rushed to form nationwide unions and go on strike. Unions, which had been illegal during the interwar years, were legalized after World War II; efforts by workers desiring unionization combined with the wishes of American authorities to bring that about.

To dampen labor unrest, keep workers loyal to their companies, and break nascent national unions, business leaders greatly extended the system of labor relations begun earlier. Increasingly, big businesses hired men graduating from high schools and colleges for lifetime employment ending only with retirement. Companies provided promotions and wage increases based mainly on seniority and a broad range of welfare services such as subsidized housing and recreational facilities. In return, employees generally remained loyal to their companies. Workers belonged only to enterprise unions, organizations based upon a single company rather than a nationwide industry or trade.

A compromise was reached between labor and management. By the mid-1950s labor challenged companies' managers less and less. Labor disturbances and strikes became rarer, usually limited to the wearing of symbolic red arm bands during the "spring offensive" when new annual contracts were negotiated. In return, in addition to providing lifetime employment and seniority-based promotions and wages, companies gave more control over the work floor to their employees: control over such matters as the layout of production, personnel transfers, and how tasks would be performed. Management and labor saw this delegation of control to workers as helping them both. Business leaders obtained the labor stability they needed for high-speed economic growth, and labor received increased security, wages, benefits, and authority over work processes.

One of the major advantages to emerge from the Japanese system of labor relations was the flexibility businesses had in using their workforces. Committed to their workers, the companies provided extensive and ongoing training and education for employees, from shop-floor workers to top-level managers. In return, businesses came to possess well-educated employees able to adjust to changing situations. More than that, workers often contributed ideas about how work processes could be made more efficient and how products might be improved. Then, too, because of their commitment to their companies, workers were unlikely to move to another firm, justifying the educational investments made in them. There was, as well, willingness on the part of Japanese workers, more than was the case with either their American or British counterparts, to undertake whatever job was needed in their firm. Unlike the situation in the United States, union-based work rules did not restrict what Japanese employees would do on the shop floor.

However, it is important to realize that this system of labor relations was limited to only a minority of workers and managers: to male employees working on a permanent basis for big businesses, perhaps one-third of Japan's industrial workforce. Smaller companies, men working on temporary assignments, and most women employees were not part of this employment system. Even in some large firms there were occasionally mutterings of dis- sent. For instance, a journalist disguised as a shop-floor worker at Toyota found that many factory workers were dissatisfied. Workers grumbled that management benefited most from Toyota's system of labor relations and complained about company tyranny in controlling the work process and in speeding up work on the assembly line.

Businesses in West Germany and China

German and Chinese businesses underwent changes that were even more wrenching than those experienced by American, British, and Japanese companies after World War II. Like Japan, Germany was occupied after the conflict. Unlike Japan, however, Germany was divided into two nations, East and West Germany. In China, the Communists, led by Mao Zedong, de- feated Chiang Kai-shek's Nationalists in a civil war that raged between 1946 and 1949. Mao declared the formation of the People's Republic of China on 1 October 1949, and Chiang and many other Nationalists retreated to Taiwan.

West German Businesses

German businesses underwent postwar experiences similar in important ways to businesses in Japan. The first impulse of the Western occupying powers — the United States, Great Britain, and France — was to democra- tize Germany economically. In the western zones of occupation (the Soviet Union controlled an eastern zone, later East Germany) cartels were broken up and wartime business leaders were removed from office. German com- panies closely associated with the nation's war effort — I.G. Farben, Krupp, and others — had their assets confiscated. As in the case of Japan, however, these efforts were short-lived. As the Cold War intensified, the Western pow- ers decided that West Germany, formed as a nation from the western occu- pation zones in 1949, would be rebuilt as an industrial nation and bastion of democracy against the Soviet Union. The Marshall Plan was put forward, in part, to aid in West Germany's recovery.

During the 1950s and 1960s West German businesses, building on foun- dations laid in the interwar years and earlier, reorganized to lead their na- tion into a period of high-speed economic growth similar to Japan's. Gov- ernment actions were significant in aiding this business redevelopment. The Law for Promoting Stability and Growth of the Economy, passed in 1967, brought to culmination earlier efforts. The law made currency stability, economic growth, full employment, and a positive trade balance official governmental goals. Nonetheless, as in the case of Japan, private initiatives were at least equally important. From the mid-1950s into the 1960s universal banks once again played important roles in providing industrial financing. Various business associations reemerged or were developed anew. Perhaps most important was the new Federation of Germany Industry, which helped coordinate national economic legislation. And, of course, individual companies rebuilt their capabilities. As companies did so, they were less likely than their British or American counterparts to adopt decentralized management or to be involved in mergers. Instead, they resembled Japanese firms more in their growth strategies and structures, and by the 1960s were taking parts of international markets away from their British competitors.

As in Japan, cooperation typically characterized relations between management and labor in Germany. A Codetermination Law of 1976 required that firms with 2,000 or more employees have supervisory boards consisting of equal number of representatives of labor and management to set grand policies for the firms. Codetermination grew out of earlier precedents, experiments with works councils in the 1920s and a 1951 codetermination law for companies in the coal and steel industries. Codetermination did not extend to medium-size and small firms, thus excluding 80 percent of Germany's workers from its coverage.

While big businesses were important, as they had been in earlier times, in West Germany's economic advance, so were small and medium-size firms (SMEs), the *Mittelstand*. (In East Germany, most SMEs in manufacturing were eliminated with the socialization of the economy, though some reappeared with denationalization in the 1990s.) Far from disappearing, SMEs remained a significant part of West Germany's business system. In the late 1990s SMEs employed 70 percent of Germany's workers, made 45 percent of all sales, and accounted for 46 percent of gross investments in business. SMEs also accounted for 57 percent of all value added by manufacturing and 30 percent of Germany's exports.

Members of the *Mittelstand* remained family businesses for the most part, with informal controls and with relatively little separation between management and family. As was true in other nations, in Germany SMEs in manufacturing prospered as makers of specialized goods for niche markets by batch-production, not mass-production, methods. Nonetheless, under pressure from growing global competition, the *Mittelstand* underwent significant changes beginning in the 1970s that have continued to the present. The SMEs became more dependent on outside financing and also somewhat more dependent on professional as opposed to family management. They often acted as subcontractors to big businesses, similar perhaps to what occurred in Japan.

Chinese Businesses

The fate of business was not clear when Communists won control of China in 1949 and, in fact, was not clarified until the late 1950s. Mao was fully occupied with putting a new government in place and the Korean War. For about five or six years, economic matters took a backseat to political, diplomatic, and military developments. However, with the Korean War ended in 1953, Mao and other Chinese Communist Party (CCP) leaders devoted themselves full-time to domestic affairs, including the socialization (state ownership) of their nation's economy. By the late 1950s virtually no private businesses remained in China.

Socialization took several forms. For peasants it meant land reform and redistribution in the early 1950s and then collectivization in the mid-1950s and later. Beginning with an Agrarian Law of 1950, land reform became the rule for China. Wealthy peasants and those who lived on rents from lands worked by others lost much of their land, which was given to poorer peasants. Peasant associations set up in the early 1950s to oversee land reforms often became farmers' cooperatives later in the decade. These cooperatives bought and sold crops and purchased inputs needed for farming, such as fertilizer. By 1956 most farmers belonged to cooperatives. Still later in the 1950s farmers were forced to join communes, which were much larger than the cooperatives. Some 26,000 communes were set up. Each controlled about 10,000 acres and had about 5,000 households as members, supposedly to bring the benefit of economies of scale to farming. Private land ownership ended.

The same trend toward state ownership was visible in industry. Influenced in part by the example of the Soviet Union, which sent numerous advisers to China, and by examples from their own nation's history, officials in the CCP stressed state ownership of business. As in the Soviet Union, plans were drawn up on five-year bases, with the first one covering 1953–57. By late 1952 the Chinese state had nationalized about 80 percent of heavy industry and about 40 percent of light industry. The state operated all of the railroads and a majority of steamships in China's home waters, and state trading companies handled nearly all of China's imports and exports. As in agriculture, the trend was away from private ownership, the free operation of markets, and toward the development of a planned economy.

The business people who had owned the enterprises received some compensation, and many of them became administrators in the state enterprises formed from their businesses. There was such a reaction against Western-style business methods that accounting was abandoned as bourgeoisie decadence, leaving the new state-owned enterprises unaccountable to anyone, at least on strictly economic grounds. Workers laboring in state enterprises had what was called an "iron rice bowl": they were rarely fired even if they performed poorly; they had low-cost, state-subsidized housing; and they received many other benefits from the state, including free medical care. These benefits made the low wages they received tolerable.

This trend toward state ownership of business in China was *not* brand new. Far from it. Modern government involvement in business dates back to at least the self-strengthening movement of the 1890s. Various forms of state aid to business continued during the years of the Republic. As we have seen, state enterprises controlled by the Nationalist government grew in importance after 1937, and they provided many of the same sorts of benefits that state enterprises did after 1949. Then, too, the Japanese army and Japanese-controlled puppet governments had directly controlled businesses in the parts of China they had occupied. And finally, the CCP had closely regulated business and agriculture in its enclaves before and during World War II. CCP economic policies after 1949 were less of a break with the past than might be imagined.

Two major results accompanied the growth in state control over business and agriculture. Continuing efforts begun by the Nationalists, the CCP, which controlled the government and which allowed no dissent from its top-down decisions about economic and social policies, stressed the need to locate industry in new areas. In 1949, 80 percent of China's industrial production remained in six coastal provinces and in the Northeast. The government mandated the development of heavy industry elsewhere in China throughout the 1950s and 1960s. Then, too, the government encouraged the formation of Town and Village Enterprises (TVEs) in the late 1950s and early 1960s, continuing a separation between large-scale heavy industry and smaller rural industries.

The economic policies put forward by the CCP brought substantial economic growth. According to a World Bank report, GNP per capita rose at 2–2.5 percent annually in 1957–77, despite a 2 percent annual increase in population. Steel production tripled, machine-tool production greatly increased, and the basis was laid for a petroleum industry. The net output of industry rose at an average of 10.2 percent annually in 1957–79. By the

1970s China possessed one of the world's largest industrial economies. On the farm, cereal production increased 3.5 percent annually in 1952–57, but at a slower 2 percent per year over the next two decades — just about enough to keep pace with China's population growth.

There were problems. Agricultural efforts were hurt by bad weather and floods in the late 1950s. Then, too, in what was billed at the time as "The Great Leap Forward," aimed at catching up with Great Britain in steel production, the CCP decreed in 1957–58 the building of backyard furnaces to make steel. Much of the resulting steel was of poor quality and unusable, but making it took peasants away from their agricultural jobs. The result of these policies — and the bad weather — was famine, in which 20–30 million Chinese died. The creation of the TVEs may have prevented even more widespread suffering by giving some peasants income alternatives to farming.

Following this disaster, agricultural production was decentralized from 1961 onward. Communes remained intact, but within them work teams were formed, corresponding roughly in size to older village workforces. However, further disruptions occurred with the "Great Proletarian Cultural Revolution," which was at its high tide in 1966–68. Only in the 1970s did the Cultural Revolution wind down, especially with Mao's death in 1976. An effort spearheaded by Mao to keep a sense of revolution alive, the Cultural Revolution took on a life of its own and led to excesses that overturned China's society and tore apart its economy. Systemic problems appeared. Like the Soviet Union, China emphasized investment in producer-goods industries at the expense of consumer-goods ones, leading to shortfalls in the making of what consumers needed and wanted. Peasants, especially, found themselves lacking the funds they needed in a centrally directed economy geared toward heavy industry.

Market-based solutions developed from the 1970s onward, with precursors dating back into the 1960s in a few regions. By 1975 peasants, though still organized in communes, had gained the right to have private plots of land. Similarly, factory workers could engage in some work for themselves and had limited rights to take part in demonstrations and strikes. Some local markets were back in operation, but extensive reforms came only from 1978 onward.

Business and the Environment: Silicon Valley

In most of the nations under examination here, policy makers hoped to create high-tech districts as engines of economic growth. In only a few cases did they fully succeed. California's Silicon Valley, which became the globe's leading high-tech district, was sometimes seen worldwide as a possible harbinger for the future of business developments. People around the United States and the world aspired to make their regions new Silicon Valleys, new high-tech regions. Silicon Valley's development in the 1950s and 1960s certainly had an upside in job generation and high-tech developments. However, it also had some lesser-known downsides in the forms of health problems for workers and environmental degradation.

Silicon Valley's Foundation

The name "Silicon Valley" came from a reporter for *Electronic News* who wrote a journalistic history of the San Francisco Bay Area's semiconductor industry in 1971. The name stuck, because the region long remained home to building computer hardware, which used silicon in great quantities. The geographic area came to include 1,500 square miles running from the outskirts of San Francisco south along the San Francisco Peninsula through Santa Clara County, with the city of San Jose at its center.

Silicon was a primary raw material used in making semiconductors and integrated circuits. Silicon transmits electricity well and is thus a semiconductor, and so could be used in making transistors, which are in effect very small switches to control the flow of electricity. In 1947 William Shockley and others at Bell Laboratories in New York invented the transistor. Seven years later, Shockley moved to Silicon Valley, where he started Shockley Transistor Laboratories. Soon, leaders of firms in Silicon Valley and Texas combined transistors with other devices on silicon wafers to make integrated circuits. Integrated circuits were capable of sending complex electrical signals from a miniaturized component. Transistors and integrated circuits quickly replaced bulky and less reliable vacuum tubes in such tasks. By the early 1970s Silicon Valley firms were assembling not just integrated circuits but also microprocessors, the hearts of personal computers.

The Development of Silicon Valley

Small and medium-size firms were the lifeblood of Silicon Valley. Nimble, ever-changing, and amorphous, these companies made the region the foremost high-tech center in the world after World War II. These companies formed a regional network, based on shared knowledge. However, there was more to the development of Silicon Valley than a collection of small and medium-size firms. A wide variety of developments came together to create the high-tech region: the work of people at nearby universities, the labors of business entrepreneurs, and federal government spending for military purposes.

Particular individuals were important. Frederick Terman was the "father" of Silicon Valley. As a faculty member in engineering, later as the dean of engineering, and finally as the provost of Stanford University, Terman pioneered in the establishment of connections between academia and industry, trained students in high-tech fields, and helped those students get started in business. Two of his best-known graduate students, William Hewlett and David Packard, formed Hewlett-Packard in 1937, using a loan of $538 from Terman to begin business. Other start-ups, often formed by Terman's students, were also important in the prewar years. Charles Litton established Litton Industries in 1932, and Sigurd and Russell Varian started Varian Associates a few years later.

Prodded by Terman, Stanford University established the Stanford Industrial Park in the early 1950s. Renamed the Stanford Research Park (SRP) in 1961, this land became the nation's first high-tech park. The SRP soon bustled with activity. In a bucolic, campus-like setting, where buildings seemed to blend into the rolling hills of the countryside, the SRP accepted Varian Associates as its first tenant, a move that successfully brought together academic researchers and business people. By 1963 the SRP housed forty-two companies employing 12,000 workers. Six years later, the SRP boasted sixty firms with almost 18,000 employees.

Military spending helped, as World War II orders aided individual companies. Hewlett-Packard saw the number of its employees jump from nine in 1940 to one hundred in 1943 and its annual sales mushroom from $37,000 to $1 million in the same years. The Cold War and the very hot Korean War further benefited California's high-tech companies. Between 1951 and 1953 California firms received $13 billion in prime defense contracts, allowing the state to displace New York as the nation's leading recipient in this regard. Aerospace ventures in Southern California received much of the funding, but those in Silicon Valley won their share. Sensing opportunities, eastern high-tech firms moved west. Lockheed Missiles and Aerospace opened a major manufacturing facility not far from Stanford University in 1956. Soon employing 28,000 workers there and at a research facility in Palo Alto, Lockheed served as a catalyst for further high-tech growth.

By the early 1970s what had been a small cluster of companies had expanded into a full-fledged high-tech district. At first, executives located their operations near Stanford University, but they soon spread them southward down the San Francisco Peninsula. Confined by natural boundaries of mountains and ocean, the companies formed a very dense network of enterprises. As Silicon Valley matured, individual entrepreneurs and small firms remained at its core, and their work helped explain the Valley's success as a high-tech district. As some of the high-tech firms developed, they "hived off" many new, smaller companies. A case in point was Fairchild Semiconductor, founded in 1957 by Robert Noyce and other scientists who broke away from Shockley Transistor Laboratories. During the 1960s employees who left Fairchild to try to capitalize on their specialized knowledge founded over two dozen semiconductor-related companies. Called "Fairchildren," these small firms added greatly to the vibrancy of Silicon Valley. Noyce himself left Fairchild to help start the firm that became Intel in 1968.

Most of the high-tech businesses were SMEs that consciously avoided vertical integration. Instead of trying to internalize all facets of their companies' work in single firms, Silicon Valley entrepreneurs got ahead by establishing a large, informal, flexible network of linked, but independent, companies. Located in one region, this agglomeration of many SMEs allowed producers to benefit from economies of scale without forming big businesses. Proximity encouraged communications among the firms and stimulated growth. Bars and restaurants, along with institutions such as professional and business associations, where scientists and entrepreneurs could meet informally, encouraged the spread of information among the firms. Then, too, job-hopping workers spread information across firm boundaries.

By the late 1970s Silicon Valley possessed nearly 3,000 electronics firms, 70 percent of which had fewer than ten employees and 85 percent of which had fewer than one hundred. It was the flexibility of the many small firms and of Silicon Valley as a whole that spelled success for decades. Between 1959 and 1976 about 210,000 new jobs were added to the region. Many of these were high-tech jobs (not all were, for some were in companies servicing the high-tech firms). Silicon Valley firms employed about 115,000 high-tech workers in 1975. By 1990 that number had jumped to 265,000.

Even so, Silicon Valley firms faced a major crisis in the mid-1980s and early 1990s, when they lost the market for semiconductors to fierce competition brought by Japanese companies. In 1980 American companies made about 57 percent of the world's semiconductors, but by 1989 their share had dropped to only 36 percent. Semiconductors had shifted from being a custom to a commodity product, in which low-cost production had become the watchword. Between 1985 and 1986 about 20 percent of the semiconductor employees in Silicon Valley lost their jobs. Silicon Valley partially recovered in the 1990s, when it boomed with the advent of commercial applications for the Internet, only to partially collapse in a "dot-com" bust as the decade closed. The Valley was recovering from those losses in the opening decade of the twenty-first century.

Environmental Problems in Silicon Valley

The economic prowess of Silicon Valley was often emulated, even though environmental problems hurt people in the region. Health issues affected production-line workers. As late as 1999 making an 8-inch silicon wafer required 3,023 gallons of deionized water (in addition to many gallons of regular water), 4,267 cubic feet of bulk gasses, 29 cubic feet of hazardous gasses, and 27 pounds of chemicals. Production processes created 3,787 gallons of waste water and 9 pounds of hazardous waste.

Unless handled very carefully, these substances harmed the health of workers, and too often few safeguards were in place, especially in the early days. Chemical fumes, corrosive acids, and other toxic substances assailed production-line workers, who were usually not warned of the dangerous situations in which they labored as they fabricated silicon wafers and assembled electronics products. According to a 1980 report by the state of California, workers in semiconductor plants suffered from illnesses at a rate three times greater than that of workers in general manufacturing. A year later a state report about conditions in California semiconductor firms revealed that nearly half of the elevated illness rates that their workers incurred came from systemic poisoning or toxic exposure.

A further investigation in 1984 summarized many of the dangers. It found that "electronics is not a sterile, clean industry" but rather one using "hundreds of potentially dangerous substances." Organic solvents used in cleaning operations caused "a range of health problems, including dermatitis; central nervous system effects, such as nausea, dizziness, and headaches; liver and kidney damage; and even cancer." Corrosive acids caused "serious burns" and "lung damage." Moreover, "other toxic substances, including gasses such as arsine and phosphine, metals such as lead and other solders, and epoxies, pose[d] additional risks." Finally, "reproductive hazards" included "radiation and various chemicals." These dangers fell heavily on a largely immigrant workforce, raising environmental-justice issues. Most of the workers in the high-tech firms were Hispanics or Asians, often women.

Environmental challenges extended beyond the workplace. Nowhere were problems worse than in the pollution of groundwater supplies. Silicon Valley drew mainly on groundwater in aquifers for its industrial and drinking water. By the early 1980s it was becoming apparent that toxic waste water from high-tech manufacturing was contaminating the aquifers. Testing by governmental authorities soon showed that sixty-five of seventy-nine companies examined had released toxic chemicals into the ground beneath them. By the late 1990s the Environmental Protection Agency had designated twenty-nine Superfund sites in the Valley, more than in any other county in the United States. Twenty-four of the sites resulted from pollution by electronics firms.

Silicon Valley experienced exuberant growth in the twentieth century, especially after World War II. Buoyed by entrepreneurial ambitions and defense spending, the region boomed as a high-tech region, the best-known and most widely imitated such district in the world. Silicon Valley had the mix of factors needed to succeed. Its very growth, however, caused problems, especially health problems for workers, which should give pause to policy makers in other regions seeking to emulate its rapid development.

Conclusions

By the close of the 1950s and 1960s large companies existed in many of the same fields worldwide: transportation equipment, metals, electrical machinery, chemicals, textiles, petroleum, tobacco processing, and stone, clay, and glass. To some degree, companies in these fields became more similar in their management, as large manufacturers moved toward bureaucratic management. The growing similarity was most pronounced in the United States and Great Britain, as large, diversified British companies adopted decentralized management directly from America.

Convergence also typified some aspects of the business systems of most of the nations we are studying. National governments and international organizations played increasing roles in economic development. The first twenty-five years after World War II were ones of tremendous economic expansion. Businesses in many industrial nations, although less so in Great Britain, benefited from the expansion of international trade. (While not a member of the Bretton Woods Agreement or the GATT, China had extensive trade with Eastern Europe and the Soviet Union from the 1950s onward, and later on with Western Europe, though not with the United States.) Big businesses usually profited more than smaller concerns. Consumer demand for large numbers of standardized goods spurred the development of large factories devoted to long production runs, and big businesses usually owned and operated those factories. As a result, in the United States the distinction between center and peripheral firms broadened, in Japan the dual economy developed apace, and in Great Britain a meaningful difference between large and small firms grew up for the first time.

Global business remained complex, as it had always been. Marked differences continued to separate businesses in the different lands. As in the past, many Japanese firms, and to some extent West German companies as well, operated as parts of constellations of businesses and did not adopt decentralized management. In general, large American companies had more levels of management than their counterparts elsewhere, run by executives increasingly trained in finance and marketing rather than in operations. In the immediate postwar decades these characteristics of American management did not hurt the companies. However, as Japan and West Germany recovered from the devastation of World War II and as global competition heated up in the 1970s and 1980s, those layers of management and a lack of knowledge about what was taking place on the factory floor acted as drags on American firms. They too often failed to respond quickly to changes in the international business situation. However, even within the United States there was diversity in the business world. The small, nimble firms composing the economy of Silicon Valley were quite capable of responding to market demands, making them the envy of policy makers around the globe.

Suggested Readings

Harold Vatter and John Walker, eds., *History of the U.S. Economy since World War II* (Armonk, 1996), and Alfred D. Chandler Jr., "The Competitive Performance of U.S. Industrial Enterprises since the Second World War," *Business History Review* 68 (Spring 1994): 1–72, offer overviews of American economic and business development since 1945. Mira Wilkins, *The Maturing of Multinational Enterprise: American Business Abroad from 1914 to 1970* (Cambridge, Mass., 1974), is the standard work on the modern development of American multinationals. Sandra S. Vance and Roy V. Scott, *Wal-Mart: A History of Sam Walton's Retail Phenomena* (New York, 1994), provides a valuable look at changes in retailing. On the continuing development of a consumer society in the United States, see Lizabeth Cohen, *A Consumer's Republic: The Politics of Mass Consumption in Postwar America* (New York, 2003).

Derek Channon, *The Strategy and Structure of British Enterprise* (Cambridge, Mass., 1973), and S. J. Prais, *The Evolution of Giant Firms in Britain* (Cambridge, 1976), are important overviews of British businesses after World War II. John Wilson and Andrew Thompson, *The Making of Modern Management: British Management in Historical Perspective* (Oxford, 2006), looks at the evolution of British management practices. Ronald Dore, *Brit-*

ish Factory-Japanese Factory: The Origins of National Diversity in Industrial Relations (Berkeley, 1973), examines factory management and labor relations. David Vogel, *National Styles of Regulation: Environmental Policy in Great Britain and the United States* (Ithaca, 1986), is comparative. Geoffrey Jones and Frances Bostock, "U.S. Multinationals in British Manufacturing before 1962," *Business History Review* 70 (Spring 1996): 207–56, is valuable.

Nakamura Takafusa, *The Postwar Japanese Economy: Its Development and Structure* (Tokyo, 1980), surveys economic changes occurring in postwar Japan. Chalmers Johnson, *MITI and the Japanese Miracle: The Growth of Economic Policy, 1925–1975* (Stanford, 1982), focuses on the roles government played in Japan's economic advance. On the business firm and its management, see Michael Cusumano, *The Japanese Automobile Industry: Technology & Management at Nissan and Toyota* (Cambridge, Mass., 1985), Kazuo Wada and Yui Tsunihiko, *Courage and Change: The Life of Kiichiro Toyoda* (Toyota City, 2002), and Thomas R. H. Havens, *Architects of Affluence: The Tsutsumi Family and the Seibu-Saison Enterprises in Twentieth-Century Japan* (Cambridge, Mass., 1994). On roles the United States played in Japan's economic ascent, see Aaron Forsberg, *America and the Japanese Miracle: The Cold War Context of Japan's Postwar Economic Revival, 1950–1960* (Chapel Hill, 2000), and Sayuri Shimizu, *Creating People of Plenty: The United States and Japan's Economic Alternatives, 1950–1960* (Kent, Ohio, 2001).

There are emerging literatures on postwar Chinese and German businesses. On Germany, see Werner Abelshauer, *Dynamics of German Industry: Germany's Path toward the New Economy and the American Challenge* (New York, 2005), Harmut Berghoff, "The End of Family Business? The Mittelstand and German Capitalism in Transition, 1949–2000," *Business History Review* 80 (Summer 2006), 263–96, Raymond Stokes, *Constructing Socialism: Technology and Change in East Germany, 1945–1990* (Baltimore, 2000), Raymond Stokes, *Divide and Prosper: The Heirs to I.G. Farben under Allied Authority, 1945–1951* (Berkeley, 1988), Steve Tolliday, "Enterprise and State in the West German Wirtschaftswunder: Volkswagen and the Automobile Industry, 1939–1962," *Business History Review* 69 (Autumn 1995), 273–350, and S. Jonathan Wiesen, *West German Industry and the Challenge of the Nazi Past, 1945–1955* (Chapel Hill, 2001). On China, see David Faure, *China and Capitalism: A History of Business Enterprise in Modern China* (Hong Kong, 2006), chapter 5, John Gittings *The Changing Face of China: From Mao to Market* (New York, 2006), chapters 6 and 7, Maurice Meisner, *Mao's China and After* (New York, 1986), and *R*. Bin Wong, *China Transformed: Historical Change and the Limits of European Experience* (Ithaca, 1997), chapter 8.

On the history of Silicon Valley and efforts to replicate it in the United States and abroad, see Martin Kenney, ed., *Understanding Silicon Valley: The Anatomy of an Entrepreneurial Region* (Stanford, 2000), Margaret Pugh O'Meara, *Cities of Knowledge: Cold War Science and the Search for the Next Silicon Valley* (Princeton, 2005), and Annalee Saxenian, *Regional Advantage: Culture and Competition in Silicon Valley and Route 128* (Cambridge, Mass., 1994).

Into the Twenty-First Century

The stable international economic system created by the Bretton Woods Agreement and the GATT eroded from the early 1970s. In 1971 President Richard Nixon, responding to pressures on the American economy and the American dollar, suspended the convertibility of the dollar into gold and other reserve requirements (this convertibility had been one of the main underpinnings of the Bretton Woods Agreement). Currency exchange rates were (and are) no longer tied to any fixed standard. The rates "float" with regard to each other according to the values placed upon them by market forces. Two years later the Organization of Petroleum Exporting Countries began rapidly increasing oil prices, an action that further disrupted the international economic situation, as did a similar move in 1979. Major recessions in the early 1970s, early 1980s, and early 1990s upset longstanding ways of doing business, challenging executives to alter their practices. So did increased international competition, made possible in part by transportation and communication advances, from jumbo jet airliners to computers to container ships. For businesses across the world the 1970s, 1980s, and 1990s were unstable decades.

Restructuring of both individual firms and of national economies became the watchword, as business and political leaders responded to the challenges they faced. The British business system, which had shown signs of weakness in earlier years, slumped in the 1970s and 1980s, but recovered to become one of Europe's strongest economies in the 1990s and early 2000s. The American business system presented a spectacle of mixed strengths and weaknesses to observers in the 1970s and 1980s, but emerged as the global giant in the 1990s and the early 2000s. Parts of the Japanese business system were caught up in the development of what became known as a "bubble" economy in the 1980s, a speculative boom based on skyrocketing real estate and stock prices, which crashed in the early 1990s. Japan then endured more than a decade of economic difficulties, experiencing some economic growth again only in the opening decade of the twenty-first century. Meanwhile, many aspects of China's business system boomed from 1978, when the government began replacing its socialistic command economy with one based on market transactions. Economic growth continued in China at a rapid rate into the early 2000s.

Changes in American Business

By the 1970s most Americans recognized that their nation faced economic problems and, more specifically, that many American businesses were not faring well in international competition. Events in the 1980s reinforced doubts Americans had about their nation's economy. A sharp recession early in the decade, combined with a high rate of unemployment coupled to inflation, troubled Americans. Trade imbalances clouded America's economic horizon. The most basic problem Americans faced was a decline in the competitiveness of their nation's businesses. After boasting trade surpluses through 1968, the United States developed an unfavorable balance of trade. These developments, along with the general uncertainty of the international economic situation, led to a restructuring of American business. That restructuring was generally successful in the 1990s and later, allowing the United States to retain its place as the globe's leading economy.

Problems in Management and Labor Relations

Many foreigners greatly admired American business management in the 1950s and 1960s. The British imported the American concept of decentralized management, and the Japanese appropriated American ideas about quality controls. This admiration was partly misplaced. Problems in managerial decision making lay at the heart of a decline in the competitiveness of American business. A basic difficulty was that too much of American industry was obsolete, for businesses failed to reinvest enough of their earnings in capital improvements. Moreover, when capital improvements were made, they were too often made in a hasty, add-on manner that failed to increase the overall production efficiency of the plants. Rather than building new, efficient factories from the ground up, business leaders added onto existing, often inefficient installations.

Adding to problems was a proliferation of levels of management in America's large multidivisional firms. Companies developed too many layers of management, making it difficult for them to respond quickly to changes occurring in their markets and economic environments. In the early 1970s General Motors had twenty major levels of management, compared to nine at Toyota. The growth in management levels divorced managers from the factory floor and placed a premium on managing by the numbers — that is, using financial reports as the way to run companies. Managers trained in finance, not operations, came to the fore.

Conflict between management and labor added to the problems American business faced. Management worried that a lack of dedication of workers to their companies and jobs was eroding labor productivity and thus business profits. There were grounds for concern. After rising at an average annual rate of 3.4 percent between 1947 and 1964, the productivity of workers in American manufacturing increased only 2 percent per year between 1965 and 1975, and just 1 percent annually during the years 1976 through 1978. In 1979 labor productivity fell by 0.9 percent, and it dipped another 0.3 percent in the following year. By way of contrast, the productivity of industrial workers in Japan climbed an average 7.4 percent annually between 1947 and 1980. However, to assert, as some observers of the American scene did, that the cause for the decline in American labor productivity was simply that workers lacked pride in their jobs and so did not work hard enough misses a crucial point: the failure of management to modernize factories meant that workers often had inefficient equipment with which to work. By 1980, for example, Japanese factories used 10,000 robots to speed their work processes, but American plants employed only 3,000.

Nowhere were the differences in the productivity between American and Japanese workers more pronounced than in heavy industry. For instance, in the early 1980s Japanese companies could produce a subcompact car for about $2,000 less than their American rivals. Part of this difference was due to lower wages in Japan, but most of it resulted from the greater productivity of Japanese workers. A Japanese subcompact car could be assembled in fourteen worker-hours, while a similar American car required thirty-three.

The Restructuring of American Business: BFGoodrich

In response to the challenges they faced, American firms, especially those in manufacturing, restructured their operations. Restructuring involved a search for profits, which in turn led to an increased focus on what business executives considered the core capabilities of their corporations. Restructuring involved still more. Business leaders often sought to make their firms more entrepreneurial in their management and more flexible in their production methods, allowing them to move away from long, standardized production runs of homogeneous products, in favor of making smaller batches of specialty products for niche markets. Thus, they emulated what some smaller industrial firms had been doing for decades.

BFGoodrich—for decades one of America's leading tire makers and a leading producer, as well, of industrial rubber products and goods made of polyvinyl chloride (PVC)—was one of the many industrial companies to restructure its operations. By the late 1960s and early 1970s Goodrich faced greatly increased domestic and foreign competition in its two major product lines, commodity PVC goods (ranging from house siding to water pipes) and car tires, setting the stage for its transformation. Between 1971 and 1995 BFGoodrich sold over $2 billion worth of its assets, while making about $1 billion worth of acquisitions (the difference went mainly to pay off huge debts incurred primarily in the 1980s).

The restructuring of BFGoodrich entailed basic changes in the firm's product lines. Goodrich found itself unable to compete in tires and rubber products, for its plants were obsolete compared to those of other firms, a legacy going back to the 1920s. Goodrich left the making of original equipment tires in 1982 and the making of replacement tires about five years later. Michelin, a French tire maker, later bought what was left of Goodrich's tire venture. Goodrich was in the 1970s and early 1980s America's leading producer of PVC, but in the early 1980s Goodrich ran into major problems in trying to control the raw materials and intermediates going into the manufacture of PVC. Faced with financial problems and growing foreign competition in the making of commodity PVC, Goodrich sought in the late 1980s and early 1990s to move into specialty, higher-margin PVC products, but this attempt only partly succeeded. In 1993 Goodrich sold nearly all of its PVC operations.

What did BFGoodrich become? By the mid-1990s Goodrich consisted of two loosely related divisions, specialty chemicals and aerospace. Both had histories at Goodrich dating back to the 1910s and 1920s, but neither became very important until the 1980s. Beginning in the mid-1980s Goodrich's executives poured hundreds of millions of dollars into acquisitions to expand aerospace operations. They tended, by contrast, to develop specialty chemicals more by internal growth. Goodrich, thus, eschewed the making of commodity products for large homogeneous markets. Instead, the company came to make specialty products for niche markets, from carbon brakes for America's space shuttle to a wide range of chemical adhesives. In the case of aerospace Goodrich provided repair and maintenance services as well. In the late 1990s Goodrich left even chemicals, becoming simply a maker and servicer of aerospace products. It moved its headquarters out of Ohio to North Carolina and changed its name from the BFGoodrich Company to the Goodrich Company.

BFGoodrich also changed its management. From centralized management it moved to decentralized management. Corporate executives pushed extensive authority over operations far down the managerial line, shedding layers of management. By 1996 BFGoodrich consisted of several dozen almost independent business units (profit centers) set up around products only loosely controlled by the corporate office. John Ong, the CEO from 1979 through 1995, explained how management worked. "No one is in control of you [the manager of a business unit], or can interfere with you. You can do the r & d the way you want, operate your plants the way you want, do marketing the way you want, do your own management hiring and firing, do your own capital spending (within generous limits). You are operating your business almost as if you owned it." These actions succeeded. While reporting mainly losses or only small profits in the 1980s, Goodrich emerged as a profitable concern in the mid-1990s.

Restructuring, such as that conducted at Goodrich, generally worked, at least for business firms. Large industrial companies, which had been losing ground to their smaller counterparts, grew in relative importance after 1991, and they did better than their foreign competitors as the 1990s progressed. Corporate restructuring made American manufacturers more efficient. Possessing flatter management structures than just a decade or two earlier, they were more focused in what they did and generally prospered. Manufacturing productivity, as measured by output per worker-hour, rose 30 percent in the United States between 1983 and 1990, far ahead of the 13 percent gain in Canada or the 19 percent increase in Germany, and not far behind the 35 percent rise in Japan.

Restructuring had a mixed impact on workers. Between 1979 and 1996 the United States' economy generated a net increase of 27 million jobs, enough to provide work for all those laid off as a result of corporate restructuring and all new job seekers. However, the availability of jobs hid a growing insecurity of work. One-third of all households had a family member who was laid off, and 40 percent more knew of a relative, friend, or neighbor who had lost a job. Moreover, while most found another job, only about one-third found a new job that paid as well as the one lost. Between 1973 and 1990 real hourly wages for nonsupervisory workers (about two-thirds of the nation's workforce) dropped 12 percent, before recovering a bit in the 1990s and later years.

Large and Small Businesses in a Restructured Economy

Despite loss in importance relative to that of big business in the 1990s, small business remained a significant segment of America's industrial economy. As in earlier decades, some small firms proved adept at exploiting niche markets with specialized products based upon short production runs. By the 1970s and 1980s, however, perhaps more was involved. Some observers have suggested that the ability of small businesses to react quickly to alterations in markets and fluctuating exchange rates helped explain their continuing significance. Then, too, the use of computers in computer-aided design, engineering, and manufacturing allowed small, independent firms to perform tasks that only larger businesses could earlier accomplish, thus allowing more direct competition with their larger counterparts. What developed in some fields were networked congeries of small industrial firms, similar perhaps to the nineteenth-century textile makers in Philadelphia or the independent steel mills in Pittsburgh in the same period. Often located near each other in specific locales, the small firms supported each other and in some fields offered a viable alternative to mass production by big businesses. As we have seen, this situation is what developed in Silicon Valley.

A hotly debated topic rife with consequences for policymakers was the issue of the roles small businesses played in job creation in modern America, especially in manufacturing. The best evidence on this controversial topic does not support the notion that small firms were outstanding as engines of growth, at least in manufacturing. Between 1972 and 1988 plants with at least one hundred employees accounted for two-thirds of job creation in America. Small manufacturers were better at *gross* job creation than larger ones. However, small manufacturers went out of existence more frequently than large companies, thus destroying more jobs. In sum, small manufacturers were no better than their larger counterparts in *net* job creation.

Nor did small businesses do particularly well in sales or services. In services, nationwide chains and groupings of banks, insurance companies, and real estate firms, often using computers to link themselves together, grew in importance. Larger companies such as Wal-Mart, Kmart, Sears, Metro International, and Daiei increased their market shares in the United States and elsewhere. Between 1987 and 1993 the market share of America's top ten supermarkets rose from about 23 percent to nearly 30 percent, the market share of the top ten specialist clothing chains rose from about 24 percent to 30 percent, the share of the top ten home improvement chains rose from about 17 percent to about 27 percent, and the top ten department store groups increased their market share from about 42 percent to about 53 percent.

The growth of Wal-Mart was dramatic. By offering consumers low prices and by operating on low profit margins, the company expanded rapidly. In the early 2000s, 100 million Americans shopped at Wal-Mart each week. Wal-Mart's annual sales came to a sum equal to $2,060 per American, on which the firm earned a profit of $75. The company was the largest retailer in the United States, Mexico, and Canada, and it was the second-largest seller of groceries in Great Britain. Wal-Mart's sales were greater than the combined sales of Home Depot, Kroger, Target, Costco, Sears, and Kmart. Wal-Mart sold more goods in one day than Target sold all year. Wal-Mart was the largest private employer in the United States and the world, employing 1.6 million people globally.

In manufacturing, sales, and services the trend in the United States' business system seemed to be toward concentration and the growth of oligopolies. True, small firms remained significant, but mainly as niche players. Larger companies used capabilities in management, production, and sales, especially in the 1990s, to move ahead in importance.

Government: Deregulation

Restructuring reached into the realm of government-business relations. Some observers of American business believed that the deregulation of business by the federal government would spur economic growth and business development. Begun especially by President Jimmy Carter and continued by President Ronald Reagan, deregulation aimed at removing what many viewed as excessive federal governmental regulations from a wide variety of industries, ranging from electric utilities to communications. What occurred in transportation and banking illustrates the many twists and turns to deregulation.

Transportation industries were the first to experience the full force of deregulation. The federal government, through the Civil Aeronautics Board (CAB), had regulated the airline industry since the 1930s, controlling both the fares that carriers could charge and the routes the airlines could fly. The reform of the airline industry began in the 1970s, especially when the CAB started to ease restrictions on routes and fares. When the results of increased competition appeared to be better service at lower costs, while the airline companies continued to enjoy profits thanks to higher passenger traffic, Congress was won over. The Airline Deregulation Act of 1978 called for the dissolution of the CAB over a six-year period, with free entry of airline companies into routes of their choosing at fares determined by competition. After deregulating the airlines, Congress turned to trucks and railroads. Economists had complained that the regulation of the trucking industry since 1935 by the Interstate Commerce Commission had resulted in gross inefficiencies. In 1980 Congress made it easier to enter the trucking business and allowed competitive forces to determine rates. Similarly, the Rail Act of 1980 allowed rail executives much greater flexibility in charting the course of their firms.

Deregulation profoundly affected banking. Deregulation combined with economic circumstances to bring about unexpected and unwanted changes in the nation's savings and loan industry. The Depository Institutions Deregulation and Monetary Control Act of 1980 created a framework in which various types of financial institutions could compete with one another for deposits and loans. Savings and loan institutions, which had traditionally made long-term loans to homeowners, entered new fields. Seeking higher returns on their loans than could be obtained in the residential housing field, they made loans for various sorts of real estate development and construction, which carried high degrees of risk. Inexperienced in these fields, and sometimes engaging in fraudulent activities, savings and loan executives often found themselves overextended. The failure of federal agencies to monitor the activities of the thrift institutions adequately made the problem worse. As a result, by 1989 some 500 of the nation's 3,000 savings and loan banks were insolvent, and Americans faced a bill of over $500 billion to protect depositors. That year Congress passed the Financial Institutions Reform, Recovery and Enforcement Act to bail out the failed thrift banks and, in effect, to reregulate the industry.

As the twenty-first century opened, it was too early to discern clearly all the effects of deregulation on the United States, but it was clear that some of those effects would be unexpected, as in the failure of the many savings and loan institutions. While supporters touted deregulation for increasing the efficiency of the American economy and for generating economic growth and jobs, critics viewed it as a government retreat from responsibility for the public welfare. Through deregulation the government was, critics maintained, washing its hands of social responsibilities and leaving many Americans unduly vulnerable to free market forces.

British Business: Decline and Revival

The decline of British business was much in the news during the 1970s and 1980s, as Americans, worried about their own nation's economic health, feared that the United States might catch what they called the "British disease." For a time, British industry declined relative to that of other nations. Great Britain accounted for 22 percent of the world's exports of manufactured goods in 1952, but only 11 percent by 1969 and a scant 7 percent in 1980. In 1983, for the first time since the Industrial Revolution had begun, Great Britain imported industrial goods greater in value than those it exported.

Still, several points need to be observed. First, this decline was only *relative* to what was occurring in other nations; the British economy continued to grow in the 1970s and 1980s. In fact, Great Britain's real Gross Domestic Product (GDP) per capita more than tripled between 1900 and 1984, and real disposable income per capita rose 46 percent between 1971 and 1992. By the 1980s nearly all households had refrigerators, washing machines, and color televisions. Car ownership stood at 224 per 1,000 people in 1971, but had risen to 380 in 1995. By way of contrast, even bicycles had been luxury items in the late nineteenth century. Second, some parts of Britain's business system continued to do very well during these decades, showing no signs of decline. Moreover, in the 1990s some segments of the British economy that had earlier slumped, including some areas of heavy industry, rebounded, making Britain's economy one of the strongest in Europe.

Business Problems

Business and economic problems were most apparent in the 1970s. British management remained parochial, with a lack of breadth and an unwillingness to take risks. This situation was not due to the more personal nature of British management than what prevailed in the United States (at any rate, by the 1980s families were no longer very important in the management of the largest British companies). Ironically, the adoption of decentralized management methods from the United States, with their many layers of managers and emphasis on financial reporting, contributed to the rigidity of some British firms.

Rigidities showed up especially in marketing. Their conservatism led British executives to place too much emphasis upon trying to sell in Britain's former colonial markets, while not paying enough attention to potentially richer markets elsewhere. Some British businesses scored marketing successes. For instance, Lipton, Boots and W. H. Smith's (both pharmaceuticals) performed well. By and large, however, effective marketing was limited to those sectors of the British economy already immune to foreign competition or was confined to industries that contributed little to employment or foreign trade. Thus, woolens and bicycles were marketed more effectively than cotton goods or automobiles.

Britain's system of education continued to be a drag on business. As in the past, the British tended to elevate the practical man who could learn on the job, at a time when the development of new science-based industries made this approach even less realistic than it had been earlier. Great Britain had a lower proportion of its population enrolled in places of higher learning than the United States. Engineering education, stressed at many of America's state-supported land grant universities, too often received scant attention in Great Britain. Underlying the conservatism of many British businesses, seen in their reluctance to adopt new production processes and to move into new products, was the poor education of their workers and managers. In the 1970s, 60 percent of German workers but a scant 30 percent of British workers possessed intermediate or vocational qualifications, that is, the equivalent of an apprenticeship or full secretarial training. In the 1980s, 85 percent of the senior managers in America and Japan held college degrees, but only 25 percent did so in Britain. Few of those British managers holding degrees had them in engineering.

Continuing Successes

Not all British industrial businesses were in trouble, even in the 1970s. Pharmaceutical companies and makers of food and drink remained world leaders. Through its development of Zantac, an anti-ulcer drug, Glaxo emerged as Great Britain's largest company in terms of market capitalization by 1992. Glaxo found ways to reduce the time needed to bring drugs to market and succeeded in marketing them well. Nor was Glaxo alone. SmithKline, Wellcome, and other pharmaceutical companies performed admirably on the world stage. In Glaxo's case, the entrepreneurial orientation of its CEO, Paul Girolami, the competitive environment resulting from American drug companies operating in Britain, and a market provided by Britain's National Health Service contributed to success.

Beyond manufacturing, some businesses in service industries did well. Great Britain lost ground relative to other nations in the provision of private services — freight, insurance, and transportation — in which the nation had once excelled. Between 1955 and 1976 Britain's share of international trade in private services dropped from 40 percent to just 15 percent. Nonetheless, even amidst this gloomy picture there were bright spots. City of London financial enterprises, long preeminent in the international equity, bond, and foreign exchange markets, expanded their roles worldwide. The deregulation of Britain's financial sector in what was dubbed the "Big Bang" of 1986 stimulated competition. For the first time in decades, merchant bankers, stockbrokers, and insurance companies could cross over financial lines to compete with one another.

Governmental Actions: The Thatcher Revolution

Despite some rays of success and hope, Great Britain's general economic position was not promising in the 1970s. In 1976 the nation had to borrow a large sum from the International Monetary Fund to stay solvent, a step usually taken only by third-world nations. In addition to business problems, there were difficulties emanating from government actions. The expansion of the welfare state after World War II was more than Great Britain could afford, given the nation's existing structure of property relations, class, and race. According to the Treasury, public spending took 60 percent of Britain's GDP in 1976 (these figures were later shown to be 10 percent too high, but even 50 percent of GDP was a very large proportion).

However, it long remained impossible politically to alter the welfare state much. Edward Heath, the leader of the Conservatives during the 1960s and early 1970s, was one of the few British politicians who clearly saw the need for alterations. His party won a surprise victory in 1970, and as prime minister Heath tried to limit welfare growth, even at the expense of cutting aid to many less fortunate members of British society. He failed. Soon viewed as a divisive figure, Heath quickly found most of his program in tatters, even before the Conservatives were swept out of office by the Labour Party in 1973–74. Harold Wilson and James Callaghan, the Labour Party leaders, promoted social harmony and economic stabilization more than limiting the state's role in providing welfare.

A sustained new approach began when the Conservatives, led by Margaret Thatcher, returned to power in the late 1970s. Thatcher was an outsider to the inner circles of political and economic power in Great Britain, just the sort of person to shake things up. Thatcher grew up in the small town of Grantham located in Lincolnshire in the Midlands, not in London; she was the daughter of a grocer, not a political or business leader; and she was a Methodist rather than an Anglican. She attended grammar school on a county scholarship and went on to Oxford, where she studied chemistry, which was unusual for women then. After graduation, she worked as a research chemist and entered the Bar. Drawn to politics, Thatcher became the leader of the Conservatives in 1975 and prime minister with a Conservative victory in 1979, the post she held until stepping down in favor of John Major, another Conservative, in 1990. Major continued Thatcher's economic policies, and even a later Labour government led by Tony Blair from 1997 into 2007 did little to alter their basic thrust. The trend was toward increased competitiveness and privatization.

Thatcher wanted to make the British economy and British business more competitive in the international marketplace. She sought to attain this end through three interrelated steps. Thatcher reduced taxes, while at the same time limiting inflation. Her preoccupation with lowering taxes and inflation marked a real shift in public policy, which earlier had stressed ending unemployment. Hit by problems beyond her immediate control in the early 1980s, Thatcher hung on grimly to her policies; and by 1983 they had borne fruit, with both inflation and unemployment down.

Thatcher also sought to check the power of Britain's trade unions, arguing that the demands of their members for hefty wage hikes contributed to inflation and priced British goods out of international markets. Added to these difficulties was the problem of work stoppages. Some 2.3 million days were lost to stoppages in 1964–67, and a whopping 6.8 million days in 1969. Since many of the strikes and stoppages took place in nationalized businesses, they directly involved the government. Legislation passed by Parliament in 1980 and 1982 placed limits on union activities, including limits on their right to strike. Even more significant in signaling a new direction was the settlement of a nationwide coal strike in 1985 (coal was a nationalized industry at the time) on terms more favorable to the government than the unions. Most important in the long term and very troubling to trade union leaders was that a shrinking proportion of Britain's industrial workers were covered by collective-bargaining agreements: over 70 percent in the early 1980s, but just over 50 percent by 1990. (Thatcher's policies were not the only reasons for the decline of trade unions. As industrial businesses, in which unions were heavily entrenched, became less important to Britain's economy, and service businesses, which were much less unionized, grew in significance, unions declined in importance. The same trend was apparent in the United States.)

Finally, Thatcher moved to end government ownership of Britain's nationalized industries, or, as they were often called, "public" industries. In the late 1970s nationalized industries accounted for 10 percent of Britain's industrial output and employed 1.75 million workers. Many were privatized by their sale via stockmarket flotations: British Aerospace and Cable and Wireless in 1981, National Freight in 1983, and Jaguar and British Telecom in 1984. Then came a host of others in the mid- and late 1980s: British Gas, British Airways, Rolls-Royce, British Airports Authority, the British Steel Corporation, and British Coal. While spurring competition and often contributing to economic revival, privatization came at a price. Often the government sold its businesses for a pittance of their actual value. For instance, British Gas was sold for £6 billion, when, according to one estimate, it was worth £16 billion. In addition, privatization often hurt workers. Some lost their jobs as the new private businesses reduced their workforces, and others found their unions under attack by the new private managers of the companies.

Large and Small Businesses

Into the 1970s British industry continued its march toward concentration. The share of manufacturing output produced by Britain's one hundred largest enterprises was 43 percent, almost one-third greater than the share of the one hundred largest firms in the United States. However, British industry's movement toward centralization ended in the 1980s and 1990s. Interestingly, the improvement in Britain's industrial productivity relative to other nations during the 1980s coincided with the decline in industrial concentration. The growth in number of small manufacturers, those with no more than 200 employees, was remarkable: from 71,000 (of a total 75,000 manufacturers in Britain) in 1971 to 133,000 (of a total 135,000) by 1988. In 1971 small manufacturers gave jobs to just 21 percent of Britain's industrial workers, but by 1988 they provided work for 31 percent.

To some extent, the growing importance of small business in manufacturing was replicated in other fields. In 1979 enterprises with fewer than 500 employees accounted for 57 percent of Britain's private sector employment, but by 1986 their share had risen to 71 percent. Contributing to the resurgence of small business were government policies favoring small firms, the spread of public attitudes favoring entrepreneurship, the development of the same flexible manufacturing techniques that helped small industrialists in the United States, the embrace of subcontracting and outsourcing by large manufacturers (similar to what had been occurring in Japan for decades), and the search for employment opportunities by people out of work in Great Britain. Even so, the overall contribution of small firms to Great Britain's economy remained less than elsewhere. Small companies, generally those with no more than 300 employees, accounted for 32 percent of Great Britain's private-sector GDP in the 1980s, compared to 46 percent in West Germany, 50 percent in the United States, and 60 percent in Japan.

West Germany and France caught up with and then surpassed Great Britain in manufacturing output per person hour between 1951 and 1979, and throughout these years the United States led the West European nations. In 1988 Great Britain still lagged the other nations, but had begun to lessen the difference. Then, in the 1990s Great Britain closed the gap and moved ahead of its European rivals. In a manner similar to what occurred in the United States, business leaders in Great Britain flattened corporate management structures and focused their firms on their core capabilities. These actions, combined with the continued privatization and deregulation of the British economy by the new centrist Labour government, made Britain's economy the strongest in Europe. A reunified Germany encountered great difficulty in reviving the economy of the region that had been Communist East Germany, and this difficulty acted as a severe drag on Germany's economy throughout the 1990s.

Even with business revival, problems continued for the British. While average income rose in the 1970s and 1980s, it was — as in the United States — unevenly distributed. There were winners and losers in Britain's uneven economic growth. The poorest 10 percent of British households suffered from a fall in real income. Those in London and southern England benefited more than those in the industrial North, exacerbating a long-standing socioeconomic rift. Job insecurity increased, again as in the United States. In 1970 unemployment stood at about 500,000, but by 1994 it was five times as great. In 1966, 84 percent of British men were economically active, by 1993 only 72 percent. One economic journalist was probably correct when he noted in 1995 that Britain had become a 30:30:40 society. That is, a privileged 40 percent of the population was secure and well-off, another 30 percent was marginalized and insecure, and a final 30 percent hovered between the two extremes.

Japanese and Chinese Businesses

Japan's high-speed economic growth slowed dramatically during the 1970s, impeded especially by the oil shocks of 1973 and 1979, which hit Japan even harder than the United States and Britain; by the collapse of the Bretton Woods Agreement, in whose wake the prices of Japan's export products soared; and by the opening of Japanese markets to foreign firms. Considerable recovery occurred in the 1980s, leading to an overheated boom in several fields, particularly real estate and stocks and bonds — what the Japanese labeled a "bubble" economy. The bubble burst in the early 1990s, and its collapse sent shock waves through Japan's business system, especially through financial institutions, many of which had invested heavily and un-wisely in securities and land. After a decade of depression in the 1990s, Japan's economy experienced considerable recovery in the early 2000s. However, that recovery was spotty and incomplete.

In China, a tentative opening of that nation's economy to market forces in the late 1970s and the 1980s and then a more complete liberalization during the 1990s led to rapid economic growth. China's GDP soared by 10 percent or more annually in the early 2000s. By keeping the value of its currency low (critics said artificially low), by paying workers wages that were low by international standards, by importing state-of-the-art technical knowledge, and by other methods the Chinese government helped business leaders develop robust exporting industries.

Changes in Japan's Business System

In the 1970s and 1980s government agencies such as the Ministry of International Trade and Industry (MITI) sought to work closely with businesses to try to move the Japanese economy into a variety of high-tech fields — biotechnology, computers with artificial intelligence, and so forth — with only limited success. As in the past, the Japanese government had great difficulty choosing industries to target for growth. Japan's industrial policy did not, in many cases, pick winners; governmental support, on the whole, went to industrial segments that grew the slowest.

However, even as the government tried to continue providing some guidance to the Japanese economy, a counter-trend began in the 1970s and 1980s and accelerated in the 1990s. As in the United States and Great Britain, efforts to deregulate the economy started. In the 1980s the government's tobacco monopoly was ended, and Nippon Telegraph and Telephone, Japan's leading communications company, was privatized. In the late 1980s and early 1990s Japan National Railways was broken up into regional railway systems and privatized. In the mid-1990s the Japanese government began deregulating the nation's banking system, allowing different types of banks to compete with one another. More generally, government ministers tried to remove barriers to competition throughout their nation's economy. In the early 2000s government efforts to stimulate competition seemed to bear fruit, as the nation's economy slowly recovered from low points to which it had fallen in the 1990s.

From the late nineteenth century to the present many large Japanese businesses, like their American counterparts, developed bureaucratic management. However, there was always also a strong streak of entrepreneurialism in Japanese business, even in big business. In the nineteenth century Iwasaki Yataro was a very strong individual instrumental in the founding and growth of Mitsubishi. Individuals were important in the 1950s and 1960s. Honda Soichiro, Ibuka Masaru of Sony, and Mitarai Takashi of Canon were a few of the innovative business leaders active after World War II. In other words, there were always elements of both individualism and groupism in Japanese business management.

In the mid-1980s and later the emphasis shifted in the direction of entrepreneurialism. Hit by the same global economic uncertainties that affected their Western counterparts, Japanese companies found that they could not afford the long time periods required for making decisions by consensus. Too often fast-moving events overtook slow-moving decisions. In the summer of 1985 the Keizai Doyukai (the Japan Committee for Economic Development), whose 1,030 members were top managers in major Japanese firms, issued a report calling for the adoption of less bureaucratic, more flexible types of management styles and structures. The Japanese even coined a term to describe the problems they saw their companies as facing: *daikigyo-byo*, or "large enterprise disease."

Managers took steps to change the ways in which they ran their firms by stressing the use of work groups that could respond quickly to alterations in a company's environment. They simplified their management structures, eliminating a multiplicity of divisions and sections, much as was done at BFGoodrich. As they altered their management methods, companies slimmed down by shedding surplus middle managers, in a manner similar to what was occurring in American and British firms. Lifetime employment was no longer a certainty for managers, not even for those in big businesses, especially from the 1990s on. Increasingly, large companies forced white-collar workers who had been passed over for promotion to take early retirement or to accept positions found for them with smaller firms, often with a hefty reduction in pay.

Relationships between companies, especially those composing *keiretsu* groupings, loosened a bit. The linkages characteristic of big businesses in the 1950s and 1960s eroded some in the face of growing global competition and economic instability. Interlocking stock ownership among companies belonging to the same *keiretsu* became somewhat less common. By the same token, *keiretsu* banks loaned a growing proportion of their funds to firms outside of the *keiretsu*; and firms seeking the lowest interest rates on loans went far afield to secure those loans. Stockholder loyalty to companies lessened, and corporate takeovers, even hostile ones, which had been almost unheard of in Japan, began. Even so, *keiretsu*, especially those composed of horizontally linked companies, remained important. Most equity ties among firms making up the six largest horizontal *keiretsu* — Mitsui, Mitsubishi, Sumitomo, Fuyo, Sanwa, and DKB — remained intact. In 1998, on average, members of those *keiretsu* owned 20 percent of each others' shares, down only slightly from the high point of 25 percent in 1981. In 1998 the six largest *keiretsu*, not including their banks and insurance companies, employed 3.2 percent of Japan's workers, down from 4 percent ten years earlier, and made 11.5 percent of their nation's sales, as compared to 13.6 percent in 1988. Vertical ties between manufacturing companies and their subcontractors remained tight in some industries, such as automaking, but became much more attenuated in others.

Small businesses remained, as in earlier times, a significant part of Japan's business system, but the picture was a mixed one. Firms with no more than twenty employees composed 78 percent of Japan's companies in 1987 and gave work to about 31 percent of the nation's employees. Small-scale manufacturers accounted for 86 percent of Japan's industrial companies in 1972 and 87 percent in 1986. Squeezed by larger companies anxious to cut costs, many smaller manufacturers sought to escape from unremunerative subcontracting arrangements by striking out on their own as truly independent firms. In sales and service, small businesses were less successful. Small firms rose from 79 percent of Japan's retail outlets in 1972 to 84 percent in 1986. However, in the 1990s the entrance of "big box" discount outlets cut into the sales of smaller firms, a situation made possible by the repeal of some of the laws previously protecting small retailers. Then too, between 1972 and 1986 small businesses dropped from 78 percent of Japan's service businesses to just 73 percent and continued to fall in relative terms in later years.

Many of the same factors that changed business management altered labor relations. The economic slowdowns, combined with an aging of their workforces, led many company managers to rethink their systems of labor relations. Many large industrial companies switched to what the Japanese called a "modified" seniority wage system, in which wages were determined by the function a person performed on the job as well as by seniority. By the mid-1980s over half of Japan's large manufacturing companies had adopted such a wage system. In the depression years of the 1990s many firms scrapped seniority wage systems altogether. Companies also hired more "temporary" workers, especially women, who were not part of the same systems of industrial relations as permanent workers. As much as 10–20 percent, and sometimes even more, of a big business's workforce became composed of these temporaries. As Japan's economy slumped in the 1990s, large numbers of qualified college graduates could not find appropriate jobs in businesses, leading some Japanese referred to them as a "lost generation."

Modern-Day Chinese Businesses

Two years after Mao Zedong's death in 1976, Chinese Communist Party (CCP) leaders began taking their nation, at first hesitantly, then more enthusiastically, into a market economy. As they did so, they also allowed foreign companies to reenter the Chinese market and build factories in China. Deng Xiaoping, a long-time member of the CCP, led China's government and economy in new directions. Under Deng's guidance, members of the CCP agreed to make economic modernization of their party and nation their major goal in late 1978. With some ups and downs, Deng held to this strategy until his death in 1997. In practice, Deng's decisions had two major consequences: centralized economic planning by the state gave way to the freer play of market forces, and foreign companies were allowed to invest in China.

In what was known as the "household responsibility system," or more simply the "responsibility system," farm families could sell surplus agricultural production in open markets, as long as they retained a certain amount of their produce for the state. The responsibility system was based on legal contracts. Farmers could also engage in sideline production, leading to an expansion of Town and Village Enterprises (TVEs) in light industry. The TVEs were not backward companies. For instance, the Stone Company made and sold a substantial number of computers by 1986. Private markets developed, and communes withered and were abandoned in 1981. According to one respected account, one-half of China's rural economy was composed of nonagricultural activities by 1987. This situation was not brand new, but can be traced back at least to policies begun in the 1950s. Changes occurred a bit later and more slowly in heavy-industry enterprises in urban areas. Throughout the 1980s the "iron rice bowl" gradually eroded, and in 1991 the government abolished guaranteed employment altogether. At about the same time, the government permitted entrepreneurs to set up private businesses, some of which grew rapidly in size and importance. As a consequence, the state-owned enterprise share of China's economy fell from 78 percent in 1978 to just 42 percent in 1996 and to only 24 percent in 2001. (The Chinese government divested itself of businesses in a variety of ways, but often did so by selling shares to individual entrepreneurs and to the Chinese public.)

As in other nations, the trend in China was toward the privatization of business, although all banks remained state-owned. Making China's emerging new business system more open was the adoption of the Accounting Law of 1993, in line with a movement toward business transparency in Japan and most Western nations at about the same time. Fourteen years later the Chinese government put in place a modern bankruptcy law. (In something of a reaction against too rapid change, the Chinese government adopted regulations setting standards for layoffs, severance, and the use of temporary workers, designed to protect the rights of laborers, in 2007.)

Even with privatization, the influence of government remained substantial, much stronger than the influence of government in any of the other nations examined in this study. For instance, China's national and provincial governments urged businesses to form various types of groups so that they might compete more effectively with Japanese *keiretsu* and Korean business groups in the global marketplace, and by 2000 some 2,655 Chinese business groups had come into existence. Three years later, twenty Chinese business groups made *Fortune's* list of the top 200 emerging-market enterprises. Whether the groups increased China's business competitiveness, however, was unclear.

The Chinese government also permitted foreign companies to trade with China. A major milestone came with the normalization of international relations with the United States, under President Richard M. Nixon, in 1972. Full diplomatic recognition of the People's Republic of China by the United States came from President Jimmy Carter in early 1979. The year before, in 1978, Japan signed a treaty of friendship with China (the two countries had exchanged ambassadors even earlier, in 1972). Increased trade quickly followed, with China's merchandise trade surplus with the United States surpassing $100 billion in 2003. The European Union's merchandise trade deficit with China amounted to $45 billion in 2005.

Many companies soon went beyond trading with China to establish factories there. They often entered China via joint ventures with Chinese companies, which assured China of the acquisition of much of the world's most advanced technology. At first, most of the foreign companies located their plants in four special economic zones created along China's coast in 1979. The four zones were designed to attract foreign investment by offering tax breaks to companies building factories there. After some rocky times in the 1980s, many of these companies achieved sustained growth in the 1990s and spread their operations to other parts of China. Foreign direct investment (FDI) in China rose from about $4 billion in 1990 to roughly $40 billion in 2000 and to over $70 billion in 2005. These amounts were much greater than the $1 billion of FDI entering Japan in 1994, the $8 billion in 2000, or the $6 billion in 2003. Annual FDI in China exceeded total FDI in all of the rest of East and Southeast Asia combined during most of the 1990s and early 2000s. Much of the FDI in China came from Taiwanese investors. In addition, in the early 2000s more than 300 of the largest 500 industrial companies in the United States had invested in production facilities in China. Nor were they alone. European and South American companies also sold their goods in China and invested in that nation. For instance, in the first quarter of 2003 Volkswagen (Brazil) sold more vehicles in China than Volkswagen sold in Germany.

The combination of foreign investments and indigenous developments created an emerging economic powerhouse in China. By the early 2000s China made 70 percent of the world's conventional toys, 60 percent of its bicycles, one-half of its shoes, and one-third of its luggage. In 2005 the Chinese purchased nearly 6 million automobiles, 27 percent of which were made in China; and they exported another 75,000 automobiles to over one hundred countries. A year later, China was the second-largest national market for cars and light trucks, after only the United States, with domestic sales amounting to 7.2 million vehicles. China accounted for about 6 percent of the globe's merchandise exports in 2003, up from just 3 percent in 1996. With a population of about 1.3 billion people in 2005, China possessed the world's second-largest economy (after the United States), if adjustments were made for purchasing-power differentials. Even so, in 2003 China's per capita income was just $1,100 — compared to Japan's $34,510, Taiwan's $13,320, and South Korea's $12,020.

However, China's expanding economy also faced serious challenges. One was quality control. In 2007 U.S. companies selling products made in China, from automobile tires to toys, had to recall those goods for not meeting American safety standards. Even more troublesome were environmental issues: polluted water, dirty air, and the desertification of land due to, among other matters, continuing deforestation. China's tenth five-year plan, covering the years 2000–2005, was supposed to reduce the amount of sulfur dioxide in the air by 10 percent, but in those years air pollution actually rose 27 percent. It was estimated that about 360,000 Chinese died prematurely each year in the early 2000s because of air pollution. There were, in addition, energy issues. China emerged in the late 1990s as one of the globe's largest oil importers, with its imports of petroleum rising from $245 million in 1999 to $964 million in 2004. It was unclear in the early 2000s if China could continue to obtain oil at prices low enough to sustain rapid economic growth. The nation also faced widening disparities of income and wealth, as urban dwellers generally did much better economically than people in the countryside, leading many farmers to move into overcrowded cities unable to readily handle the population influx. Social unrest — including protests, strikes, and riots — resulting from these various challenges suggested that economic advances for China as a whole were fast outrunning gains perceived by significant portions of the nation's population.

One of the industries the Chinese sought to develop was tourism. Chinese were ardent tourists. The Chinese government began authorizing trips abroad in 1997, and in 2006 about 31 million Chinese traveled beyond mainland China (two-thirds made it only as far as Hong Kong or Macao, however). The number of Chinese traveling beyond mainland China was expected to grow, according to the World Tourism Organization, to about 50 million by 2010 and to perhaps 100 million ten years later. About 6 million Chinese were true international tourists in 2006. Many who traveled abroad did so mainly to shop, skimping on hotel accommodations in order to be able to spend more on foreign brand-name products. How to capture the tourism market and its consumer spending attracted the attention of the Chinese governmental officials and Chinese entrepreneurs alike in the early 2000s.

The Business of Tourism and the Environment

By the 1980s and 1990s tourism was one of the globe's largest industries, especially as measured by employment. By some accounts it was the largest industry. Moreover, tourism was often praised, like high-tech industries, for being a "green," environmentally friendly industry. The reality was more complex. Tourism was certainly important for the United States. In 1995 travel and tourism was the nation's third-largest retail industry, behind only automobile and food sales, generating $430 billion in expenditures. In the same year, travel and tourism ranked second only to health care as the largest source of jobs in the United States and was among the top three employers in thirty-four states, including many western states. Tourism saved parts of the American West from economic stagnation in the wake of job losses due to declines in logging, mining, ranching, and farming. However, the economic gains derived from tourism came with social and environmental price tags attached.

Tourism: A Devil's Bargain

Tourism in the American West and around the world was a double-edged sword, or, as one historian has labeled it, "a devil's bargain." Tourism created jobs, sometimes by the thousands, in regions that otherwise might not have had them; but many of those jobs were poorly paid entry-level positions with little chance of advancement. Tourism also usually left considerable "footprints," significant impacts on host communities and their environments. Tourism often strained local infrastructures, raising questions about land use, water rights, transportation facilities, and the generation of electrical power. Most fundamentally, the growth of tourism raised questions about community development and identity. Residents in the American West often lost control of their locales to outsiders, suffered from unwanted changes in their lifestyles, and experienced unexpected alterations in their physical and cultural environments. From nineteenth-century developments near the Grand Canyon to the building of high-rise hotels in modern Las Vegas, tourism was a transforming force.

In America's Trans-Mississippi West tourism was both a blessing and a curse. It brought prosperity to some people in areas in economic decline, but not all benefited. Around 1900 railroads boomed tourism in the Grand Canyon area for America's newly emerging economic elite. With the coming of railroads, local, small-scale tourist developments gave way to larger, more heavily capitalized, and more highly organized ones controlled by outsiders. Nor was that all. Native American culture was commodified. The Hopi, who sold trinkets and interacted with tourists at the Grand Canyon, came to be seen as the "standard" Indian tribe of the Southwest. The Havasupai, who did neither, were ignored and marginalized. In the Southwest, Santa Fe was a city in economic decay that embraced tourism. The boosting of culture through systematic advertising, emphasizing the city's Spanish past, highly romanticized in tourist publications, was of prime importance. Tragically, Hispanics actually living in Santa Fe benefited little. Dude ranching in Jackson Hole, Wyoming, was another form of early-day tourism out west. In this industry relative newcomers — "neonatives" — quickly wrenched economic control away from the original inhabitants. Neonatives then worked to preserve the scenery and local fauna, an approach that ran counter to the wishes of old-time ranchers who desired unregulated development. This dichotomy was replicated in many other western tourist regions.

Tourism grew rapidly in the first four decades of the twentieth century. The availability of automobiles and highway travel boosted tourism, especially in national parks. Recreational tourism for a broad cross-section of Americans replaced more culturally oriented elite tourism, particularly in the 1920s. Small-time tourist operators found new economic opportunities, but only for a short time. Skiing became an important form of recreational tourism in Steamboat Springs, Colorado, and Sun Valley, Idaho. Sun Valley especially revealed the characteristics of a modern tourist economy, as locals lost out to outsiders in resort development.

Following World War II, tourism boomed even more in importance for the West. Better roads, increased personal incomes, and more leisure time gave Americans more chances to explore their nation. Recreational tourism became the norm, with ski resorts sprouting like mushrooms throughout the Mountain West. As in earlier resort areas, local economic development quickly yielded to control by newcomers. The dramatic growth of Las Vegas was a prime example of the rise of entertainment tourism in the American West, a successor to heritage (cultural) tourism and recreational tourism, which took place after World War II. The trend was toward national corporate control, a movement not even mobsters could resist, as most sold out to national hotel and resort operations in the 1970s and later. Local residents benefited from job creation, but suffered from a high cost of living as housing prices soared.

Conclusions

Tentative conclusions may be drawn about the future of business. The economic shocks and instabilities of the 1970s, 1980s, and 1990s spurred global business restructuring. Executives adjusted their management methods to meet new situations developing within their nations and abroad with varying degrees of success. Restructuring involved more than business firms, for it included alterations in government-business relations as well. Government regulation of business — and in Great Britain, Japan, and China government ownership of business — lessened, as governments tried to spur business development through the creation of more competitive environments. As is so often the case, far from all of the results of restructuring were predictable, as the international marketplace remained complex and ever-changing.

In fact, one of the few things that was predictable was precisely the continued complexity of the global economy. Anyone searching for easy answers to questions about international business was bound to be disappointed.

National business systems are not monolithic; nor are the interactions of their many parts with each other or with the business systems of other nations simple. Moreover, as in the past, businesses have been evolving as their economic, political, and cultural environments have changed and will continue to do so in the twenty-first century, making it necessary to look beyond the individual business firm to understand fully business successes and failures.

Suggested Readings

On the development of important high-tech industries in the United States and the world, see Alfred D. Chandler Jr., *Shaping the Industrial Century: The Remarkable Story of the Evolution of the Modern Chemical and Pharmaceutical Industries* (Cambridge, Mass., 2005), and Alfred D. Chandler Jr., *Inventing the Electronic Century: The Epic Story of the Consumer Electronics and Computer Industries* (Cambridge, Mass., 2005). Mansel G. Blackford and K. Austin Kerr, *BFGoodrich: Tradition and Transformation, 1870–1995* (Columbus, 1996), is a case study. Richard H. K. Vietor, *Contrived Competition: Regulation and Deregulation in America* (Cambridge, Mass., 1994), looks at the deregulation of American business through a series of case studies. On business regulation and deregulation, see also Mark H. Rose, Bruce E. Seeley, and Paul F. Barrett, *The Best Transportation System in the World: Railroads, Trucks, Airlines, and American Public Policy in the Twentieth Century* (Columbus, 2006), and David L. Mason, *From Buildings and Loans to Bail-Outs: A History of the American Savings and Loan Industry, 1831–1995* (Cambridge, 2004). On Wal-Mart's recent development, see Charles Fishman, *The Wal-Mart Effect* (New York, 2006).

Michael Dintenfass, *The Decline of Industrial Britain, 1870–1980* (London, 1992), provides a provocative introduction to the many problems that afflicted the British business system. Geoffrey Jones, "Great Britain: Big Business, Management, and Competitiveness in Twentieth Century Britain," in *Big Business and the Wealth of Nations* (Cambridge, 1997), ed. Alfred D. Chandler Jr., Franco Amatori, and Takahi Hikino, is illuminating. Ray Oakey, Roy Rothwell, and Sarah Cooper, *Management of Innovation in High Technology Firms* (New York, 1988), compares the development of high-tech firms in parts of the United States, Scotland, and England. Charles Dellheim, *The Disenchanted Isles: Mrs. Thatcher's Capitalistic Revolution* (New York, 1995), is a balanced examination. John Stanworth and Colin Gray, eds., *Bolton 20 Years On: the Small Firm in the 1990s* (London, 1991), surveys the development of small business in Great Britain during the 1970s and 1980s. D. J.

Storey, ed., *The Small Firm: An International Survey* (New York, 1983), is a collection of essays on small businesses and their relation to big businesses around the world.

Rodney Clark, *The Japanese Company* (New Haven, 1979), James C. Abegglen and George Stalk Jr., *Kaisha: The Japanese Corporation* (New York, 1985), and W. Carl Kester, *Japanese Takeovers: The Global Contest for Corporate Control* (Cambridge, Mass., 1991), look at Japanese business in the 1970s and 1980s. For a case study of small business development, see D. H. Whittaker, *Small Firms in the Japanese Economy* (New York, 1997), about small manufacturers in one part of Tokyo. On Japan's bubble economy and the problems of the 1990s, see J. Robert Brown, *The Ministry of Finance: Bureaucratic Practices and the Transformation of the Japanese Economy* (Westport, Conn., 1999), and William W. Grimes, *Unmaking the Japanese Miracle: Macroeconomic Politics, 1985–2000* (Ithaca, 2001). Janet Hunter and Cornelia Storz, eds., *Institutional and Technological Change in Japan's Economy: Past and Present* (Abingdon, 2006), is broad in scope. Douglas A. Farnie et al., eds., *Region and Strategy in Britain and Japan: Business in Lancashire and Kansai, 1890–1990* (London, 2000), is an especially valuable comparative study.

For overviews on economic developments in modern China, see David Faure, *China and Capitalism: A History of Business Enterprise in Modern China* (Hong Kong, 2006), chapter 5, John Gittings, *The Changing Face of China: From Mao to Market* (Oxford, 2005), Peter Hessler, *Oracle Bones: A Journey Through Time in China* (New York, 2006), and Oded Shenkar, *The Chinese Century: The Rising Chinese Economy and Its Impact on the Global Economy, the Balance of Power, and Your Job* (Upper Saddle River, N.J., 2005). Robyn Meredith, *The Elephant and the Dragon* (New York, 2007), compares recent business developments in China and India. Dei-Jin Chang, ed., *Business Groups in East Asia: Financial Crisis, Restructuring, and New Growth* (Oxford, 2006), contains a useful essay on *keiretsu* by Christina Ahmadjian and a valuable essay about Chinese business groups by Donghoon Hahn and Keun Lee. On tourism in China, see Pal Nyiri, *Scenic Spots: Chinese Tourism, the State, and Cultural Authority* (Seattle, 2006). On the consequences of economic growth for China's environment, see Elizabeth C. Economy, *The River Runs Black: The Environmental Challenge to China's Future* (Ithaca, 2004), and Judith Shapiro, *Mao's War Against Nature: Politics and the Environment in Revolutionary China* (Cambridge, 2001).

On the history of tourism in the American West, see Hal K. Rothman, *Devil's Bargains: Tourism in the Twentieth-Century American West* (Lawrence, 1998), and David M. Wrobel and Patrick T. Long, eds., *Seeing & Being Seen:*

Tourism in the American West (Lawrence, 2001). For a case study, see Mansel G. Blackford, *Fragile Paradise: The Impact of Tourism on Maui, 1959–2000* (Lawrence, 2001). Valene L. Smith, ed., *Hosts and Guests: The Anthropology of Tourism* (Philadelphia, 1989), is a broad-ranging work. On the business of tourism, see Philip Scranton and Janet F. Davidson, eds., *The Business of Tourism: Place, Faith, and History* (Philadelphia, 2007).

Conclusion
Convergence and Divergence
in World Businesses

In the mid-1990s an American firm sought to introduce the drink Snapple, which was very popular in the United States, to the Japanese market. The attempt failed. Part of the problem lay in the outlets through which Snapple was marketed, Seven-Eleven stores. The stores had limited shelf space, and when Snapple did not immediately catch on with the Japanese public, store managers took it off their shelves. However, an even more basic difficulty was cultural. Many Japanese preferred to drink clear liquids and so passed by the opaque Snapple. And so we conclude this study with a realization that business both shapes its external environment and is shaped by that environment. At no time was that situation clearer than at the beginning of the twenty-first century. Businesses, especially multinational companies (MNCs), affected the lives of people worldwide, but those same businesses were in turn influenced by the social, economic, and political environments in which they operated.

The Spread of Multinational Companies

During the 1990s MNCs remained, as they had been for over a century, important agents of change in world business. They spread forms of business methods from nation to nation. In the 1980s Ford Motors flew some of the foremen and workers from its Mexican plants to Hiroshima. There they were trained in new production methods on Mazda's assembly lines — Ford owned a large share of Mazda — preparatory to introducing them to Ford's Mexican factories. However, even MNCs had to adjust to local environments and cultures to operate effectively. MNCs were important for all the nations examined in this study, at no time more so than in the 1990s and early 2000s.

Great Britain was still a leading nation in terms of foreign direct investment (FDI) overseas. In 1990 Britain held 15 percent of the world's outward direct foreign investment (mainly sums invested in overseas industrial plants), second only to the United States, which held 26 percent, and ahead of Japan, with 12 percent, and Germany, which had 9 percent. This continued importance of British businesses in FDI was a leading example of British business success. Conversely, MNCs operating within Great Britain were important sources of that nation's industrial revival. Japanese makers of cars and electronics goods, along with many American, German, French, and Swedish firms, found it profitable to manufacture a wide variety of goods in British factories for sale in Great Britain and in markets beyond that nation. These MNCs were generally more efficient than their British counterparts; in 1987 they accounted for about 18 percent of the gross value added in British manufacturing but were responsible for only about 13 percent of manufacturing employment in Britain.

Similarly, Japanese businesses generally succeeded in transferring their production methods to America, illustrating persuasively that those techniques were not embedded in Japanese culture and society. Japanese firms in the automobile, automotive supply, steel, rubber, and consumer electronics industries brought their production methods to American transplants. In 1990 companies in these industries owned about one-half of the 1,275 Japanese plants in America, and those factories employed nearly three-quarters of the 300,000 Americans working for Japanese firms in the United States. In the 1980s and 1990s Japanese companies, ranging from Honda Motors to Nisshin Steel and to Bridgestone Tires, built an integrated, self-reinforcing industrial complex in the American Midwest, increasingly including scores of transplanted Japanese subcontractors.

Japanese transplants succeeded in some of the very industries that American businesses exited. They did so by putting in place business methods markedly different from their less successful American competitors: labor recruitment and payment systems that bound workers to their companies, the use of production teams, the rotation of jobs among workers, the adoption of worker ideas in process and product advances, reliance on just-in-time production systems, which reduced inventories to a minimum, and other matters. Even so, as two investigators found in the late 1980s, transplant factories were not paradises. Overwork, repetitive-motion injuries, poor race relations, and other problems plagued them.

Just as foreigners invested in the United States, so did Americans invest abroad as part of the development of the post–World War II global economy. A growing American presence in Japan was part of this overseas expansion of American business. Americans who visit Japan are struck by the pervasiveness of familiar corporate names: IBM, Coca-Cola, McDonald's, Kentucky Fried Chicken, to list a few. By 1984 there were 1,000 firms that were either wholly or substantially owned by Americans doing business in Japan, and in that year the largest 200 had gross sales of $44 billion. Even so, much remained undone. In 1984, 80 of the 200 largest American manufacturing and mining companies had no major operations in Japan.

American companies operating with success in Japan were in a wide range of industries. For example, the Japanese drank more Coca-Cola than anyone else in the world, except Americans and Mexicans. Yet this was only part of Coca-Cola's Japanese business. Altogether, Coca-Cola Japan produced 60 percent of Japan's carbonated beverages. IBM Japan was the number three computer maker in Japan (after Fujitsu and Nippon Electric Company), employed 16,000 people, and had annual sales in Japan of $2 billion. McDonald's Japan had gross sales of over $400 million annually. By the mid-1990s it had over 2,000 outlets in Japan. The Ministry of Education complained that because of the influence of fast foods Japanese school children were forgetting how to use chopsticks! Like IBM Japan, some successful U.S. ventures in Japan were high-tech firms — Yamatake-Honeywell, Yokogawa-Hewlett-Packard, and Texas Instruments — but many are not — Johnson Wax, Yamazaki-Nabisco, and Japan Tupperware.

No single factor ensured success for the American companies operating in Japan. Most successful American companies were persistent and patient, willing to forgo short-term gains in favor of profits over the long haul. It typically required five to ten years before a profit was earned. Even McDonald's, which took off very quickly, needed three years to break out of the red. Japan Tupperware required three changes in its top management and nine years of experimentation before setting up a successful distribution system. By the same token, Japanese companies setting up manufacturing operations in America were willing to wait ten years or more before earning profits. In addition, successful American companies were willing to take risks. Coca-Cola entered Japan in 1946 as a yen company, meaning that it was not allowed to convert yen earned in Japan into dollars for repatriation home to the United States; the company gambled that it would be allowed to convert its yen to dollars at a later date, as proved to be the case.

Successful American firms adjusted to Japanese culture and Japanese ways of doing business. Adjustment sometimes entailed entering Japan as a joint venture with a Japanese company and only later setting up a wholly owned subsidiary. The Japanese partner could smooth the way with banks, government officials, and product distributors. It often meant placing Japanese in positions of power and having just a few Americans on the scene, adopting Japanese as the official company language, using open offices preferred by the Japanese because they can confer with each other more easily than in work spaces made up of private offices (Texas Instruments and Warner Lambert tore out partitions separating private offices to create open work spaces), and adopting in part the Japanese systems of hiring and keeping employees. However, being Western could help in some situations: college-educated women overlooked by Japanese companies except as temporaries gladly went to work for U.S. firms in Japan. Some of these same steps were taken by American firms operating successfully in China during the 1990s and later. They often entered China via various sorts of joint ventures, tried to adjust to Chinese culture (while also remaining American), and were patient.

MNCs were far from limited to the United States, Japan, and Great Britain in their origins as the twenty-first century opened. Indian and Chinese MNCs were, the British magazine *The Economist* observed in the spring of 2007, "starting to give their rich-world rivals a run for their money." The journal noted, for example, that Indian firms, led by Hindalco and Tata Steel, had purchased thirty-four foreign companies at a cost of almost $11 billion. Moreover, Brazilian and Russian MNCs had invested even more abroad. These companies were, the journal claimed, "a pack of fast-moving, sharp-toothed new multinationals . . . emerging from the poor world."

One of the world's most important MNCs was (and is) Unilever. Unilever's expansion speaks to the importance of MNCs in the global economy, especially in consumer goods. Based in Great Britain and the Netherlands, it is primarily a manufacturer and seller of branded, nondurable consumer goods. Unilever produces items that in 2005 could be found in about one-half of the world's households. It was the world's largest ice cream, tea, and margarine company, and one of the world's largest home and personal-care companies. In 1990 Unilever's officers estimated that their firm accounted for almost 1 percent of the total personal-consumption sales in the world.

Unilever originated in a 1929 merger of the British firm of Lever Brothers, a large British soap maker, with the company Margarine Unie of the Netherlands, a maker of margarine. Linking the two firms was their use of palm oils as their basic raw material. The oils came from palm trees that the companies grew at plantations in Africa and the South Pacific. From the outset, then, Unilever was a diversified firm. It extended its global reach throughout the 1920s and 1930s, by building or acquiring factories throughout Europe, the United States, Canada, Australia, India, Thailand, Indonesia, China, Argentina, and Chile. Further expansion occurred in the 1940s and 1950s, with Unilever opening factories in still more nations around the world, especially as it moved deeper into food production. Unilever also owned the United Africa Company, a major division, operating it almost like an independent company throughout much of the African continent. The United Africa Company produced palm oils, but also served as a large trading company, importing a broad range of consumer durables into emerging African markets. The United Africa Company was much like Japanese *sogo shosha*.

From the 1929 merger came an unusual management structure of Unilever, its rule by a troika of executives. This three-person top management team consisted of the chairman of the British part of the firm with offices in London, his Dutch counterpart with offices in Rotterdam, and a third person appointed by the Board of Directors. Only very recently has that troika been abandoned in favor of the more conventional top management set-up of president and vice-president: one from Britain, the other from the Netherlands, alternating every few years.

In the early 1960s about two-thirds of Unilever's sales were made in Europe, another one-tenth in the United States, and the remainder in the rest of the world. It was already a global firm and became still more international over the next four decades. Starting with a very diverse base of raw materials and products, Unilever continued to seek growth in new products and activities, both through innovation and by acquisitions. Loosely linking the various parts of the company was the notion, promoted by management, of Unilever as a "knowledge-based" company.

In the 1960s and 1970s Unilever's management came face-to-face with the need to establish a management structure appropriate for its growing range of products and global markets. Like so many companies in the 1960s, Unilever continued to diversify, bringing out many new brands of personal-care products (shampoos, perfumes, and cosmetics), soaps, and detergents for many segmented markets. It also increased its emphasis on food products, creating virtually from scratch a frozen-food industry in Europe. Ice cream became an important branded product for Unilever for the first time. Unilever operated fish and chips shops across England and parts of Europe, even vertically integrating backward to own fishing fleets. Altogether, in the late 1960s Unilever embraced around 500 operating companies.

As it diversified, Unilever put in place a decentralized management system, building on the beginnings of one already established before World War II. Unilever's officers developed the idea of what they called "coordination" from the 1950s into the 1970s, setting up major product divisions globally. By 1967 there were coordinations, or product divisions, in such fields as foods, detergents, toilet preparations, and chemicals, mainly in

Western Europe. However, there were also regional divisions. Businesses in the United States and Canada were run separately, as were the operations of the United Africa Company. The latter expanded to include businesses worldwide, operating as a real company inside a company. As might be expected, McKinsey & Company helped design Unilever's decentralized structure, finalized in 1974. At the same time, Unilever also modernized its financial systems by requiring standardization in reporting.

Between 1974 and 1984 Unilever faced challenges in the world economy to which it responded inadequately. There was a lingering recession in the mid-1970s, energy shocks in 1973 and 1979, another recession in the early 1980s, growing worldwide competition in consumer goods, and restrictions placed on foreign-business operations in newly independent countries in Africa and the South Pacific. In trying to meet these challenges, Unilever failed to keep up with the growth of its rivals, such as Proctor & Gamble. Unilever was simply too cumbersome, especially in its troika-style management, to move quickly enough in difficult times, leaving its sales and profits about the same in 1983 as they had been in 1971.

However, from 1984 into the 1990s, led by new management (the troika was abandoned), Unilever embarked on a transformation, which was largely successful. The firm's officers defined their company's core competencies as being mainly in consumer goods — food, laundry detergents, and personal-care items — and sold those parts of the company that did not fit into these categories. They pulled back from the overdiversification of earlier years. Between 1983 and 1987 Unilever sold over seventy companies and then bought over seventy different companies. Most dramatic was the demise of the United Africa Company. Parts of it were sold off, and other parts were folded into other divisions of Unilever.

By 1987 Unilever had sales of $21 billion, upon which it earned a net profit of $1.4 billion. As had been hoped, profits reached levels of benchmark firms such as Proctor & Gamble. Approximately 60 percent of profits and sales were made in Europe, about 20 percent in the United States, and another 20 percent in the rest of the world. Unilever's core products in food, detergents, and personal-care accounted for 90 percent of its sales. By 1987 Unilever was organized almost wholly along product lines. Nineteen years later, Western Europe accounted for 34 percent of Unilever's sales, North America 22 percent, Asia and the Pacific 18 percent, Latin America 13 percent, and the rest of the world the remainder. Profit margins stood at a respectable 14 percent.

In large part, Unilever succeeded through its marketing. How Unilever developed its brands in global markets and how it sought to reach workable balances between centralization and decentralization in marketing were especially important. Unilever opted mainly for decentralized marketing. The company downplayed its corporate name (unlike Nestle, Colgate Palmolive, Kraft, and Heinz) and played up its many individual brand names. As part of this effort, as early as 1972 Unilever had over thirty market research units, all operating at regional and product levels, not at the corporate level. Unilever opted for segmented marketing on a global scale, much as General Motors had done within the United States in the 1920s. For instance, in the 1970s Unilever gave consumers choices among its margarine brands: the Blue Brand conveyed images of "mothercare"; the Becel and Flora brands touched on fears of heart disease; and the Rama brand was a premier taste brand conveying feeling of pleasure. In the 1980s further segmentation occurred. Unilever launched butterlike brands, such as Krona in England, and low-fat spreads as lifestyle choices, such as the Latta brand in Sweden. Much the same type of market segmentation occurred in ice cream, other foods, and personal-care products.

Unlike many companies, Unilever paid close attention to newly developing markets around the world and succeeded in them. In the late 1950s Unilever decided that whatever the political risks, there would be growing numbers of potential consumers in developing markets as income levels rose. It succeeded for several reasons. It was often the first MNC on the scene and it tried hard to get local participation in investment, often in joint ventures. Unilever's aim was to be an invisible MNC, leading it to localize top management in different nations. As early as 1966 only 8 percent of its 2,965 overseas managers were expatriates. Unilever refused to bribe government officials, but worked closely with them in other ways, and was very persistent. Unilever's range of brands helped. For example, most people could soon afford its hard soaps, moving on later with higher incomes to buy its detergents and shampoos.

The Development of Regional Trading Blocs

Even as MNCs seemed to bring businesses and people in different lands closer together, trends in trade were contradictory. On the one hand, British and American policy makers led in promoting the liberalization of trade through the GATT Agreement, which from 1947 on sought with considerable success to lower barriers to trade. In 1995 the GATT became the World Trade Organization (WTO), which continued to promote trade liberalization worldwide. China joined the WTO, with American support, in late 2001. Although some actions of the WTO proved to be controversial in the late 1990s and early 2000s, leading to protests against the organization, there can be little doubt that its policies helped increase world trade, regional specialization, and movements toward the establishment of comparative advantages in many countries.

On the other hand, the development of regional trading blocs seemed to create barriers to trade. While flows of trade, people, and funds across national boundaries within regional blocs were eased, flows across boundaries separating the blocs were restricted. As the 2000s opened, the results of the formation of the trading blocs remained uncertain. Would they eventually stimulate free trade worldwide, leading, perhaps, to prosperity for many nations? Or, conversely, would they restrict trade, except for trade among their members, and contribute to growing disparities of national income and wealth? Three trading blocs were of most importance: North America, Europe, and Asia.

Following World War II, American policy encouraged the economic integration of Western European economies as a way of strengthening the region during the Cold War. Many European leaders, especially Robert Schuman, France's foreign minister, began to think of economic integration, first in coal and iron production and later in other fields, as a way of ensuring that no Western European nation would ever again wage industrialized war against its neighbors. Dreams became reality with the signing in 1951 of a "Treaty of Paris" by representatives of West Germany, France, Italy, and the Benelux nations. The treaty established the European Coal and Steel Community. In 1957 representatives of the same six nations formed the European Economic Community (EEC), soon known as the Common Market. With the revival by the 1960s of the West German economy and a rising level of prosperity across Europe, leaders began to consider more ways of achieving a closer economic union and some political integration.

The European Union (EU), which grew out of the EEC and was originally composed of twelve nations, was the result. Members of the EU integrated their markets by ending most tariff barriers in 1992–93, thus creating the world's largest unified market, one of 380 million people. Member nations allowed the free movement of goods, people, and capital across national boundaries. A major purpose of the formation of the EU was to protect European nations from foreign competition, whether from the United States, Japan, or elsewhere, and many American business leaders viewed the EU as "Fortress Europe." By the late 1990s and early 2000s European nations were also moving, although only with considerable difficulty, toward the adoption of a single currency (Great Britain was one nation that rejected this move) and a European constitution and parliament. By 2007 twenty-seven nations, stretching from Finland in the north to Cyprus in the south and from Portugal in the west to Romania and Bulgaria in the east, composed the EU, and negotiations were under way to admit Croatia, Macedonia, and Turkey.

Meanwhile, the United States set about developing a trading bloc for North America. The North American Free Trade Agreement (NAFTA) began to take shape in 1989, when the United States and Canada signed a Comprehensive Free Trade Agreement, which lowered trade barriers. Almost immediately economic benefits appeared to flow as a result of the agreement. Merchandise shipments between the United States and Canada rose 35 percent between 1987 and 1991, and each nation gained about 2 million jobs as a result. In 1992 the United States and Canada expanded NAFTA to include Mexico. As trade restrictions eased, the three nations, which had a combined population of about 360 million people in the early 1990s, began to form a large unified market for goods and services. By 1992 Mexico was the United States' third-largest market, after Canada and Japan.

However, the creation of NAFTA did not occur without adding to uncertainty in the economies involved. American banks and insurance companies, long frozen out of Mexico, looked forward to benefiting from the arrangement. American manufacturing was relocating into Mexico well before NAFTA to take advantage of the lower wage scales south of the border, but NAFTA accelerated that trend. Consequently, some American industrial workers and their political leaders saw the establishment of NAFTA as a political decision that threatened to erode their job security and standard of living. It was not surprising, then, that organized labor in the United States generally opposed NAFTA.

Reacting to the formation of NAFTA and the EU, Japan stepped up its backing for the creation of an Asian trading bloc. First proposed by Australia, this bloc, tentatively called the Asian Pacific Economic Cooperation, was to be composed of Japan, Australia, and the nations making up the Association of Southeast Asian Nations (ASEAN)—Thailand, Singapore, Malaysia, Indonesia, Brunei, and the Philippines. However, by the early 2000s no such comprehensive trading bloc had developed. Japan proved unwilling to provide wholehearted backing, and the depression that blanketed Japan for the decade of the 1990s ended its efforts. Then too, some of the ASEAN nations had closer economic ties to the United States than to each other and did not want to endanger those connections. Enmities from World War II separated nations as well. Instead, many Asian nations worked out bilateral free trade agreements (FTAs), signing some seventy of them between 1997 and 2007 alone. In 2004, for example, China and the ASEAN reached an FTA on goods, and three years later they signed one covering services.

Similarities and Differences in World Business

This book has stressed the importance of the interaction between business and its political environment as partially explaining the ways in which firms developed from preindustrial times to the present. Although, as we have repeatedly seen, certain economic and technological factors led to changes in the world of business, the differing environments of business in the five nations covered in this study ensured that those changes would be varied.

In preindustrial times, Great Britain, the United States, Germany, Japan, and China possessed expanding commercial economies, not stagnant economies. In part, the growth of these economies resulted from political frameworks that were generally conducive to economic integration and development. Nonetheless, when compared to the economies that developed with industrialization, those preindustrial economies were primitive. The low volume and slow pace of business allowed merchants to carry on their businesses in traditional ways. Personal trust based on family ties and friendships was the key to preindustrial business. Business was a personal affair practically devoid of managerial hierarchies.

Industrialization quickened the pace of economic life. Industrial revolutions dramatically sped up the production of goods and increased their output exponentially. The throughput of business rose tremendously. As companies sought to cope with this increased throughput, big business began developing. In time, large companies with managerial hierarchies replaced the simpler merchant houses of earlier days, and the personal business world of the merchant gave way to the more impersonal business world of the industrialist. However, because of differences in the politics, cultures, and social systems of the nations — as well as economic differences — big businesses developed at different paces and took significantly different forms in different nations. And, in all five nations small businesses persisted as important economic forces, with company networks of various sorts remaining significant. Although Great Britain was the first nation to industrialize, it trailed behind many of the nations to possess a large number of big businesses. Vertically integrated companies, the norm among large manufacturing firms in the United States, were much less common elsewhere.

Both similarities and differences continued to appear in individual companies and in the business systems of the various nations after 1920. Big businesses, already entrenched in America, Germany, and Japan, continued their development and grew up in Great Britain and China for the first time. However, despite some convergence in world business, differences remained marked. No one would mistake the multi-divisional decentralized companies of the United States and Great Britain for the types of big businesses that existed in Japan, China, or Germany. Indeed, differences in managerial styles and structures long continued to impede business negotiations and the formation of joint-ventures throughout the world — and do so to the present day.

Suggested Readings

George Fields, *From Bonsai to Levi's* (New York, 1983), stresses the importance of understanding cultural differences for business executives hoping to succeed in international marketing. Martin Kenney and Richard Florida, *Beyond Mass Production: The Japanese System and its Transfer to the U.S.* (New York, 1993), and Abe Tetsuo, ed., *Hybrid Factory: The Japanese Production System in the United States* (New York, 1994), examine the operations of Japanese industrial multinationals in the United States. For the reverse story, see Mark Mason, *American Multinationals and Japan: The Political Economy of Japanese Capital Controls, 1899–1980* (Cambridge, Mass., 1992), and Robert Christopher, *Second to None: American Companies in Japan* (New York, 1986). For the history of Unilever, see Geoffrey Jones, *Renewing Unilever: Transformation and Tradition* (Oxford, 2005). On MNCs, more generally, see Geoffrey Jones, *The Evolution of International Business: An Introduction* (New York, 1996). On the origins of the EU, see John Gillingham, *Coal, Steel, and the Birth of Europe, 1945–1955* (Cambridge, 1991).

Index

Accounting: in preindustrial times, 21, 22, 25, 31; during industrialization, 66, 74–75, 91, 102; during 1920s and 1930s, 141, 143, 148, 155, 190; in post–World War II period, 203, 221; in late twentieth/early twenty-first centuries, 249

Advertising, 140, 142–43, 148, 213

Africa, 33

Africa Company, 18–19

Agrarian Law of 1950, 220

Agriculture, 11–13, 28, 34, 47–49, 82, 130, 220–22, 248

American business: and big business, 2, 66, 69, 83, 86–94, 98–104, 108, 117, 140–41, 147, 190, 194, 198, 200, 227, 236, 237, 267; and company structure, 2, 87–89; and industrialization, 37, 39–41, 47; and markets, 39, 40, 51, 53, 54, 86–89, 139–43, 145, 147, 194, 195, 197, 236; and raw materials, 48; and capital investment, 49–50, 83, 87, 146; and labor supply, 51, 61; and small business, 61, 62, 95–99, 104–5, 119, 140, 146–47, 194, 198–99, 200, 223, 225, 228, 233, 236, 237; and throughput of business, 62, 73, 88; and accounting, 74; government role in, 93, 97–101, 149, 150, 194–95, 224, 237–38, 253; and interwar period, 139–52; and urban planning, 161–63; and international economy, 194–200; and Silicon Valley, 222–27; in late twentieth/early

twenty-first centuries, 231, 232–38; restructuring of, 232, 233–38; and tourism in West, 251, 252–53; and multinational corporations, 258–60; in preindustrial era, 266. *See also* Colonial American business

American Civil War, 40, 50

American Federation of Labor (AFL), 103, 125

American Revolution, 8, 39

"American System" of manufacturing, 56

American Tobacco Company, 73, 92–94, 95, 101

Artisanal industries, 13, 16, 28–32, 45, 46, 54, 61, 82, 125, 130

Asano, 110

Associationalism, 149, 195

Association of Southeast Asian Nations (ASEAN), 265–66

Austin Motors, 154, 160

Australia, 33

Autarchy, 191, 193

Automobile industry: in United States, 54, 140–41, 147, 152, 154, 176, 196, 233, 258; and mass production, 140, 153, 160; in Great Britain, 154, 160, 161, 166; in Germany, 163; in Japan, 176, 177, 210, 211–12, 233, 247, 258; in China, 250

Ayukawa Yoshisuke, 172

Baku-han system, 9

Banking: in China, 10, 54, 55, 135, 187,

188, 249; in Great Britain, 19, 21, 72, 77, 78–80, 98, 122, 158–59, 166, 205, 240–41; and Colonial American merchants, 23; in Japan, 42, 107–10, 113–15, 117, 121–22, 158, 172, 209, 216, 245, 247; in Germany, 44, 49, 80, 82, 83, 98, 122, 136, 158, 163, 219; and capital investment, 49; in United States, 79, 98–100, 122, 148, 200, 236, 238, 265

Beijing, China, 127, 185

BFGoodrich Company, 234–35, 246

Big business: in United States, 2, 66, 69, 83, 86–94, 98–104, 108, 117, 140–41, 147, 190, 194, 198, 200, 227, 236, 237, 267; in Germany, 63, 80–81, 83, 136, 164, 219, 267; in Great Britain, 69–77, 83, 108, 136, 152, 154, 155, 157, 161, 201, 202–4, 228, 266; in China, 107, 133–36, 266; in Japan, 107–18, 122, 136, 170–73, 177, 180–82, 190, 210–12, 214–17, 227–28, 246–48, 267

Bills of exchange, 21–22, 23, 25

Biotic interchanges, 32–34

Blair, Tony, 242

Bonsack, James, 93

Bonsack machine, 57, 73, 93

Boston, Mass., 12, 16, 28

Boxer Rebellion, 127

Bretton Woods Agreement, 193–94, 195, 202, 231, 244

Brewing industry, 71–72

Bridgestone Tires, 258

British-American Tobacco, 132, 187

British business: effects of industrialization on, 2, 37, 63; in preindustrial period, 7, 8–9, 11, 12–13, 18–22, 266; and raw materials, 8–9, 48, 71, 72; and markets, 38, 45, 51–53, 64–66, 70–73, 83, 161, 203; government role in, 38–39, 99, 153, 159–60, 201–2, 241–43, 253; and timing of industrialization, 45, 46–47; and

capital investment, 49, 72, 77, 79–80, 83; and labor supply, 50–51; and process of industrialization, 55–56; and small business, 63–69, 77, 83, 117, 136, 153, 158, 161, 165, 204–5, 243, 266; and big business, 69–77, 83, 108, 136, 152, 154, 155, 157, 161, 201, 202–4, 228, 266; and throughput of business, 71, 73, 77; industrial leaders of, 75; and interwar period, 152–63; and urban planning, 161–63; and international economy, 200–206; in late twentieth/early twenty-first centuries, 231, 238–44; and multinational corporations, 257–58, 260–61. See also Colonial American business

British Coal, 243

British Empire, 7, 8–9, 18, 21, 202

British Gas, 242–43

British Petroleum, 204

British Steel Corporation, 202, 243

British Telecom, 242

British West Indies, 14

Bubble Act, 19, 39

Buckeye Steel Castings Company, 96–98, 104, 105

Buick Company, 141, 142

Bureaucratic management, 91–92, 114, 115, 117, 122, 136, 155, 215, 227, 245–46

Business development, modern and traditional forms of, coexisting, 1–2, 4, 37, 45, 46, 69

Business management: in United States, 2, 86, 91–92, 94, 117, 139–45, 147, 190, 194, 196–97, 198, 227, 228, 232–33, 235; in preindustrial period, 31; during industrialization, 63, 66, 69, 72, 73–75, 86, 91–92, 94, 107, 112, 114–17, 122, 123, 132, 135; in Great Britain, 69, 72, 73–75, 117, 145, 152, 155–57, 158, 159–60, 165, 166, 203–4, 239–40, 261; in Japan, 107,

112, 114–17, 122–23, 136, 174–75, 177, 180–81, 214–16, 228, 246, 247; in China, 132, 135, 190; in 1920s and 1930s, 139–45, 147, 152, 155–57, 163, 165; in Germany, 163, 219, 228; in post–World War II period, 196–97, 198, 203; in late twentieth/ early twenty-first centuries, 232–33, 239–40, 261; differences between, impeding joint-ventures, 267

Business Round Table, 195

Butterfield & Swire, 166

Cable and wireless, 242

Cabot, Sebastian, 19

Cadbury Brothers, 71

Callaghan, James, 241

Canada, 235, 265

Canals, 13, 17, 39, 41, 52, 53, 67

Canary Islands, 33

Capital investment: and industrialization, 47, 49–50, 61; in Japan, 47, 50, 108, 212; in Great Britain, 49, 72, 77, 79–80, 83; in United States, 49–50, 83, 87, 146; in China, 55, 131, 133

Carnegie, Andrew, 56, 75, 88, 92, 100

Carnegie Steel, 50, 88, 92, 95, 100, 103, 104, 190. *See also* United States Steel Corporation

Cartels: in United States, 66, 101; in Great Britain, 66, 101, 159, 201; in Germany, 80–81, 82, 83, 101, 136, 163, 164, 218; in Japan, 170–71, 177, 178

Carter, Jimmy, 237, 249

Carter, Robert "King," 20

Chain stores, 78, 98, 147–48, 160, 178, 198–99, 212–13

Chandler, Alfred D., Jr., 61–62

Chemical industry, 48, 56, 80, 109, 119, 145, 156, 170, 171

Chiang Kai-shek, 31, 129, 184–86, 218

Chinese business: share of global economic production, 2; economic

power of, 2–3; evolution of, 4; in preindustrial times, 10–11, 12, 13, 14, 26, 28–32, 266; and artisanal industries of Zigong, 28–32, 54, 107; and economic modernization, 29, 44, 54, 126, 127–30; government role in, 31, 126–31, 134, 184–88, 220–22, 248–49, 253; effect of political disunity on, 44, 186; and proto-industry, 46, 54; and capital investment, 50; and industrialization, 54–55, 126–36; and raw materials, 55; and small business, 55, 107, 131, 136; and big business, 107, 133–36, 266; and markets, 130, 188, 248; and Japanese military aggression, 169, 184, 185, 187, 189, 221; in interwar period, 184–90; forms of, 188–90; and Communist control, 220–22; in late twentieth/early twenty-first century, 232, 245, 248–51; and multinational corporations, 260

Chinese Communist Party (CCP), 44, 185, 189, 208, 218, 220–22, 248

Cigarette industry, 57, 71–73, 88, 92–94, 131

City Planning and Urban Building Laws of 1919, 183

Civil Aeronautics Board (CAB), 237–38

Cleveland Gatling Gun Regiment, 97

Coal industry, 46, 48, 55, 66, 70, 80, 210

Coats Sewing, 154

Coca-Cola, 258–59

Codetermination Law of 1976, 219

Cold War, 194, 208, 210, 218, 224, 264

Colonial American business: British control over, 7; and preindustrial period, 8–9, 11; raw materials in, 8–9, 48; commercial agriculture in, 12, 13; trade within, 14, 17, 39; and trade with Great Britain, 14, 20; urbanization of, 16; population growth in, 17; merchants of, 19, 22–24; and transatlantic economy,

Federal Fishery Conservation and Management Act, 60
Federal Reserve Act of 1913, 100
Federation of British Industries, 153
Federation of Germany Industry, 219
Feudal business systems, 3
Financial Institutions Reform, Recovery and Enforcement Act, 238
First Industrial Revolution, 45, 46, 48, 51
Fish, over-fishing, 58, 59–61
Ford, Henry, 54, 140, 154
Ford Motors, 140, 141, 145, 153, 176, 257
Ford of Great Britain, 154
Foreign direct investment (FDI): and British business, 166, 204, 257–58; and American business, 197, 204, 257–59; and German business, 204, 211, 258; and Japanese business, 207–8, 211, 250, 258; and Chinese business, 250
Fourth Industrial Revolution, 45
France, 38, 52, 69, 206, 244
Franchising, 105
Free trade agreements (FTAs), 266
Fuji, 211
Furukawa, 110, 175
Fuyo, 247

Geneen, Harold, 197
General Agreement on Tariffs and Trade (GATT), 193–95, 202, 207, 231, 263
General Dynamics, 198
General Electric, 145, 153
General Incorporation Act of 1893, 42–43, 108, 113
General Mills, 1
General Mobilization Law of 1938, 182
General Motors, 140, 141–45, 152, 153, 155, 157, 176, 197, 203, 212, 232, 263
General Motors Acceptance Corporation, 140

German business: and industrialization, 2, 37, 44, 47, 63, 80–83; in preindustrial period, 7–8, 266; effect of political disunity on, 11, 38; and banking, 49; and Japanese industrialization, 57; and big business, 63, 80–81, 83, 136, 164, 219, 267; and small business, 63, 81–82, 83, 164, 219–20; and interwar period, 163–65; and foreign direct investment, 204, 211, 258; and international economy, 218–20; and international competitiveness, 235
Girolami, Paul, 240
Glaxo, 240
Gleason Company, 118
Globalization, as political construction, 191
Global market, 145. *See also* International competitiveness; International economy
Global trading blocs, 263–66
Goodspeed, Wilbur, 97
Goodwin and Company, 93
Goodyear Rubber, 141
Government-business relations: in China, 31, 126–31, 134, 184–88, 220–22, 248–49, 253; in Great Britain, 38–39, 99, 153, 159–60, 201–2, 241–43, 253; in United States, 93, 97–101, 149, 150, 194–95, 224, 237–38, 253; in Japan, 99, 100, 121, 124, 153, 170, 176–78, 180, 182, 208–10, 245, 253; in Germany, 163, 164
Great Atlantic and Pacific Tea Company (A&P), 98, 147, 148
Great Depression of 1930s: and Philadelphia textile production, 96; and interwar period, 139, 169; and decentralized management, 145; and rationalization movement, 149, 159, 164, 171; and welfare state, 150; and labor relations, 152; and urban

International Telephone and Telegraph (ITT), 197
Internet, 226
Interstate Commerce Commission (ICC), 100, 101, 238
Interwar period: political environment of, 4; economic environment of, 139; and American business, 139–52; and British business, 152–63; and German business, 163–65; and Japanese business, 169–84, 209, 216; and Chinese business, 184–90
Ireland, 32, 51
Iron industry: in Great Britain, 46, 48, 56, 67, 69, 70; in United States, 48, 61, 96, 104; in Japan, 48–49, 109; in Germany, 80; in China, 131
Isao Nakauchi, 213
Italy, 69, 206
Itoh, C., Company, 118
Iwasaki Hisaya, 113
Iwasaki Koyata, 113, 114–15
Iwasaki Yanosuke, 113
Iwasaki Yataro, 27, 112–13, 246

Jaguar, 242
Japanese business: and industrialization, 2, 35, 37, 41–45, 46, 57; in preindustrial period, 9–10, 11, 12, 13, 14–15, 24–27, 34–35, 266; and handicraft industry, 13, 16; and capital investment, 47, 50, 108, 212; and raw materials, 48–49; and labor supply, 52; and markets, 53, 54, 110, 207; government role in, 99, 110, 121, 124, 153, 170, 176–78, 180, 182, 208–10, 253; and small business, 107, 118–19, 120, 136, 164, 173–74, 177–78, 181, 182, 190, 207, 212, 217–18, 247; and big business, 107–18, 122, 136, 170–73, 177, 180–82, 190, 210–12, 214–17, 227–28, 246–48, 267; U.S. role in, 112, 115, 173, 195, 207, 208; and

urban zoning, 163, 183; in interwar period, 169–84, 209, 216; and urban planning, 182–84; and international economy, 206–18; in late twentieth/early twenty-first centuries, 231–32, 244–48; and multinational corporations, 257–60
Japan Industrial Club, 126
Japan Nitrogen, 171
Jiangnan Arsenal, 131
Jimmu (emperor of Japan), 9
Johnson Wax, 259
Joint Stock Acts of 1856, 66
Joint-stock companies, 18–19, 22, 39, 43, 78–79, 108, 114–15, 122, 174
Jomukai, 215

Kan koba, 120–21
Kawasaki, 110
Keiretsu, 112, 115, 211, 214, 216, 246–47, 249
Kikkoman, 173–76, 207
Korea, 44, 249
Korean War, 195, 208, 220, 224
Korvette, E. J., 199–200
Kresge, S. S., 200
Kyoto, Japan, 14, 16, 24, 25
Kyushu, Japan, 48

Labor relations: in Great Britain, 51, 75–77, 153, 159–60, 242; in United States, 51–52, 56, 76, 102–4, 146, 150–52, 196–97, 233; in Japan, 52, 122, 124–26, 170, 180–81, 216–18, 233, 247–48; in Germany, 82, 163–64, 219; in China, 132, 186
Labor supply, and industrialization, 37–38, 45–46, 47, 50–52, 57, 61
Labor unions, 103, 104, 125, 150–52, 159–60, 180–81, 186, 196–97, 201, 242
Labour Party, 201, 241, 244
Lane, Thomas, 20
Las Vegas, Nev., 252, 253

Law for Promoting Stability and Growth of the Economy of 1967, 218–19
Law of the Sea Conferences, 60
Leeds, England, 21
Levant Company, 19
Lever, William, 162
Lever Brothers, 260
Liaodong Peninsula of China, 44
Liggett and Myers Tobacco Company, 93
Lineage estates, in China, 10–11, 30–32, 54
Lipton, 78, 239
Litton, Charles, 224
Litton Industries, 224
Liverpool, England, 15, 162
Lockheed Missiles and Aerospace, 224
London, England, 15, 18–21, 71–72, 79
London and North Western Railroad (LNWR), 74
Lopez, Aaron, 23–24
Los Angeles, Calif., 162, 183
Lowell, Mass., 61, 96, 134

Machinery-making industry, in United States, 146, 198
Machines, and industrialization, 37, 45, 49, 57, 71–72, 73
Machine tool industry, in Japan, 178, 182
Maize, 32–33
Major, John, 241–42
Major Industries Control Law of 1931, 170, 178, 182
Manchester, England, 15, 70
Manchester Exchange, 67
Manchuria, 44, 169, 170, 185
Manufacturing: in United States, 47, 49, 62, 87, 94, 95, 97, 105, 139, 140–41, 146–47, 194, 196, 198, 200, 201, 211, 233, 235, 236, 237, 244, 265; in Japan, 47, 107, 108–9, 115, 117, 118–19, 170, 177–78, 210–12,

216, 247; and capital investment, 49; innovations in, 55; in Great Britain, 63, 95, 152, 154, 158, 165, 166, 201, 202, 204, 206, 239, 243–44, 258; in Germany, 101, 163, 219, 244; in China, 131. *See also* Mass production
Mao Zedong, 185, 189, 218, 220, 222, 248
Marden, Orden Swett, 124
Margarine Unie, 260
Marketing systems: and economies of scope, 87; and vertical integration, 88, 120; and big business, 98, 140; and zaibatsu, 117; and foreign businesses, 121; in interwar period, 163, 178–79; conservatism in, 239–40; and multinational corporations, 262–63
Markets: and British business, 38, 45, 51–53, 64–66, 70–72, 83, 161, 203; and American business, 39, 40, 51, 53, 54, 86–89, 139–43, 145, 147, 194, 195, 197, 236; and industrialization, 47, 52–54, 61, 71, 72; and Japanese business, 53, 54, 110, 207; and Chinese business, 130, 188, 248; and decentralized management, 139, 145. *See also* Domestic commerce; Trade
Market segmentation, 142
Marshall Plan of 1948, 195, 218
Marubeni Company, 118
Mass production: development of, 46, 103–4; and vertical integration, 88; and cigarette industry, 92; and big business, 102, 147, 205; and automobile industry, 140, 153, 160; and labor relations, 151, 152; and mergers, 153; and international economy, 198
Matsukata Deflation, 43
Matsukata Masayoshi, 43, 209
Matsushita Electric Industrial, 215
Maypole, 78

period, 7–11, 22, 24, 266; in Colonial
America, 8–9, 11, 39; in Japan, 9–10,
11, 41–44, 45, 108, 123, 170, 180;
in China, 10–11, 184–88, 220; and
industrialization, 38–45, 62, 136; in
United States, 39–41, 45, 99–104
Population growth: in Great Britain,
17, 50, 52, 64; in Japan, 17, 53, 184,
207; in China, 17, 54, 127, 250; in
Europe, 32; in United States, 53, 64
Prince Hotels, 214
Printing machinery industry, in China,
132–33
Proctor & Gamble, 262
Production: effects of industrializa-
tion on, 37, 56–57, 61; in United
States, 56–57, 86–89, 97, 105, 149,
198, 226, 232, 233; in Great Britain,
70, 72, 153, 166, 205; in Japan, 170,
171, 174, 175, 181, 212; and multi-
national corporations, 197; in China,
221. *See also* Mass production
Progressive period, 100, 149
Promissory notes, 22, 23
Protestantism, 24
Prussia, 8, 38
Pure Foods and Drug Act of 1906, 100
Puritanism, 24

Qing dynasty, 10, 29, 54, 127–28, 129,
131
Quality control, 46, 232, 250

Rail Act of 1980, 238
Railroads: in Japan, 39, 43, 53, 74,
213–14, 245; in United States, 39,
40–41, 50, 58, 74, 87, 92, 97, 98, 100,
238, 252; in Great Britain, 39, 52–53,
67, 73, 74–75; in China, 131, 186,
220
Rationalization movement: in United
States, 148–49, 150, 170–71; in Great
Britain, 153, 155, 156, 157–59, 165,
170, 200–201, 202, 204; in Germany,

164; in Japan, 170–71, 177, 178, 181,
209; in China, 187; purpose of, 191
Raw materials, 8–9, 16, 45–49, 55, 61,
71, 72, 88, 89, 142
Reagan, Ronald, 237
Regionalism: in preindustrial period,
11, 12–17; development of, 34, 41; in
Great Britain, 52–53, 54, 64, 65, 67,
71, 73, 82, 155, 160; in Japan, 53, 54,
178; in United States, 53, 61, 95, 141;
in Germany, 82; in China, 133–36
Responsibility system, 248
Restoration Settlement of 1689, 7
Restrictive Trade Practices Act of 1956,
202
Restrictive Trade Practices Act of 1968,
202
Retailing: in Great Britain, 77–78, 153,
160–61, 165, 205; in Germany, 82,
164–65; in United States, 98, 147–48,
198–200; in Japan, 120–21, 178, 212,
213
Rhodesia, 204
Right-to-work laws, 196
Rikagaku Industrial Company, 172–73
Riken Industrial Group, 172, 173, 174,
177
Ringi system, 215
R.J. Reynolds Tobacco Company, 93
Robinsons, 70
Rolls-Royce, 243
Roosevelt, Franklin D., 149–50
Royal Dutch Shell, 204
Russia, 19, 260
Russo-Japanese War (1904–5), 44, 125,
185
Ryukyu Islands, 43

Saga domain, 10
Saison Group, 214, 215
Sakhalin Island, 44
Sales businesses: in Great Britain,
77–80, 205; in Germany, 82; in
United States, 88, 89, 95, 98–99, 105,

Unilever Company, 154, 155, 260–63
Union of South Africa, 204
United Africa Company, 261, 262
United Auto Workers, 152
United Cigar Stores, 93
United Nations, 60, 193
United Rubber Workers, 1552
United States Steel Corporation, 83, 87, 96. *See also* Carnegie Steel
United Steel Company, 158, 165
United Steelworkers, 152
Urbanization: in preindustrial period, 11, 12, 15–17, 22; and Japanese merchants, 27; continued growth of, 34; and big business, 98; and Japanese industrialization, 120; and Chinese industrialization, 130
Urban planning, 161–63, 182–84
Urban zoning, 162–63

Vancouver, George, 33
Varian Associates, 224
Vauxhall Motors, 153
Veblen, Thorstein, 100
Vertical integration: and salt making in Zigong, 30–32; in Germany, 63, 80, 158; in Great Britain, 71, 78, 118, 158, 159; in United States, 88–89, 93, 94, 101, 108, 117, 119, 120, 136, 148, 158, 177, 225, 266; in Japan, 118, 119, 120
Vickers, 155
Virginia, 33
Virginia Company, 19
Volkswagen, 250

Wal-Mart, 148, 200, 236, 237
War Industries Board, 149, 150
Warner Lambert, 260
Water power, 16, 48, 49, 55, 61, 68
Wedgwood, Josiah, 15
Weimar Republic, 163, 164
Welfare capitalism, 77, 103, 151, 152
Welfare state, 150, 201, 205, 241

West Germany, 211, 218–20, 228, 244. *See also* German business
Whitley, William, 78
Wholesalers, 64, 71, 88, 98, 120, 179, 199, 212
W. H. Smith, 239
William Douglas and Partners, 70
Willing, Thomas, 23
Wills, W. D. & H. O., Company, 73, 93
Wilson, Harold, 204, 241
Women as workers, 52, 125, 134, 218, 248, 260
Woolworth, 147
Woolworth, F. W., 98
Work process: and industrialization, 37, 38, 46; in Great Britain, 51, 75, 76–77, 102, 160; in United States, 51–52, 102–4; in Germany, 82; in China, 134; in Japan, 181, 258
World Bank, 193
World Tourism Organization, 251
World Trade Organization (WTO), 263–64
World War I: and Japan, 44, 119, 169, 171; and labor relations, 126, 151; and government-business relations, 149, 153, 163
World War II: and steel industry, 96; and government-business relations, 150, 164; and labor relations, 152; and British chemical industry, 156; and Japan, 170, 182, 184

Yamatake-Honeywell, 259
Yamazaki-Nabisco, 259
Yang-Chou, China, 11
Yangzi River delta, China, 54, 55
Yasuda, 110, 172
Yawata Iron and Steel Company, 43, 49, 50, 57, 171
Yellowstone National Park, 59
Yokogawa-Hewlett-Packard, 259
Yokohama, Japan, 26
Yuan Shikai, 129

Zaibatsu: rise of, 107–17; development of, 108–10, 136; and sogo shosha, 110–11; trends in evolution of, 111–15; management of, 115–17, 122, 158, 174–75; industrial development, 118; and Japan Industrial Club, 126; Chinese business compared to, 135; and banking, 158; in interwar period, 170, 171–73, 180; new, 171–73, 190, 211; and anti-zaibatsu sentiment, 180; and American intervention, 207, 208. See also *Keiretsu*

Zhang Jian, 133–36

Zigong, China, salt making in, 28–32, 54, 107